Space and Sound in the British Parliament, 1399 to the Present

Space and Sound in the British Parliament, 1399 to the Present

Architecture, Access and Acoustics

Edited by

J.P.D. Cooper and Richard A. Gaunt

WILEY

for

THE PARLIAMENTARY HISTORY YEARBOOK TRUST

Library of Congress Cataloging-in-Publication Data
Library of Congress Cataloging-in-Publication data is available for this book

ISBN 9781119564171

A catalogue record for this title is available from the British Library
Set in 10/12pt Bembo
by Aptara Inc., India
Printed and bound in Singapore
by Markono print Media Pte Ltd

1   2019

CONTENTS

NOTES ON CONTRIBUTORS

Jennifer Caddick is a PhD student at the University of Nottingham, supervised by Dr Gwilym Dodd and Dr James Bothwell and supported by the AHRC-funded Midlands3Cities Doctoral Training Partnership. Her thesis on 'The Distribution of Royal Patronage to the Gentry in the Minority of Henry VI, 1422–1437' explores the late-medieval conceptualisation of patronage, the assumption of processes normally reserved for the royal prerogative by senior political figures, and the gentry's engagement with the crown through patronage networks. Jennifer completed her MA in medieval studies and BA (Hons) in history at the University of York submitting dissertations on 'Sermons, Speakers, and Physical Spaces in English Parliamentary Openings, 1399–1484' (2016) and 'Parliament and Legislation in the Reign of Henry VII' (2015).

Catriona Cooper is a digital archaeologist and a buildings specialist who is currently working as a post-doctoral researcher on the AHRC-funded 'Listening to the Commons' project at the University of York. Her research interests lie in exploring the multisensory experience of the past through the implementation of digital technology. She undertook her PhD at the University of Southampton in collaboration with the National Trust, exploring lived experience in late medieval buildings through the use of digital techniques. She then spent two years working as a buildings archaeologist for a commercial archaeological unit.

J.P.D. Cooper researches and teaches 16th-century British history at the University of York. Since 2013 he has been principal investigator of the AHRC-funded projects 'St Stephen's Chapel, Westminster', and 'Listening to the Commons', exploring the architecture, political culture, ceremony and soundscapes of the Palace of Westminster between 1292 and the present day, in partnership with the UK parliament. A Leverhulme-funded collaboration with Elizabeth Hallam Smith is examining St Stephen's cloister. Previous publications include *Propaganda and the Tudor State* (Oxford, 2003); *Henry VIII: Arms and the Man* (2009), co-edited with Thom Richardson and Graeme Rimer; and *The Queen's Agent: Francis Walsingham at the Court of Elizabeth I* (2011), the last of which was serialised on BBC Radio 4. He is a fellow of the Society of Antiquaries, a fellow of the Royal Historical Society, and honorary historical consultant to the Royal Armouries. He enjoys talking about his research on 'Today in Parliament'.

Leanne-Marie Cotter undertook her PhD at Cardiff University before joining the Crick Centre at the University of Sheffield as a post-doctoral research associate on the ESRC-funded project, 'Shrinking the State', examining the coalition government's public bodies reform agenda. She has worked as a researcher for The Bevan Foundation, an independent think-tank which inspires social justice in Wales through research, publications and events, and as a researcher for Cuts Watch Cymru, a network of charities and voluntary organisations monitoring how reforms to the welfare system impact people in Wales. In 2018 she took up a position as influencing manager for Mencap.

Matthew Flinders is professor of politics at the University of Sheffield and founding director of the Sir Bernard Crick Centre for the Public Understanding of Politics.

Richard A. Gaunt is associate professor in modern British history at the University of Nottingham, where he has taught since the year 2000. A fellow of the Royal Historical Society, and a former council member of the Historical Association, he has published widely on aspects of British politics, electioneering and political culture between c.1780 and c.1850. Major works include *Sir Robert Peel: The Life and Legacy* (2010) and two volumes of selections from the diaries of the 4th duke of Newcastle: *Unhappy Reactionary: The Diaries of the Fourth Duke of Newcastle, 1822–1850* (Nottingham, 2003) and *Unrepentant Tory: Political Selections from the Diaries of the Fourth Duke of Newcastle, 1827–1838* (Woodbridge, 2006). A further volume, covering the period 1839–50, is forthcoming. Dr Gaunt has been co-editor of *Parliamentary History* since 2013.

Elizabeth Hallam Smith was, until 2016, director of information services and librarian at the house of lords. She is currently researching the history of St Stephen's cloister and St Mary Undercroft at the Palace of Westminster. Her many published works include the history of the Domesday Book and of the Chapter House record office at Westminster Abbey. She currently holds a Leverhulme Trust emeritus research fellowship, based in the houses of parliament and at the University of York.

Sarah Richardson is associate professor of British history at the University of Warwick. She writes widely on political and gender history including *The Political Worlds of Women: Gender and Politics in Nineteenth-Century Britain* (Abingdon, 2013).

Paul Seaward is currently British Academy/Wolfson Foundation research professor at the History of Parliament. From 2001 to 2017 he was the director of the History of Parliament, and before that spent 13 years as a clerk in the house of commons. His current project, 'Reformation to Referendum: A New History of Parliament', is an investigation of the history of parliament over 500 years as an institution based around the themes of time, space, memory, community, and leadership. He has written on parliamentary history in general, on English politics, political thought and history writing in the later 17th century, and on the life and work of the statesman and historian, Edward Hyde, earl of Clarendon. His most recent publications include a selection from Clarendon's History of the Rebellion for Oxford World's Classics, and an edition of Thomas Hobbes's *Behemoth* for the Oxford edition of Hobbes's works.

Miles Taylor is professor of modern history at the University of York. Between 2008 and 2014 he was director of the Institute of Historical Research in London. He is currently completing a history of parliamentary representation in Britain since the 18th century. His recent books include, as editor, *The Age of Asa: Lord Briggs, Public Life and History in Britain since 1945* (Basingstoke, 2015); and as author, *Empress: Queen Victoria and India* (New Haven, CT, 2018).

Architecture and Politics in the Palace of Westminster, 1399 to the Present

J.P.D. COOPER 🆔 AND RICHARD A. GAUNT 🆔

1

On 27 April 1940, an editorial column in *The Times* reflected on the passage of 100 years since Sarah Barry, wife of the architect, Sir Charles, had laid the foundation stone of the new Palace of Westminster. For what would turn out to be such a momentous building, the event had been surprisingly low-key. No royal or parliamentary dignitaries were in attendance, nor was any inscription carved to mark the occasion. A century later, no one seemed to know where the foundation stone could be found. Following the 'almost surreptitious ceremony', Barry had returned to multiple controversies surrounding the fitting out of the two houses of parliament, the payment of his salary, and the cracking of the bell affectionately known as Big Ben. And yet a building which had begun in unceremonious wrangling was now, in 1940, 'one of the best liked and most distinctive in the world'. More than that, to many people, 'it has come to symbolize the democratic system of government to which it was dedicated and which we are fighting to maintain'. The long, disheartening, but ultimately triumphant, struggle of Charles Barry, suggested *The Times* leader writer, might be taken as a good omen for the difficult days ahead.[1]

Those who heeded the advice of *The Times* would all too soon have experienced a different kind of omen. Bombing raids in September and December of that year damaged the Commons lobby and St Stephen's Cloister and left a huge crater in Old Palace Yard. Worse was to follow during the weekend of 10–11 May 1941, when an incendiary attack ignited an inferno within the Commons chamber itself.[2] But here, too, there was powerful and positive symbolism to be found. The survival of the Speaker's Bible amidst the furnace of the Commons took on an almost mystical significance, while a bomb embedded in the Lords had somehow failed to detonate. Photographs of Prime Minister Winston Churchill inspecting the ruined chamber strengthened the sense that (to quote the title of an influential GPO Film Unit documentary) 'London can take it'. Big Ben continued to chime. An identification between the architecture of parliament and the 'British values' that it represents is perhaps not so surprising during the height of the Blitz. In fact, the association between Westminster and resistance to assaults on democracy continues to develop

---

[1] 'A Century at Westminster', *The Times*, 27 Apr. 1940, p. 7. The laying of the foundation stone is described in C. Shenton, *Mr Barry's War: Rebuilding the Houses of Parliament After the Great Fire of 1834* (Oxford, 2016), 100–1.

[2] Chris Bryant, *Parliament the Biography: Reform* (2014), 180.

new forms of expression, whether in the reconstruction of the Jubilee Room following an IRA bomb in 1974, the unveiling of a plaque in the Commons chamber to Jo Cox MP, or the flowers gathering along the railings where PC Keith Palmer lost his life in 2017 while protecting parliament from attack.[3]

The Palace of Westminster is habitually spoken of in superlatives: a masterpiece of Victorian engineering and 'the greatest building programme in Britain since the Middle Ages'; as instantly recognizable as the Great Pyramid, the Taj Mahal or the Eiffel Tower; its clock tower designed by A.W.N. Pugin, 'one of the most famous landmarks in the world ... the crowning glory of the Palace'.[4] These are descriptions of the houses of parliament as reconstructed following the devastating fire of 1834, but an awareness of the building's deeper history underpins the connection that is often made between parliament as a place and as a representative ideal. The fact that the house of commons occupied, and came of age in, the converted medieval royal chapel of St Stephen was not forgotten at Westminster, where the lower House was referred to as St Stephen's well into the 19th century.[5] An older Palace of Westminster still endures within the carcase of the building constructed by Barry and Pugin, magnificently on show in Westminster Hall but surviving, too, in less publically visible spaces: the rededicated chapel of St Mary Undercroft (once the lower chapel of St Stephen's), and the two ranges of Henry VIII's cloister that escaped the incendiary attack of 1941.

Less tangible, but every bit as important as the physical survivals of the pre-1834 Palace of Westminster, are the customs and procedures bequeathed by that older building. Parliaments had assembled at Westminster (both the palace and the abbey) since the term had been coined in 1236. Medieval peers and commons gathered in spaces decorated to vaunt the splendour of English monarchy: the Painted Chamber for state openings, the Queen's or Parliament Chamber where the Lords debated, and the chapter house of Westminster Abbey (the Commons' meeting place during the reigns of Edward III and Richard II) with its tiles depicting the arms of Henry III.[6] In 1548, the Commons acquired a permanent foothold within the royal palace, when St Stephen's Chapel was converted for its exclusive use; MPs transacted their business in the presence of medieval heraldry and the royal arms over the Speaker's chair.[7]

The notion that parliament assembled on royal ground persisted, and has still not entirely gone away. In 1841, Prime Minister Robert Peel, speaking in the temporary house of commons, affirmed that 'the new building, when completed, would comprise a part of her

---

[3] See Rachel Cunliffe, 'There's Nothing More London than its Resilience in the Face of Terror', 24 Mar. 2017, available at *http://www.cityam.com/261591/theres-nothing-more-london-than-its-resilience-face-terror* (accessed 8 Aug. 2018).

[4] Shenton, *Mr Barry's War*, 5; David Cannadine, 'The Palace of Westminster as Palace of Varieties', in *The Houses of Parliament: History, Art, Architecture*, ed. Christine Riding and Jacqueline Riding (2000), 11; Rosemary Hill, *God's Architect: Pugin and the Building of Romantic Britain* (2007), 481–2.

[5] On St Stephen's Chapel and the Commons chamber, see J.P.D. Cooper's essay in this volume.

[6] David Harrison, 'Parliaments, MPs and the Buildings of Westminster in the Middle Ages', in *Westminster II: The Art, Architecture and Archaeology of the Royal Palace*, ed. Warwick Rodwell and Tim Tatton-Brown (Leeds, 2015), 139, 144; John Goodall, 'The Medieval Palace of Westminster', in *Houses of Parliament*, ed. Riding and Riding, 55; Alasdair Hawkyard, 'From Painted Chamber to St Stephen's Chapel: The Meeting Places of the House of Commons at Westminster until 1603', *Parliamentary History*, xxi (2002), 67–9. The Commons moved into the refectory of the abbey later in Richard II's reign.

[7] See J.P.D. Cooper's essay in this volume.

Majesty's ancient palace of Westminster'.[8] The appearance of continuity in parliamentary ceremony can be striking, as indeed (we might argue) is the intention of those charged with maintaining it. To a Tudor historian, television footage of Queen Elizabeth II at a state opening – crowned, making her speech from a throne to the seated Lords and standing Commons – irresistibly recalls depictions of her predecessor, Elizabeth I, in parliament. The precise relationship between the present and the past, however, demands to be interrogated. In what ways has the Palace of Westminster shaped the practice and the presentation of the British parliament? What has been inherited, and what imagined or invented? Can we say with confidence, as one recent political science study has it, that the ceremonies of the house of commons 'are ancient and not much changed'?[9] The architectural framework within which parliamentary ritual takes place has actually altered a good deal since the 16th century, while the social context has shifted beyond recognition. If the succession of history can sometimes be difficult to measure, however, there is no doubting the importance of the perceived link with the past.[10]

Investigating the interplay between architecture and politics in the British parliament over the *longue durée* invites a multidisciplinary approach. Since 2012, the University of York has hosted a series of linked research projects funded by the Arts and Humanities Research Council and the Leverhulme Trust, assembling a team of historians and art historians, archaeologists, and experts in digital modelling and acoustics, to trace the visual and political culture of key spaces within the Palace of Westminster since the 13th century. Manuscript archival research has combined with the study of textual and visual sources and analysis of surviving architecture and material culture, to inform the digital reconstruction of St Stephen's Chapel as a place of worship and subsequently as the house of commons. Acoustic mapping of the pre-1834 chamber and the ventilator space above the ceiling where women listened to Commons' debates has enabled new strata of political experiences to be explored.[11]

Bringing these projects into dialogue with complementary research focusing on Westminster and parliament – including recent investigations of the art and archaeology of the medieval palace, political science research on gendered ceremony and ritual in parliament, and the continuing endeavours of the History of Parliament Trust – enables the following four themes to be categorised.[12] The ensuing discussion should be understood within the context of major trajectories of change in the parliamentary environment since the later

[8]Hansard, *Commons Debates*, 3rd ser., lix, col. 1014: 30 Sept. 1841; see Matthew Cragoe, 'Sir Robert Peel and the "Moral Authority" of the House of Commons, 1832–41', *English Historical Review*, cxxviii (2013), 55–77.

[9]Faith Armitage, 'The Speaker, Parliamentary Ceremonies and Power', *The Journal of Legislative Studies*, xvi (2010), 335.

[10]Roland Quinault, 'Westminster and the Victorian Constitution', *Transactions of the Royal Historical Society*, 6th ser., ii (1992), 79–104.

[11]'The Building Accounts for St Stephen's Chapel, Palace of Westminster, 1292–1366', Leverhulme Trust (2012–14), principal investigator, Professor Tim Ayers; 'St Stephen's Chapel Westminster: Visual and Political Culture 1292–1941', AH/K006991/1 (2013–17), principal investigator, Dr John Cooper; 'Listening to the Commons: The Sounds of Debate and the Experience of Women in Parliament c. 1800', AH/P012094/1 (2017–18), principal investigator, Dr John Cooper; 'The Cloister and Undercroft of St Stephen's Chapel Westminster, 1348–2020', Leverhulme Trust (2017–19), principal investigators, Dr Elizabeth Hallam Smith and Dr John Cooper.

[12]*Westminster: Art, Architecture and Archaeology*, ed. Rodwell and Tatton-Brown; 'Gendered Ceremony and Ritual in Parliament', Leverhulme Trust (2007 11); History of Parliament, available at *http://www.historyofparliamentonline.org/* (accessed 29 Oct. 2018).

medieval period including the growth in the power of the Commons *vis-à-vis* the Lords, the broadening of the franchise to include women and previously unrepresented groups of men, the dwindling prerogative of the crown, and the growth of antiquarian and artistic interest in Westminster as an historic site.[13]

2. *Architecture and Political Culture in the Commons and the Lords*

Buildings are configured as spaces for particular social purposes, but can also define the actions and interactions which occur within them.[14] The old Palace of Westminster acquired its function as a legislative and debating space by virtue of its role as a royal residence and seat of power in the capital. The law courts in Westminster Hall, the revenue-gathering machinery of the exchequer and the validation supplied by the assembly of parliament were all part of the dominion exercised by the medieval crown, concentrated in a complex of buildings which also proclaimed the spiritual status of English monarchy in St Stephen's Chapel and Westminster Abbey. The fact that parliament met in royal space, very evidently in the medieval and Tudor periods, but also into modern times, needs to be factored into our understanding of the institution and its members.[15] In fact, the post-1834 palace took every opportunity to refer – even to defer – to the splendour of monarchy. The Sovereign's Entrance created by Barry at the base of Victoria Tower dwarfed the former Royal Entrance created by Sir John Soane. Tudor roses designed by Pugin accentuated the 'Gothic or Elizabethan' style which had been specified for the building by the select committee of 1835.[16] Architectural and art historians have noted the didactic quality of the new Palace of Westminster: in the vision of Charles Barry 'a sculptured memorial of our national history', richly furnished with statues of kings and queens, royal coats of arms and heraldic glass and tiles.[17] David Cannadine has dated the modern revival of British royal ritual and 'invented, ceremonial splendour' to the 1870s and 1880s.[18] If this chronology is correct, then the Westminster backdrop for that restaging of monarchy had already been manufactured half a century earlier.[19]

---

[13] For some representative work in this area, see Wallace Notestein, *The Winning of the Initiative by the House of Commons* (1926); Valerie Cromwell, 'The Losing of the Initiative by the House of Commons, 1780–1914', *Transactions of the Royal Historical Society*, 5th ser., xviii (1968), 1–23; *The Advent of Democracy: The Impact of the 1918 Reform Act on British Politics*, ed. Stuart Ball (Chichester, 2018); Archibald S. Foord, 'The Waning of "The Influence of the Crown" ', *English Historical Review*, lxii (1947), 484–507; Rosemary Hill, ' "Proceeding like Guy Faux": The Antiquarian Investigation of St Stephen's Chapel Westminster, 1790–1837', *Architectural History*, lix (2016), 253–79.

[14] See Catriona Cooper's essay in this volume.

[15] In 1965, the Commons' Speaker became the monarch's principal custodian of the Palace of Westminster, although the chapel of St Mary Undercroft remains in the care of the lord great chamberlain as a Royal Peculiar.

[16] Hansard, *Lords Debates*, 3rd ser., xxviii, col. 774: 15 June 1835; Sean Sawyer, 'Sir John Soane and the Late Georgian Origins of the Royal Entrance', in *Houses of Parliament*, ed. Riding and Riding, 136–47; Shenton, *Mr Barry's War*, 203–4.

[17] *The Houses of Parliament*, ed. M.H. Port (New Haven, CT, 1976), 232.

[18] David Cannadine, 'The Context, Performance and Meaning of Ritual: The British Monarchy and the "Invention of Tradition, c. 1820–1977" ', in *The Invention of Tradition*, ed. Eric Hobsbawm and Terence Ranger (Cambridge, 1992), 161.

[19] Sawyer dates 'renewed royal ritual' at Westminster to Soane's Scala Regia, ante room, and royal gallery of 1822–4: Sawyer, 'Late Georgian Origins of the Royal Entrance', 141.

The value of bringing the history of parliament into more sustained conversation with architectural and art history is clearly demonstrated by the case of the Painted Chamber. Situated within the medieval privy palace and used for the ceremonial coming together of king, Lords, and Commons, for the opening of parliament, this former royal bedchamber was covered with murals depicting St Edward the Confessor, paired secular and sacred virtues, and Old Testament scenes relevant to the practice of kingship. As argued by Jennifer Caddick, these images functioned not simply as a demonstration of royal power but also as potent reminder of the qualities expected in a good king, thus enabling parliamentary dialogue to take place. Sermons drew on the murals for emphasis, for instance the 1427 opening address on the mutual obligations of rulers and subjects based on 2 Maccabees.[20] A similar argument has been made for the royal iconography in the early modern house of commons, the crowned mace carried by the serjeant-at-arms in procession and the royal arms above the Speaker's chair acting to legitimate loyal criticism of crown policy and thus allowing parliament to do its work.[21]

One of the most intriguing, and elusive, aspects of the relationship between architecture and politics in the British parliament relates to the first dedicated house of commons chamber. Edward VI's reassignment of the recently-dissolved St Stephen's Chapel to the use of the citizens, burgesses, and knights who made up the lower House was probably practical rather than ideological in origin: a solution to the problem of where to accommodate the Commons now that the abbey refectory had been demolished, and what to do with a redundant place of catholic worship adjoining Westminster Hall. Whatever its reasoning, the decision had political consequences that were profound and long-lasting. Between 1548 and 1834, the Commons assembled in a converted royal chapel: overpopulated and overheated (notwithstanding a series of ingenious and bizarre experiments in improving ventilation from 1701) but at the same time more the members' own space than previous meeting places of the Commons had been, and strategically sited at the juncture between the public and privy apartments of the Palace of Westminster. In the words of Chris Bryant, the Commons chamber had acquired 'a personality of its own'.[22] Following the fire of 1834, the burnt-out shell of St Stephen's was pulled down to make way for St Stephen's Hall in the new Palace of Westminster.[23] But if Barry's house of commons occupied a different footprint from the former chamber, it also recalled the lost chapel in its shape, its layout and its gothic style; another link in the chain between past and present at Westminster.

Two of the features which, for better and worse, have come to define the practice of the British parliament are oppositional debate and voting by division; both were shaped by the inherited architecture of the first house of commons chamber. The temptation might be simply to attribute these twin developments to the move into St Stephen's Chapel, but the reality is somewhat more complex. The custom of voting by division dates back at

---

[20] See Jennifer Caddick's essay in this volume.

[21] See J.P.D. Cooper's essay in this volume.

[22] See Elizabeth Hallam Smith's essay in this volume; Chris Bryant, *Parliament the Biography: Ancestral Voices* (2014), 158.

[23] Plans devised by J.C. Buckler and William Railton, placed second and fourth in the competition to design the new Palace of Westminster, would have retained St Stephen's Chapel in some form. Barry also showed some interest, but in 1838 opted to demolish the remaining structure above ground to make way for St Stephen's Hall: Alexandra Wedgwood, 'The New Palace of Westminster', in *Houses of Parliament*, ed. Riding and Riding, 113–15; Shenton, *Mr Barry's War*, 78.

least to the 1523 parliament meeting at Bridewell Palace and Blackfriars as described by the chronicler, Edward Hall.[24] Whether a recent innovation or older in origin, the practice assumed new meaning after 1548, when St Stephen's Chapel and antechapel were converted to become the Commons chamber and the lobby, respectively. As argued by the St Stephen's Chapel research project, it seems likely that the 14th-century timber pulpitum was adapted to demarcate the limits of the chamber.[25] The spatial influence of the former chapel is clear in the description of voting by division supplied by the Elizabethan MP, John Hooker: members affirming a bill filed into the lobby before being numbered by tellers 'one by one' on their return to the chamber.[26] When the Palace of Westminster was replaced following the fire of 1834, separate division lobbies for both the Commons ('aye' and 'no') and the Lords ('content' and 'not content') were included within the specification.[27] The reconstruction of the Commons chamber in 1948–50 gave Giles Gilbert Scott the opportunity to widen the lobbies, once again perpetuating the ancient custom of voting by division.[28]

As for oppositional debate and the characteristically British party system, the early practice was for privy councillors to sit on both sides of the chamber close to the Speaker, rather than as a single group of government front benchers.[29] Moreover, the Commons inhabited St Stephen's for two centuries before a recognizable version of the modern party structure emerged. John Neale may thus have been too eager to see the Elizabethan house of commons as the direct ancestor of the modern elected legislature.[30] Nevertheless, that perception of continuity with the past, and specifically the sense of connection between the architecture of the Commons and the political culture that it has fostered, has been a vital factor in shaping the modern British parliament. In January 1945, Prime Minister Winston Churchill welcomed a report of the select committee on the rebuilding of the Commons which he had effectively instructed two years earlier to privilege continuity over innovation. The fact that the replacement chamber would, once again, lack the capacity to seat all its members was an asset to democracy, preserving 'that freedom and that sense of urgency and excitement to which our Parliamentary proceedings have owed a great deal in the past'. Churchill's reasoning was explicit, both in its appeal to history and its model of politics. Post-war Britain needed to return to the 'heavy party fighting' which an oblong chamber encouraged and a semicircle would hinder. Using language reminiscent of the 18th century 'Age of Party', Churchill looked forward to a future 'when the House will be torn with fury and faction and full vent will be given to the greatest passions'. The archway between the lobby and the chamber, which had taken on 'an appearance of antiquity' thanks to the ferocity of the 1941 fire, should be preserved as a monument to the ordeal

---

[24] Alasdair Hawkyard, *The House of Commons 1509–1558: Personnel, Procedure, Precedent and Change* (Chichester, 2016), 332–3.

[25] See J.P.D. Cooper's essay in this volume.

[26] *Parliament in Elizabethan England: John Hooker's Order and Usage*, ed. V.F. Snow (New Haven, CT, 1977), 169.

[27] *Houses of Parliament*, ed. Port, 33.

[28] Gavin Stamp, ' "We Shape Our Buildings and Afterwards Our Buildings Shape Us": Sir Giles Gilbert Scott and the Rebuilding of the House of Commons', in *Houses of Parliament*, ed. Riding and Riding, 154.

[29] *Hooker's Order and Usage*, ed. Snow, 164.

[30] Neale's comparison between the 16th and the 20th centuries is discussed in J.P.D. Cooper's essay in this volume.

that the palace had survived.[31] On this, too, Churchill got his way: the scorched stonework remains a poignant stopping-point on tours of parliament to this day.

3. *Access and Space in Westminster*

Accessing parliamentary space has been a key element in campaigns to achieve full, fair and equal representation over the past six centuries. This has usually been defined in terms of having the legal ability to stand for parliament, thereby giving rights of access as duly elected representatives. The long campaign for catholic emancipation before 1829, and the protracted struggle to achieve female enfranchisement before 1928, provide ready evidence of this trend.[32] However, running alongside this technical definition of legal access has been a series of (sometimes informal) endeavours to make parliament more accessible in other ways: as a space which, though technically under royal control was not circumscribed by it; as a space which was open and accountable to external scrutiny through reporting its proceedings in newspapers and broadcast media, hence Barry's provision of a gallery for reporters and the incorporation of microphones in the seats in the 1950 chamber; or, most significantly of all, as a space which women could freely enter and observe on equal terms with men. As highlighted by the 'Voice and Vote' exhibition in Westminster Hall in 2018, the last of these remains an active political agenda.[33]

Lacking anything akin to modern notions of representation, medieval and Tudor parliaments did not conceptualise access in terms of social class or gender. Within and around the Palace of Westminster, however, access was plainly an active political issue. The Painted Chamber where parliaments opened remained royal space, with admission granted or denied by the king. Patterns of movement within the pre-modern palace are difficult to locate in the records, but certain moments can be reconstructed. In 1341, the archbishop of Canterbury, John Stratford, currently out of favour with Edward III, was stopped at the north door of Westminster Hall by officers of the king's household and made to answer charges in the adjacent exchequer building. He was then allowed to proceed across the hall, up the steps and past the entrance to the upper chapel of St Stephen, into the Lesser Hall where he was halted once more by serjeants-at-arms at the door to the Painted Chamber.[34]

For an opening of parliament, the Commons (having assembled in Westminster Hall) were temporarily allowed to move between the open and privy spaces of the palace in order to reach the bar of the Painted Chamber. But their lesser social status than the Lords was signalled by their exclusion from the accompanying mass – or procession and sermon, following the Reformation – at the abbey.[35] Some other patterns of movement within the palace can be traced. MPs heading for the Commons chamber generally made use of the

[31] Hansard, *Commons Debates*, 5th ser., cdvii, cols 1003–6: 25 Jan. 1945; see also Miles Taylor's essay in this volume.

[32] See Antonia Fraser, *The King and the Catholics: The Fight for Rights 1829* (2018); *Advent of Democracy*, ed. Ball.

[33] Andrew P. Sparrow, *Obscure Scribblers: A History of Parliamentary Reporting* (2003); see also *https://www. parliament.uk/get-involved/vote-100/voice-and-vote/* (accessed 8 Aug. 2018).

[34] Harrison, 'Parliaments, MPs and the Buildings of Westminster', 138–9.

[35] See Jennifer Caddick's essay in this volume, fig. 2; *Proceedings in the Parliaments of Elizabeth I*, ed. T.E. Hartley (3 vols, 1981–5), i, 68.

stone staircase up to the west door of the former upper chapel, although those wanting to avoid the petitioners congregating by the steps could approach the House via the court of requests; other access routes may have existed.[36] Elizabethan conferences between the lower and the upper Houses took place on the latter's terms, with MPs made to stand in the outer part of the Parliament Chamber until the Lords was ready to treat with them.[37] Another factor in the movement of MPs around the palace was the arrival of Robert Cotton's library of manuscripts in the 1620s, housed in a building previously owned by the clerk of the parliaments. Cotton House, as it was renamed, was situated between the former St Stephen's Chapel and the Painted Chamber. Its collection of parliament rolls, copies of Magna Carta, treatises, and legal records, became a valuable resource for MPs. A covered gallery was constructed opposite the courtyard, for ease of access between the Commons and the Lords.[38]

Chris Kyle and Jason Peacey have drawn attention to the public accessibility of the Palace of Westminster in the early modern period: the lobbyists and petitioners, lawyers and their clients, traders and sightseers who thronged Westminster Hall and the Commons' lobby and the courts of law which shared the site.[39] Taverns and alehouses – Heaven and Hell, Purgatory and Paradise – catered for the crowd. The fact that Guy Fawkes and his accomplices were able to rent space within the palace and stack nearly a ton of gunpowder in readiness for the opening of the 1605 parliament, apparently without generating suspicion, illustrates the point.[40] Though often passed over in historical accounts, these Westminster crowds included numerous women. The Gunpowder Plotters' chance came when a coal merchant named Ellen Bright vacated her premises located underneath the Lords chamber.[41] Female booksellers and stationers traded in Westminster Hall in the 1640s and 1650s.[42] Other women in early modern Westminster included the wives of MPs and peers, residents of the private dwellings within the palace, domestic staff, and elite visitors to parliament. Women may have been denied the vote, but it does not follow that they had no access to Westminster politics. In 1649, several hundred women demanded that parliament release the leaders of the Leveller movement. Four years later, the religious controversialist and haberdasher, Katherine Chidley, 'boldly knocked on the door' of the Commons to present a petition of more than 6,000 female signatures in support of John Lilburne. Rebuffed by an MP arguing that 'they being women and many of them wives, so that the Law tooke no notice

[36] A reference in 1611/12 to 'beatinge downe a way in the wall' of the former cloister buildings may refer to the creation of the corridor from Westminster Hall to the Commons that was supposedly used by Charles I and his soldiers, and appears on 18th-century plans: TNA, E 351/3246. I am grateful to Dr Elizabeth Biggs for her advice on this point; see also Andrew Thrush, 'Topography', in *The History of Parliament: The House of Commons, 1604–1629*, ed. Andrew Thrush and John P. Ferris (6 vols, Cambridge, 2010), i, section vii; Chris Kyle, 'Parliament and the Palace of Westminster: An Exploration of Public Space in the Early Seventeenth Century', *Parliamentary History*, xxi (2002), 86–7.

[37] *Proceedings in the Parliaments of Elizabeth I*, ed. Hartley, i, 459–60; see J.P.D. Cooper's essay in this volume.

[38] C.G.C. Tite, 'The Cotton Library in the Seventeenth Century and its Manuscript Records of the English Parliament', *Parliamentary History*, xiv (1995), 121–38.

[39] Kyle, 'Parliament and the Palace of Westminster'; Jason Peacey, 'To Every Individual Member: The Palace of Westminster and Participatory Politics in the Seventeenth Century', *Court Historian*, xiii (2008), 127–47.

[40] Mark Collins, 'The Topography of the Old Palace of Westminster, 1510–1834', in *Westminster: Art, Architecture and Archaeology*, ed. Rodwell and Tatton-Brown, 217–18.

[41] Mark Nicholls, 'Fawkes, Guy (bap 1570, d 1606)', *ODNB*.

[42] Peacey, 'Palace of Westminster and Participatory Politics', 129.

of them', they smartly replied that some of them were not wives, and those who were had husbands with swords to defend the liberties of the people.[43]

Historical research on women's access to parliament gathers pace, although there is work still to do. As Sarah Richardson points out, the suffrage movement of the early 20th century has tended to obscure the longer history of women's presence at Westminster.[44] Elite women had traditionally been able to listen to debates in the Lords, from behind curtains either side of the throne and later from a gallery designed by Soane as part of his refurbishment of the palace in the 1820s; admission to the House itself had to wait until 1958 (under the Life Peerage Act) and 1963 (for hereditary women peers). Female access to the Commons was more contested. An attempt by the Speaker in 1778 to eject women from the public galleries was subverted by the duchess of Gordon and others who continued to attend dressed as men. By 1818 it was possible for well-connected women to watch debates through a ventilator in the Commons' ceiling, where the 14th-century stonework of the former upper chapel contrasted with the wainscoted chamber below. Variously likened to a chimney, a shed and a sentry box, the ventilator panels had apertures through which the front benches, mace, and clerks, could be seen. Access was regulated by social status and gender: tickets were issued to MPs by the serjeant-at-arms, while green baize benches hinted at a semi-official space. One observer referred to her fellow watchers as 'dowagers and damsels'. But women also played a role in managing the ventilator space, particularly the Speaker's wife who took precedence when she was present.[45] As a means for women to access and comment on parliamentary politics, the ventilator set a precedent that could not be denied. A compartment was provided for women to observe the temporary house of commons constructed after the 1834 fire, while the replacement chamber opened in 1852 included a Ladies' Gallery: another way in which the old Palace of Westminster influenced the new.

4. *Acoustics and Performance*

A criticism soon levelled against the Ladies' Gallery in the new house of commons was its poor acoustic by comparison with the former ventilator space. According to Lady Shelley's account in 1818, the ventilator had funnelled the sound of debate 'so perfectly that, with attention, not a word is lost'. But now latticework grilles screened female observers from the MPs below, reminiscent (so one critic claimed) of the custom of purdah in Muslim households; 'something between a bird-cage and a tea-caddy' was another verdict.[46] Since the Ladies' Gallery was not considered to be part of the house of commons, the rule of silence applied to the men-only strangers' gallery was not enforced. Conversation among the listening women implies political engagement, but could also make it difficult to hear what was being said in the chamber. Not every woman spoke in criticism of the Ladies'

[43]Ian J. Gentles, 'Chidley, Katherine (*fl.* 1616–1653)', *ODNB*.

[44]See Sarah Richardson's essay in this volume.

[45]See Sarah Richardson's essay in this volume; Amy Galvin-Elliott, 'From Suffragette to Citizen: An Exploration of Female Experience of Parliamentary Spaces in Long Nineteenth-Century Britain', University of Warwick PhD, in progress.

[46]See Elizabeth Hallam Smith's essay in this volume; see Sarah Richardson's essay in this volume; *Houses of Parliament*, ed. Port, 168.

Gallery: the correspondent of *The Lady* wrote that 'we can hear all the good speeches', and when members chose to mumble to themselves 'I daresay, we don't lose much'.[47] Women clearly made the best of the space, remaining in place when the strangers' gallery was cleared and able to dress and behave as they wished away from the male gaze. But the grille obstructed sight as well as sound, and to many it became a potent symbol of women's exclusion from politics. On 29 October 1908, Muriel Matters and Helen Fox padlocked themselves to the metalwork with the cry 'We have been behind this grille too long!', a protest which Nirmal Puwar characterises as 'an auditory and bodily arrangement of political "noise" as an affront to what was sayable in the soundscape (inside and outside) of legitimate political space'.[48] The grille was finally removed in 1917, as the Representation of the People Act was making its way through the Commons.[49]

Disruptive noise and debate have long gone together at Westminster. The jeering, theatrical coughing, and animal noises, detailed in Paul Seaward's account of the pre-1834 house of commons, were a familiar feature of the parliamentary soundscape.[50] One of our earliest references to the Commons' meeting in St Stephen's Chapel described the space as 'made like a Theater'.[51] John Hooker may have been thinking of a stage for academic disputations rather than the playhouses soon to appear along the South Bank, but his description captures the performative element of politics all the same.[52] Noisy commentary was a feature of the early modern Commons chamber, just as it was in the theatre. Speakers were cheered, chaffed, and heckled, according to the popularity of their topic and the skilfulness of their speech. Elizabethan sources make repeated reference to 'murmur' as a signifier of discontent, frequently accompanied by coughing, throat-clearing, and mocking laughter.[53] A quick-witted orator could sometimes turn this around: when a speech by London recorder, William Fleetwood, met with unwelcome laughter, he reduced the House to silence with a memory of a ghastly execution witnessed as a boy.[54] Noise (and silence) had a particular role to play in the acclamation of a new Speaker, for instance in 1597 when MPs 'hawked and spat' at the announcement of an unpopular choice.[55] As Jason Peacey reminds us, gesture was another means to affirm or to intimidate in the Commons chamber – the pointed finger, the calculatedly wry smile, even the act of fidgeting – albeit more of a challenge to recover from the records.[56]

[47] See Sarah Richardson's essay in this volume.

[48] Nirmal Puwar, 'The Archi-texture of Parliament: Flaneur as Method in Westminster', *The Journal of Legislative Studies*, xvi (2010), 302.

[49] Images and photos of the Ladies' Gallery and grille in the Parliamentary Art Collection, available at *https://www.parliament.uk/about/living-heritage/transformingsociety/electionsvoting/womenvote/parliamentary-collections/ladies-gallery-grille/* (accessed 8 Aug. 2018).

[50] See Paul Seaward's essay in this volume.

[51] *Hooker's Order and Usage*, ed. Snow, 163.

[52] For the continuing currency of this analogy, see Richard A. Gaunt, 'Sir Robert Peel as "actor-dramatist"', in *Politics, Performance and Popular Culture: Theatre and Society in Nineteenth-Century Britain*, ed. Peter Yeandle, Katherine Newey and Jeffrey Richards (Manchester, 2016), 216–236.

[53] See J.P.D. Cooper's essay in this volume.

[54] *Proceedings in the Parliaments of Elizabeth I*, ed. Hartley, ii, 109.

[55] *Proceedings in the Parliaments of Elizabeth I*, ed. Hartley, iii, 227.

[56] Jason Peacey, 'Disorderly Debates: Noise and Gesture in the 17th Century House of Commons', *Parliamentary History*, xxxii (2013), 71–2.

Reconstructing the soundscapes of the pre-20th-century British parliament is no easy task. The problem is not so much evidential (parliamentarians and their audiences did comment on the audibility of debates) as interpretative. Sound and hearing are subjective and personal. Anyone who has experienced an academic conference, a church sermon, or a public speech, will understand that what is said, and what is heard, are not always the same to all people. As research conducted by the University of York has established, positioning within a space can significantly affect the experience of listening and hearing. Working from a specially-constructed digital model of the 18th-century house of commons, Catriona Cooper has demonstrated that some seats in the chamber would have been able to hear speeches more clearly than others. Furthermore, the positions in the Commons that were the most politically and socially prominent (notably the Speaker's chair and the front benches) were not necessarily those with the best listening experience. Her work reveals that, if you wanted to hear what was being said in the old house of commons, it could sometimes pay to be a back bencher.[57]

As Catriona Cooper makes clear, the use of technology is not a scientific substitute for historical research. Digital reconstructions are models, to be assessed and critiqued. Taken in tandem, however, archival work and digital modelling can help to make sense of differing perceptions of the soundscape of the old house of commons, from John Wilson Croker and Philip Howard (opponents of any change to the chamber, which they described in 1833 as having good acoustics) to Colonel Frederick Trench and Benjamin Wyatt (supporters of an enlarged chamber, and suspicious that the ventilator was drawing sound away from the ears of members). In fact, there is evidence to suggest that the listening experience of women in the ventilator space was superior to at least some of the men in the chamber below, which would also account for the dismay with which the Ladies' Gallery was later viewed.[58] This is how the replica ventilator was presented to the public at the 2018 'Voice and Vote' exhibition in Westminster Hall, using the sound of historic debates recorded in the current Commons chamber and then digitally engineered to reproduce the effect of listening through the ventilator in the 1820s and 1830s.[59]

The politics of sound carried from the old to the new Palace of Westminster, by way of the temporary post-fire accommodation which the Commons had been enjoying in the Lesser Hall. MPs disliked the first iteration of their replacement chamber and voted with their feet, blaming the high roof for swallowing their voices; Barry was made to lower the ceiling.[60] The question of sound resurfaced 100 years later when the Commons considered how to replace the chamber destroyed in the bombing of 1941. Once again, their debate was inflected by the experience of meeting in temporary housing, this time in Church House (referred to as the 'annexe') and afterwards in the house of lords. A few voices were raised, including Nancy Astor's, in favour of an imaginative or even radical rethinking of the shape of the Commons. But it was Churchill's that prevailed: the British way of

---

[57] See Catriona Cooper's essay in this volume.

[58] See Catriona Cooper's essay in this volume; *Houses of Parliament*, ed. Port, 13; see Paul Seaward's essay in this volume; see Elizabeth Hallam Smith's essay in this volume.

[59] The University of York 'Listening to the Commons' team would like to thank Mr Speaker, members of both Houses, and parliamentary staff who enabled these recordings to take place in the Commons chamber.

[60] *Houses of Parliament*, ed. Port, 146–9.

politics was conversational and confrontational, and the new chamber should reproduce the old.[61]

5. *Ceremony, Ritual and Space*

For Christine Riding and Jacqueline Riding, Westminster is 'the pre-eminent "theatre of state"', a stage for national history since the 11th century.[62] The theatricality of the British parliament provokes many reactions, ranging from affectionate and patriotic appreciation of the deep history of the Palace of Westminster, through guarded acceptance of the value of dignified surroundings and ceremony in spite of its anachronism in the modern world, to outright opposition and even derision. That the national politics of the United Kingdom is conducted in a 20th-century makeover of a Victorian building which was itself a reimagination of a lost medieval royal palace, is a fact which will undoubtedly be thrown into relief by the 'Restoration and Renewal' programme at Westminster over the coming years.[63]

However they are perceived, there is no denying the significance of the traditions and rituals which continue to supply the rhythm of the Palace of Westminster. Some are grand set pieces, most obviously the state opening of parliament with its royal pageantry, symbolic challenge to black rod's authority, and disorderly progress of the Commons to hear the queen's speech in the Lords. Others take place daily when the Houses are in session: the processions of the Commons' Speaker (preceded by the serjeant-at-arms) and the Lord Speaker (attended by black rod), followed by prayers in the two chambers. Elements of this parliamentary ritual are deeply historic. The election of a Commons' Speaker, and the serjeant with the mace carried across his shoulder, are both recognizable in the descriptions of Elizabeth I's parliaments supplied by MPs and antiquaries, John Hooker and William Lambarde; probably they pre-date the move into St Stephen's Chapel.[64] Other traditions are of more recent invention. The lying-in-state of Edward VII in Westminster Hall set a precedent for the British royal family which has been maintained thus far, and was extended to include Winston Churchill in 1965. The office of Lord Speaker dates only from 2005, when the Constitutional Reform Act separated the legal and legislative powers traditionally held by the lord chancellor; a version of the chancellor's court dress was retained. Other such examples of managed modernisation include the appointment of the first serjeant-at-arms from an ethnic minority (2016) and the first lady usher of the black rod (2018), illustrating the capacity of parliamentary ceremony to adapt while retaining its essentials.[65]

To visitors, parliamentary staff, politicians, and broadcasters, the ceremonial life of the Palace of Westminster marks an apparently deep set of connections with the past. Shouts of 'Speaker!', and 'Hats off, strangers!', from police officers in traditional uniform, and the hush

---

[61] Stamp, 'Scott and the Rebuilding of the House of Commons', 150–2; see Miles Taylor's essay in this volume.

[62] Christine Riding and Jacqueline Riding, 'Theatre of State', in *Houses of Parliament*, ed. Riding and Riding, 8.

[63] The latest developments can be followed at *https://restorationandrenewal.parliament.uk/index.html* (accessed 8 Aug. 2018).

[64] *Hooker's Order and Usage*, ed. Snow, 173; *William Lambarde's Notes on the Procedures and Privileges of the House of Commons (1584)*, ed. Paul L. Ward (House of Commons Library Document no 10, 1977), 56–9.

[65] For developments up to 2010, see *Ceremony and Ritual in Parliament*, ed. Shirin M. Rai (Abingdon, 2011).

that falls over a bustling central lobby when the Speaker's procession comes in sight, create a compelling impression of the dignity and antiquity of parliament – or at least its claims to both those qualities. In the words of one political scientist, parliamentary ceremonies and rituals merit examination 'not simply as historical backdrops but as operative frames of power in public life'.[66] Interviews with members and senior parliamentary officials, for instance, have highlighted the perceived 'civilising effect' of ceremony on the behaviour of the Commons and what might be lost if it were dispensed with.[67] The appeal to history is recognized by supporters and critics alike. Chris Bryant MP introduces his affectionate but iconoclastic history of parliament with a warning against the 'self-regarding mythology' that it has acquired over the centuries; the phrase 'the mother of parliaments' has been particularly misunderstood.[68] Paul Seaward also cautions us that we know surprisingly little about the 'real origins' of practices generally taken as sacrosanct in parliament: the procession of the Commons' Speaker, bowing to the chair, and dragging the conventionally unwilling new Speaker to his or her place.[69] The Commons' mace is a case in point, variously interpreted as a marker of royal authority and a representation of the authority of the House.[70]

Historical analysis of parliamentary ceremony has tended to focus more on the Lords than the Commons, a function of the proximity of the upper House to the royal court and the social superiority of peers and bishops over elected representatives. From 1510, the processions to and from Westminster Abbey to open parliament are described in a series of accounts by the royal heralds.[71] In 1512–13 a fire damaged the king's apartments at Westminster, within a few years resulting in a longer and more public processional route from Henry VIII's new palace of Whitehall. The young Edward VI made the journey back to Whitehall by barge, setting a trend for water transport. Mary I was carried on a litter, while Elizabeth travelled variously on horseback, in a coach, or by sedan chair, as well as by barge. The streets of Westminster were richly dressed for a parliamentary opening, recalling the celebration of a royal coronation. With some variation (security fears in 1679 prevented Charles II from riding in procession), the royal and noble pageantry of the state opening continued in similar vein until Victoria's withdrawal following the loss of Prince Albert; the splendour of monarchy was then revived by Edward VII and his successors.[72]

In nearly all of this ceremonial, members of the Commons were observers at best. At the 1593 state opening, the door to the Parliament Chamber remained shut, preventing many MPs from hearing the lord keeper's speech; they 'murmured so loude' that the queen

[66]Shirin M. Rai, 'Analysing Ceremony and Ritual in Parliament', *The Journal of Legislative Studies*, xvi (2010), 285.

[67]Armitage, 'Speaker, Parliamentary Ceremonies and Power', 333–4.

[68]Bryant, *Ancestral Voices*, 16–17.

[69]Paul Seaward, 'Institutional Memory and Contemporary History in the House of Commons, 1547–1640', in *Writing the History of Parliament in Tudor and Early Stuart England*, ed. Paul Cavill and Alexandra Gajda (Manchester, 2018), 214.

[70]See J.P.D. Cooper's essay in this volume.

[71]David Dean, 'Image and Ritual in the Tudor Parliaments', in *Tudor Political Culture*, ed. Dale Hoak (Cambridge, 1995), 243–71; Henry S. Cobb, 'The Staging of Ceremonies in the House of Lords', in *Houses of Parliament*, ed. Riding and Riding, 30–47.

[72]Jason Peacey, 'The Street Theatre of State. The Ceremonial Opening of Parliament, 1603 60', in *Managing Tudor and Stuart Parliaments: Essays in Memory of Michael Graves*, ed. Chris Kyle (Chichester, 2015), 155–72.

herself commanded the door to be opened.[73] Traditionally, the Lords has been the house of magnificence. In one important respect, however, the ritual life of the Commons has been neglected until now. For centuries, MPs have prayed together at the start of each day's business: for the welfare of monarch and nation, for peaceful and good government, and for their own wisdom and integrity in the service of the common wealth. The earliest evidence discovered so far dates from Elizabeth's reign, though it is quite possible that members were carrying on a practice which had begun with the introduction of the English prayer book in Edward VI's reign or, indeed, before the Reformation.[74] By the 1570s, members of the Commons were reciting the prayer book litany, kneeling in their stalls and led by the Speaker or the clerk. In 1597, the parliamentary diarist, Hayward Townshend, transcribed a prayer for parliament from the clerk's book, which would one day be echoed in the petition 'for the high court of parliament' included in the Book of Common Prayer.[75] The act of praying together must have been a powerful counterpoint to the noise and the barracking that had already come to characterise debate in the Commons. The fact that their prayers were said in the converted shell of St Stephen's Chapel, a catholic place of worship reformed by the power of the monarch in parliament, can only have made the experience more pointed.

More than any other aspect of its role as the national legislature, the ritual and ceremony of the British parliament are embedded in the building itself. David Cannadine has explained how the splendid stage created for Queen Victoria by Barry and Pugin, 'more a celebration of royal majesty and ordered hierarchy than of political freedom or legislative autonomy', in course of time became a picture gallery for a whig narrative of history. Scenes from the civil war and the Glorious Revolution thus tempered the display of Tudor royal majesty elsewhere in the palace.[76] The use of art to alter the meaning of the Palace of Westminster continues to evolve. In 2016, an illuminated glass and metal sculpture celebrating women's suffrage was installed in the archway leading from Westminster Hall to St Stephen's Hall. Designed by Mary Branson, 'New Dawn' changes colour in rhythm with the tide on the Thames to represent the ebb and flow of hopes for women's political enfranchisement.[77] How parliamentary culture will change when members and officials are required to decant from the Palace of Westminster, and are physically separated from the inherited architecture and artwork which structure and justify the British model of national politics, is one of the most interesting questions to ask of the Restoration and Renewal programme.

6. *Conclusion*

The relationship between architecture and politics in the Palace of Westminster is complex and multilayered; an interaction of many factors over a span of more than eight centuries. Neither this one essay, nor the many others that it points towards, can do the subject full

---

[73] *Proceedings in the Parliaments of Elizabeth I*, ed. Hartley, iii, 62.

[74] See J.P.D. Cooper's essay in this volume.

[75] *Proceedings in the Parliaments of Elizabeth I*, ed. Hartley, iii, 230.

[76] Cannadine, 'The Palace of Westminster as Palace of Varieties', 16–17, 20.

[77] ' "New Dawn": Celebrating Women's Suffrage', available at *https://www.parliament.uk/newdawn* (accessed 29 Oct. 2018).

justice. By creating a framework of analysis, however, we can hope to focus attention on some of the principal connections between the houses of parliament and the spaces in which they have met. Some of these associations derive from the physical structure of the palace at different stages in its development: the occupation and adaptation of St Stephen's Chapel by the Commons after 1548; the accidents of architecture and science which produced a ventilator that early 19th-century women then colonized as an access route to politics; the highly-charged proximity of debate in the Commons chamber which (so Churchill believed, at least) precipitated a uniquely British way of democratic governance. Other connections between place and politics depend more on Westminster as a repository of shared ceremony and memory, perceptions of history and the maintenance (and invention) of tradition. As Chris Bryant warns us, we need to remain alert to the element of caprice in all of this; what he calls the 'haphazard history' of parliament, 'a story of the vagaries of chance' rather than the working out of some inevitable plan.[78]

Destruction has repeatedly played its part in that Westminster story: most famously in 1834, prompting the creation of Britain's first purpose-built legislature, but also in 1512–13 (when Henry VIII abandoned the Palace of Westminster following a fire, thus accelerating its transition towards becoming the seat of government) and in 1940–1 (prompting the conscious decision to keep the shape of parliament the way it was, influencing the tone of politics to this day). Such moments of destruction enable us to see what parliament represented to commentators at the time. By the early 1830s, the Commons chamber had become symbolic of the corruption of the pre-reform political establishment: dark and gloomy, crammed with placemen and the products of rotten boroughs, in the words of Scottish journalist James Grant, 'a second edition of the Black Hole of Calcutta'.[79] Pugin saw its burning as an act of cleansing, exulting in the collapse of modern brick and cement while 'the old walls stood triumphantly amidst this scene of ruin'.[80] By way of contrast, the Commons chamber that Pugin and Barry went on to create was viewed with far more affection when it, in turn, fell victim to fire. Concluding a 1943 debate on how to replace the lost chamber, the postmaster general personified the house of commons as having 'died' in a democratic struggle that had begun with the Reform Act and was now a fight against tyranny.[81]

The Palace of Westminster is under threat. Roofs are leaking, stonework decaying. Pipework, cabling and other services are often antiquated and sometimes unrecorded on any available plans. Infestations are not uncommon. Successive reports have drawn increasingly urgent attention to the possibility of a catastrophic failure in the structure or another major fire. These are just some of the challenges faced by the Restoration and Renewal programme in the palace. Another is, of course, how to recreate the Commons and Lords chambers under the full decant of members which will be required if the programme is to be completed within an acceptable timescale.

In an article taking the long view on windows of opportunity to build a parliament that is 'fit for purpose', Leanne-Marie Cotter and Matthew Flinders ask if lessons can be learned from previous experiences of restoring and renewing the Palace of Westminster. Her analysis

[78]Bryant, *Ancestral Voices*, 20.

[79]See Paul Seaward's essay in this volume.

[80]Hill, *God's Architect*, 128–9.

[81]Hansard, *Commons Debates*, 5th ser., cccxciii, col. 472.

contrasts the successful expansion of elements of the parliamentary estate (notably the addition of committee rooms and office space in Portcullis House, opened in 2000) with 'woeful under-investment' in the main palace site. Citing a range of evidence, from high-pressure steam leaks to an architectural environment which fosters an 'Oxford Union' style of debate unpalatable to female members in particular, their bleak conclusion is that the palace is, indeed, unfit for purpose.[82] Their advice to those responsible for implementing restoration and renewal, not least the need to accept the importance of modernisation and the costs that it will bring, is compelling. Plainly, parliament needs to think, and to consult, about what is necessary for the future of the Palace of Westminster. Questions of access and of transparency are likely to be of paramount importance. Portcullis House is now generally regarded as a success story, but its early days were plagued with unwelcome media attention on the costly trees in the atrium and the loss of public access to MPs, who could now approach the main palace site via a tunnel under the road.[83] As a UNESCO World Heritage Site and an international beacon of British influence, the Palace of Westminster is clearly a tremendous asset to parliament. The challenge facing the Restoration and Renewal programme is to balance the historic art and architecture of the palace with the requirements of a modern legislature, combining access to the public with protection from terrorist attack. The future British parliament deserves nothing less.

---

[82] See Leanne-Marie Cotter and Matthew Flinders's essay in this volume.

[83] 'Raise Portcullis', *The Times*, 7 Nov. 2000; Caroline Shenton, 'Fixing Westminster', *London Review of Books*, 16 Nov. 2017, p. 33.

The Painted Chamber at Westminster and the Openings of Parliament, 1399–1484[*]

JENNIFER CADDICK

The aim of this article is to investigate the use of the Painted Chamber in the Palace of Westminster as a parliamentary space in the 15th century, focusing on 41 openings of parliament held there between 1399 and 1484. It will examine the history and images of the Painted Chamber and the procedures of the opening of parliament through a combination of historical, art historical, and archaeological sources, scholarship and methodologies. It will argue that the Painted Chamber and the openings of parliament therein were tools used by the crown to establish a dynamic between itself and the Commons in which the crown claimed its right to authority but also encouraged a political dialogue. Furthermore, it will argue that this need for dialogue was a response to the growing political influence of the Commons.

Keywords: ceremony; medieval; Painted Chamber; Palace of Westminster; parliament; parliamentary opening; 15th century

1

The period 1399 to 1484 marks a tumultuous phase in English political history. It saw a broad range of political pressures including the reigns of six kings and two minority kingships,[1] the continuation of the Hundred Years War, and the Wars of the Roses. According to the rolls of parliament,[2] a total of 50 parliaments were held between 1399 and 1484, and, of these, 41 were opened in the Painted Chamber at Westminster.[3] It was the only space to be used repeatedly for this purpose during this period. Given the evident significance of this building to contemporaries, it is perhaps surprising that the Painted Chamber at Westminster has not been extensively studied as a parliamentary space. Instead, it has been more broadly interpreted in terms of its development and earlier functions as the King's Chamber. One of the most comprehensive insights into the development of the Painted

[*]I would like to express my gratitude to the AHRC-funded Midlands3Cities Doctoral Training Partnership for its continued support. Thanks also to Dr John Cooper, Dr Richard Gaunt, and Dr Gwilym Dodd, for their feedback on earlier drafts of this article, and Dr Craig Taylor and Dr Kate Giles, for their guidance in producing the dissertation upon which this article has been based.

[1]This assumes Edward V's reign to have been legitimate due to the established practice of hereditary inheritance of the crown if unchallenged by the 15th century.

[2]*The Parliament Rolls of Medieval England, 1275–1504*, ed. Chris Given-Wilson *et al.* (16 vols, Woodbridge, 2005) [hereafter cited as PROME], Volumes IV, VIII– XV.

[3]PROME explicitly describes 39 of these openings as being held in the Painted Chamber. Further research by the editors of PROME provides a total of 41.

Chamber is Paul Binski's *The Painted Chamber at Westminster*.[4] However, Binski's primary focus on the iconography of the space in Henry III's reign means that there is considerably less information about the Painted Chamber's later parliamentary functions.[5] The same can be said of Christopher Wilson's contribution to the British Archaeological Association's volume on the Palace of Westminster, which focuses on the 13th-century renovations to the building.[6] The Painted Chamber has also featured as a case study in scholarship on a variety of topics, for example Amanda Richardson's access analysis work and Thomas Beaumont James's earlier work on medieval English palaces.[7] While each of these forms of research can inform our understanding of the parliamentary Painted Chamber, there remain few studies specifically on this topic.

The Painted Chamber was positioned in the southern or 'privy' Palace of Westminster.[8] It stood to the south-east of Westminster Hall from which it was separated by St Stephen's Chapel and the Lesser Hall. It measured 24.5m long by 7.9m wide, with a height of 9.7m.[9] Initial renovations to the existing Norman structure began under Henry III in the 13th century and were completed under Edward I within the first decade of the 14th century.[10] Originally the King's Chamber,[11] the room was known as the Painted Chamber (sometimes referred to as the *camera depicta*) from the 14th century, due to the extensive murals which adorned its walls.[12] These murals depicted a variety of themes and specific scenes, including images of St Edward the Confessor,[13] triumphant virtues,[14] and Old Testament scenes from Maccabees, Kings, Judges, and Samuel.[15] Between the late medieval period and the late 1700s the walls of the Painted Chamber were whitewashed, although little is known about the motivations behind this decision or when precisely it occurred.[16] The wall paintings were uncovered again around the turn of the 19th century and, fortunately, were copied by

[4] Paul Binski, *The Painted Chamber at Westminster* (1986).

[5] Binski, *The Painted Chamber*, 2–3, 35.

[6] Christopher Wilson, 'A Monument to St Edward the Confessor: Henry III's Great Chamber at Westminster and its Paintings', in *Westminster II: The Art, Architecture and Archaeology of the Royal Palace*, ed. Warwick Rodwell and Tim Tatton-Brown (2017), 152–86. Wilson also provided the main point of opposition to Binski's view that Henry III would not have commissioned the Maccabees cycle in the Painted Chamber due to its usage against him by baronial opponents: Wilson, 'A Monument to St Edward the Confessor', 172–3.

[7] Amanda Richardson, 'Gender and Space in English Royal Palaces c. 1160–c. 1547: A Study in Access Analysis and Imagery', *Medieval Archaeology*, xlvii (2003), 134–9, 150–3; Thomas Beaumont James, *The Palaces of Medieval England, c. 1050–1550: Royalty, Nobility, the Episcopate and their Residences from Edward the Confessor to Henry VIII* (Oxford, 1990), 73–7, 92, 105–6.

[8] On the term 'privy' and the function of the privy palace within the medieval palace of Westminster, see below, pp. 27–8.

[9] Binski, *The Painted Chamber*, 9.

[10] Binski, *The Painted Chamber*, 5–6.

[11] Wilson, 'A Monument to St Edward the Confessor', 153–4.

[12] 'Edward III: Parliament of April 1343, Text and Translation', ed. Seymour Phillips and W.M. Ormrod, in PROME, Volume IV, 329. The Painted Chamber is referred to as '*la chaumbre Depeynt*'.

[13] Binski, *The Painted Chamber*, 114–5.

[14] Binski, *The Painted Chamber*, 114–5.

[15] Binski, *The Painted Chamber*, 115–23.

[16] H.M. Colvin, 'Westminster Palace', in H.M. Colvin, R.A. Brown, J.M. Crook, M.H. Port *et al.*, *The History of the King's Works* (6 vols, 1963–82) [hereafter cited as KW], i, 536–7. Maintenance works occurring around the Painted Chamber, and the continued use of the space by this name during the 1400s, suggest the whitewashing was a later occurrence.

antiquarians before they were destroyed in the 1834 fire.[17] Today, the main sources available for the study of the Painted Chamber are the four extant ceiling panels, as well as the copies of its murals produced by antiquarians, plans of the room, and documentary evidence which signals its former use and importance within the palace complex.[18]

Consequently, the Painted Chamber provides a unique challenge to those who would wish to study it. An increasing trend towards interdisciplinary research, however, and the digital recreation of St Stephen's Chapel achieved through the Virtual St Stephen's Project,[19] suggest that there remains the possibility for a fuller understanding of the features and functions of the Painted Chamber at Westminster in the late medieval period. This article aims to build upon the existing corpus of research to investigate the Painted Chamber during the openings of parliament between 1399 and 1484. It will argue that, at a time when kings were not expected to speak directly to parliament,[20] the parliamentary openings were a tool through which the crown could establish a specific dynamic between itself and the Commons. Within this dynamic the crown was dominant, but not autonomous. A political dialogue was seemingly encouraged between the crown and its representatives such as the lord chancellor, and the Commons.

2. *The Need for Political Dialogue*

Before the argument that the Painted Chamber and openings of parliament were tools for encouraging dialogue can be made, it is necessary to examine the motivations behind the crown's decision to construct such a dynamic. The core argument of this section, therefore, is that the increasing political influence of the Commons during this period necessitated the construction of a co-operative dynamic. The Commons had been summoned to every parliament called by the king since the early 14th century, and the fact that it was an established part of parliament by the 15th century has been widely accepted.[21] For example, private petitions were increasingly addressed directly to the Commons, with this becoming usual practice by the time of Henry VI's reign.[22] This evidences the fact that the growing influence of the Commons was noticeable to those outside parliament, as well as those within its institutional confines. Under Edward IV, the Commons' Speaker was provided with a serjeant-at-arms by the king, to wait on him during ceremonies and lead him in

---

[17]KW, i, 536–7.

[18]John Cherry and Neil Stratford, *Westminster Kings and the Palace of Westminster* (1995), 17–22. Two of the extant ceiling panels are held by the British Museum, the other two are held by Sir John Soane's Museum. William Capon's detailed plans and watercolour views of the Painted Chamber's interior were produced in 1799. Charles Stothard and Edward Crocker produced a number of watercolour copies of the wall paintings around 1819. Capon and Stothard's plans and copies are held by the Society of Antiquaries of London. Crocker's are held by the Ashmolean Museum, University of Oxford.

[19]See Cooper and Gaunt's essay in this volume.

[20]Phil Bradford, 'A Silent Presence: The English King in Parliament in the Fourteenth Century', *Historical Research*, lxxxiv (2011), 209–11.

[21]A.L. Brown, 'Parliament, c. 1377–1422', in *The English Parliament in the Middle Ages*, ed. R.G. Davies and J.H. Denton (Manchester, 1981), 138; A.J. Pollard, *Late Medieval England 1399–1509* (Harlow, 2000), 237.

[22]Gwilym Dodd, *Justice and Grace: Private Petitioning and the English Parliament in the Late Middle Ages* (Oxford, 2007), 157, 167.

processions.[23] In 1489 judges ruled that legislation was invalid unless the Commons had assented to it, thereby legally ensuring the position and influence of the Commons within parliament.[24] The development of the Commons' influence can be linked to both the need of the crown to avoid accusations of tyranny,[25] and their ability to grant taxation,[26] a characteristic which was particularly important in the early 15th century when money was regularly required to fund warfare.

This extended influence would not, however, have necessitated the careful construction of a dynamic between the king and Commons unless it had also posed a challenge to the will of the crown in parliament. The parliament of March 1406 provides a key example of the Commons using its own influence to question the prerogative of the crown. Ongoing conflict with France, Wales, and Scotland had drained the crown's resources,[27] and the Commons was open in its criticism of Henry IV.[28] The Commons would not vote on grants of taxation unless the king's council could prove that its spending could be controlled, and it insisted that the appointed treasurers of war present their accounts for auditing.[29] The grant of taxation was then further delayed until the king agreed to be supervised in his rule by a council nominated in parliament.[30] Another example can be witnessed in the November 1449 parliament. Henry VI's government had been weakened by the king's poor health and the continued defeat of the English army in France. The king's chief minister, William de la Pole, requested a vote of confidence be held, but the Commons 'through … their speaker … accused and impeached' him.[31] Henry VI was forced to intercede directly, the result being that de la Pole was 'neither declared nor charged'.[32]

This is not to suggest that all kings fostered the same dynamic with the Commons, and the topic of the relationship between the two has been debated extensively by historians.[33]

---

[23] A.R. Myers, 'Parliament, c. 1422–1509', in *The English Parliament in the Middle Ages*, ed. Davies and Denton, 181.

[24] Michael Hicks, 'King in Lords and Commons: Three Insights into Late Fifteenth-Century Parliaments, 1461–85', in *People, Places and Perspectives: Essays on Later Medieval & Early Tudor England in Honour of Ralph A. Griffiths*, ed. Keith Dockray and Peter Fleming (Stroud, 2005), 150.

[25] Gwilym Dodd, 'Conflict or Consensus: Henry IV and Parliament, 1399–1406', in *Social Attitudes and Political Structures*, ed. Tim Thornton (Stroud, 2001), 254.

[26] Pollard, *Late Medieval England*, 237.

[27] A.J. Pollard, 'The Lancastrian Constitutional Experiment Revisited: Henry IV, Sir John Tiptoft and the Parliament of 1406', *Parliamentary History*, xiv (1995), 104–5.

[28] Dodd, 'Conflict or Consensus', 242.

[29] Pollard, 'The Lancastrian Constitutional Experiment Revisited', 105.

[30] Simon Payling, 'The House of Commons, 1307–1529', in *A Short History of Parliament: England, Great Britain, the United Kingdom, Ireland & Scotland*, ed. Clyve Jones (Woodbridge, 2009), 76–7.

[31] 'Henry VI: Parliament of November 1449, Text and Translation', ed. Anne Curry and Rosemary Horrox, in PROME, Volume XII, 94. For an overview of the process of impeachment for William de la Pole see Michael Hicks, *The Wars of the Roses* (2010), 66–8.

[32] 'Parliament of November 1449, Text and Translation', ed. Curry and Horrox, 106.

[33] For a more comprehensive view of the history of politics and parliament see Jean-Philippe Genet, 'Politics: Theory and Practice', in *The New Cambridge Medieval History. Vol. 7: c.1415–c.1500*, ed. Christopher Allmand (Cambridge, 1998), 1–28. For an example of divergent views on the general relationship between king and parliament, see J.W. McKenna, 'The Myth of Parliamentary Sovereignty in Late-Medieval England', *English Historical Review*, xciv (1979), 503; John Watts, *Henry VI and the Politics of Kingship* (Cambridge, 1996), 19–20; Michael Hicks, 'What was Personal about Personal Monarchy in the Fifteenth Century?', in *The Image and Perception of Monarchy in Medieval and Early Modern Europe*, ed. Sean McGlynn and Elena Woodacre (Cambridge, 2014), 8–22.

Henry IV came into conflict with his own parliaments,[34] but they never evolved into a threat to his rule,[35] and Henry V enjoyed a largely amicable relationship with his parliaments.[36] Edward IV's reign, by contrast, has been described as an uninspiring phase in English parliamentary history.[37] Over the course of the period 1399 to 1484 it can, despite the different approaches of individual kings, be broadly accepted that the Commons had an established role in parliament, and that it held enough influence as a collective to challenge the authority of the king when it was required. It is this combination of features which made it necessary for the crown to at least appear to foster a dialogue with the Commons.

3. *The Painted Chamber as a Physical Space*

The history of the Painted Chamber, and the images for which it was named, were key to the presentation of a more co-operative dynamic between crown and Commons. The concept of the past, particularly in terms of lineage, was of great importance to individuals and institutions during this period, but it was especially significant to the crown.[38] Mark Ormrod has emphasized the point that the medieval political present was processed and understood through the past.[39] The role of lineage in 15th-century conceptions of royal power can be seen in the suspension of aspects of governance during the minority rule of Henry VI,[40] and the emphasis that those kings who took the throne through deposition or conquest placed on their own royal lineage.[41] The specific significance of the Norman kings is demonstrated in the parliament rolls. The regnal year provided at the beginning of each parliament roll was connected through the phrase 'since the conquest' to the events of 1066,[42] defining and preserving a king's place in history in relation to the beginning of Norman rule. There was no right to the throne in the 15th century that was expressed without emphasizing the continuation of a lineage which could be traced back to the Norman Conquest. The Painted Chamber's spatial connection to the lineage of the crown, and especially to the Norman kings, was of great importance to the identity of the reigning monarch and the justification of his right to be king. It not only memorialised the king's predecessors but, in doing so, formed part of his self-identity as a ruler.[43]

---

[34] Michael Brown, *Disunited Kingdoms: Peoples and Politics in the British Isles 1280–1460* (Harlow, 2013), 245.

[35] Chris Given-Wilson, *Henry IV* (2016), 157.

[36] Christopher Allmand, *Henry V* (1992), 366.

[37] Charles Ross, *Edward IV* (1997), 341.

[38] Mark Ormrod, 'Richard II's Sense of English History', in *The Reign of Richard II*, ed. Gwilym Dodd (Stroud, 2000), 99.

[39] Ormrod, 'Richard II's Sense of English History', 99.

[40] Watts, *Henry VI*, 114–5.

[41] E.g., Henry IV claimed his descent from Henry III, and Edward IV from Edward III: see Given-Wilson, *Henry IV*, 144–7, and Hicks, *The Wars of the Roses*, 14–5 respectively.

[42] E.g., 'in the second year of the reign of King Henry the fourth since the conquest' ('*l'an du regne le roy Henry quart puis le conquest second*'), in 'Henry IV: Parliament of January 1401, Text and Translation', ed. Chris Given-Wilson, in PROME, Volume VIII, 98; see also 'in the eighth year of the reign of Henry the sixth since the conquest' ('*anno regni regis Henrici sexti post conquestum octavo*'), in 'Henry VI: Parliament of September 1429, Text and Translation', ed. Anne Curry, in PROME, Volume X, 376.

[43] This is similar to Richard II's view of Westminster Hall as expressed in Ormrod, 'Richard II's Sense of English History', 100–1.

The Painted Chamber was a physical representation of this history and lineage. As a building, it pre-dated the Norman Conquest and had remained part of the Palace of Westminster throughout the Norman period.[44] It had been passed through generations of ruling monarchs in an unbroken chain since the 11th century. For this reason alone, it must have been deeply significant to the self-identity of kings as a tangible link to the past, and an enduring symbol of this line of rule. Kings in the 15th century controlled this space as their ancestors had done and, in their possession of the Painted Chamber and other buildings within the Palace of Westminster, joined a long-standing narrative of English kingship. It was not that the Painted Chamber of itself imbued the crown with authority; rather it was an undeniable material representation of the history and lineage which legitimised the crown's authority and its right to rule. In holding any parliamentary proceeding within this space, therefore, the crown was surrounding members of parliament with a representation of its fully-legitimised regnal authority.

If the history of the Painted Chamber was a testament to the authority of the king, then the wall paintings for which it was named more precisely reflected the dialogue which was being encouraged within it during the openings of parliament between 1399 and 1484. These images invoked themes such as kingship, tyranny, and warfare, and blended the secular with the religious. In Figure 1 the virtue *Largesce* can be seen standing victorious over Covetousness as part of the triumphant virtues series depicted in the window splays of the Painted Chamber. The other triumphant virtue clearly depicted in Charles Stothard's copies was Gentleness, labelled as *Debonereté*, overcoming Wrath.[45] In the lower half of the chamber walls there were images of Edward the Confessor.[46] The Old Testament sequences along the top half of the north, south, and east walls of the Painted Chamber provided examples of warlike scenes predominantly taken from Maccabees and Kings.[47]

In one sense, these images remained symbolic of the power of the crown through the sense of spectacle which this room created. While there is little evidence to suggest that much work was undertaken in the Painted Chamber during the 15th century, H.M. Colvin's *The History of the King's Works* details the retiling of the adjacent chapel, and suggests that some of the windows may have been installed during the reign of Edward IV.[48] There is also evidence that tapestries with an image of the Trojan armies were commissioned in Henry VII's reign.[49] Evidently, the building was deemed not only useful but suitable to be seen by contemporaries. This was a building which had benefited from a great deal of royal investment. By 1245, Henry III's keepers of the king's works at Westminster had seen more than £7,000 pass through their hands since 1216.[50] Although this cannot all be linked to the renovation of the Painted Chamber, according to Colvin it does denote a major building programme within the Palace of Westminster.[51] In 1259, Master William

[44] Cherry and Stratford, *Westminster Kings and the Medieval Palace of Westminster*, 2.

[45] Binski, *The Painted Chamber*, 41. There is another virtue within Stothard's copies which could be fortitude, but this image does not include descriptive text.

[46] Binski, *The Painted Chamber*, 14 (Fig. 2), 37 (Fig. 3).

[47] Binski, *The Painted Chamber*, 83 (Fig. 4).

[48] KW, i, 537.

[49] Stephen Farrell, 'The Armada Tapestries in the Old Palace of Westminster', *Parliamentary History*, xxix (2010), 422–3.

[50] KW, i, 494.

[51] KW, i, 494.

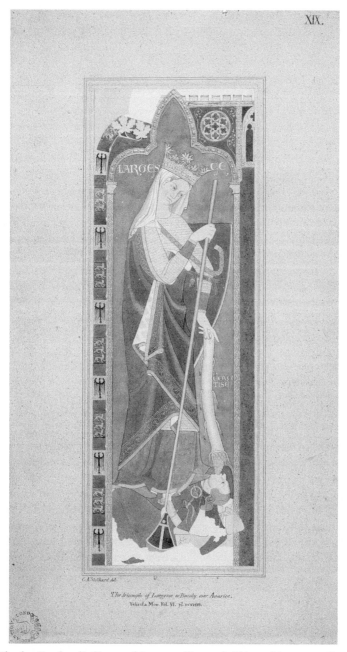

Figure 1: Charles Stothard's Copy of *Largesce* (Bounty) Triumphing over *Covoitise* (Covetousness) from *Vestuta Monumenta*. By kind permission of The Society of Antiquaries of London.

the Painter was paid £2 3s. 10d. for a painting of a Tree of Jesse on the mantel of the newly-built fireplace.[52] Repair work undertaken on the palace under Edward II, including tiling in the Painted Chamber, amounted to £3,000 in total.[53] While contemporaries might not have known precisely how much money had been invested in the Painted Chamber, it remained an ostentatious display of wealth which could then easily be linked to power. Again, there is an element of lineage to be considered here. The inheritance of a building such as the Painted Chamber was an additional legitimisation of the power which the crown's predecessors had possessed and passed down.

These images, however, were simultaneously an indicator of the pressures of kingship and the personal characteristics which members of parliament could expect from the king. The triumphant virtues provide an overt example of this. Figure 1, which depicts *Largesce* overcoming *Covoitise*, is a clear sign that the king was expected to give freely: a willingness to be generous triumphs over a selfish sense of materialism. The message was perhaps particularly striking in parliament, where petitioners' requests for the crown's intervention could be received and responded to.[54] It was a reminder that the king was bound to demonstrate largesse at a time when petitions were only assented to within the parliament rolls with the phrase 'the king wills it' or similar.[55] By the 15th century the Commons had adopted the presentation of its own petitions to the king and Lords in order to formalise some of their initiatives as legislation.[56] The opening of parliament in the Painted Chamber reminded the crown as well as the Commons of the expectations placed on the person of the king, thereby providing the Commons with a point of reference and even leverage when making its own requests.

A similar argument can be made about other images within the Painted Chamber which, as far as can be determined from evidence at this time, remained uncovered. The depictions of Edward the Confessor would have resonated with both king and Commons, offering a clear depiction of an individual against whom the reigning king could be judged.[57] As both saint and king, the example of Edward must have been particularly striking. This would have been furthered by the fact that the site on which the Painted Chamber was built was historically linked to Edward the Confessor.[58] More easily applicable to the political climate of the 15th century, perhaps, would have been the bands from Maccabees which adorned the upper walls and showed a series of battles. The scenes from I and II Maccabees pictured the tyrannical rule of Antiochus, and the role of Judas Maccabeus in leading the revolt against Antiochus's rule.[59] In depicting Antiochus, these images showed to viewers a type of warfare which was justifiable and so less likely to be held in contrast with the image of the virtue of Gentleness displayed in the windows. It also demonstrated that effective military leadership was something valued in a ruler at a time when the Hundred Years War,

---

[52]KW, i, 497.

[53]KW, i, 507.

[54]Dodd, *Justice and Grace*, 311.

[55]E.g., 'Parliament of November 1449, Text and Translation', ed. Curry and Horrox, 146.

[56]E.g., 'Parliament of November 1449, Text and Translation', ed. Curry and Horrox, 106–45; see also Dodd, *Justice and Grace*, 187, 193 (Table 6.1).

[57]Binski, *The Painted Chamber*, 114. These images include the coronation of St Edward, and St Edward gifting his ring to St John the pilgrim.

[58]Wilson, 'A Monument to St Edward the Confessor', 169.

[59]Binski, *The Painted Chamber*, 115–9, 122–3.

and subsequently the Wars of the Roses, made the need for strong military direction from the king particularly important.

Underpinning the potential impact of these images in terms of aiding a dialogue between kings and Commons is the concept of service which determined that different parts of society worked in constant dialogue with one another. Rosemary Horrox has argued that service was a 'symbiotic relationship' between lords and servants.[60] These sentiments, however, could also be broadened and applied to the relationship between king and Commons. The symbiotic nature of service in the 15th century meant that, if the king was owed obedience and service by the Commons, then it was only given on the understanding that there would be a return on their loyalty and service. While some of this return could be provided in terms of favour and influence, or even material goods, it would also need to be continually repaid by the crown through the provision of good kingship. The images in the Painted Chamber were particularly potent, therefore, in allowing a dialogue to be fostered between king and Commons because they provided contemporaries with a visual representation of the virtues and skills which any king would need to embody to fulfil this social contract of service. The Maccabees sequence may also have provided a clear warning for kings in its justification of an uprising if a king's rule became tyrannous, as Antiochus's had. The fact that these images had been inherited from Henry III and Edward I, through whom the reigning king derived his right to rule, applied an additional dimension of pressure.

If the king failed to fulfil the expectations outlined in the images of the Painted Chamber, then parliament could question his capability as a king. One of the clearest examples of this occurred during the opening of Henry IV's first parliament in Westminster Hall in 1399. Thomas Arundel, archbishop of Canterbury, accused Richard II of leading England 'to the brink of ruin', and praised Henry IV as a 'wise and prudent man' who had been sent to save England.[61] For the main theme of his sermon, Arundel took words from I Maccabees: 'It behoves us to ordain for the kingdom' where the king should not be 'governed by his own will'.[62] Arundel's address illustrates the fact that the king could be held to a particular standard, in this case seeking wise counsel for governance, a theme echoed on the walls of the nearby Painted Chamber.

4. *During the Openings of Parliament*

It seems clear from the history and fabric of the Painted Chamber that, as a space, it resonated a necessary balance between the authority of the king and the need for the crown to maintain a dialogue with the Commons. The same can be said of the specific way in which the Painted Chamber was used during the openings of parliament.[63] Parliamentary openings would set the tone for the forthcoming parliament and, by the 15th century, were largely

---

[60] Rosemary Horrox, 'Service', in *Fifteenth-Century Attitudes: Perceptions of Society in Late Medieval England*, ed. Rosemary Horrox (Cambridge, 1994), 66. A similar point was argued by Harriss, in G.L. Harriss, 'The King and his Subjects', in *Fifteenth-Century Attitudes*, ed. Horrox, 14.

[61] PROME describes England as being '*en point de perdicioun*' and Henry IV as sent by God for the good governance of the realm: 'Henry IV: Parliament of October 1399, Text and Translation', ed. Chris Given-Wilson, in PROME, Volume VIII, 9.

[62] 'Parliament of October 1399, Text and Translation', ed. Given-Wilson, 9.

[63] The opening of parliament is considered to be that which is recorded in PROME under 'The Opening of Parliament' heading, and which ends with the naming of the triers and receivers of petitions.

formulaic. The significance of this occasion, and of ceremony and ritual more broadly, has been highlighted by multiple scholars. Clifford Geertz's influential work on political culture provided an early example, when he argued that the ceremony could be utilised to create a sense of centralisation.[64] Referring specifically to the presentation of sermons at court, Pasi Ihalainen provided a similar argument. Sermons could be used either to 'define the [community's] collective political and social values', or to 'advance the politico-religious cause of the group'.[65] The concept of unity is essential to each argument and can certainly be seen in the apparent attempts by the crown to foster a dialogue with the Commons through the opening of parliament.

When held at Westminster, the opening of parliament would begin with the movement of the lords spiritual and temporal, and the selected representatives of the Commons, into the Painted Chamber. Harrison has provided useful insights into the ways in which individuals may have moved through the Palace at Westminster for the opening of parliament from the 14th to the 16th century. This movement was an essential aspect of developing the desired dynamic between crown and Commons. The king, or a representative of the king, and the lords spiritual and temporal initially met for a service in a nearby chapel, before they moved into the Painted Chamber.[66] The chapel used, however, remains uncertain due to a lack of information regarding the procession into the Painted Chamber during the 15th century.[67] There were several options within close vicinity of the Painted Chamber including St Mary le Pew, and St Stephen's Chapel. One option with evidence of usage just outside of this period, however, is Westminster Abbey. The diaries produced by the Colchester burgesses on the 1485 parliament describe the movement of the king and Lords to Westminster Abbey for mass before the opening of parliament.[68] In contrast, the Commons would be required to gather in Westminster Hall before being summoned to the Painted Chamber for the opening of parliament.[69] According to the November 1384 parliament roll, while the king was enthroned and the Lords seated in their robes in ranked order, the Commons stood at the bar.[70] It is possible that this remained the case in the 15th century. Once the opening was completed, the Commons would be dismissed to elect its Speaker and would most commonly conduct its own business in the refectory or chapter house of Westminster Abbey.[71] The Lords and king would move into the nearby Queen's Chamber to continue with their own proceedings.[72]

---

[64] Clifford Geertz, 'Centre, Kings and Charisma: Reflections on the Symbolics of Power', in *Rites of Power: Symbolism, Ritual and Politics since the Middle Ages*, ed. Sean Wilentz (Philadelphia, PA, 1985), 15.

[65] Pasi Ihalainen, 'The Sermon, Court and Parliament, 1689–1789', in *The Oxford Handbook of the British Sermon 1689–1901*, ed. Keith A. Francis and William Gibson (Oxford, 2012), 230.

[66] David Harrison, 'Parliament, MPs and the Buildings of Westminster in the Middle Ages', in *Westminster II: The Art, Architecture and Archaeology of the Royal Palace*, ed. Warwick Rodwell and Tim Tatton-Brown (Leeds, 2015), 139.

[67] Henry S. Cobb, 'Descriptions of the State Opening of Parliament, 1485–1601: A Survey', *Parliamentary History*, xviii (1999), 303–4.

[68] Cobb, 'Descriptions of the State Opening of Parliament', 304; Harrison, 'Parliament, MPs and the Buildings of Westminster', 139; P.R. Cavill, *The English Parliaments of Henry VII, 1485–1504* (Oxford, 2009), 21–2.

[69] Harrison, 'Parliament, MPs and the Buildings of Westminster', 139.

[70] Brown, 'Parliament, c. 1377–1422', 121–2; 'Richard II: Parliament of November 1384, Text and Translation', ed. Geoffrey Martin and Chris Given-Wilson, in PROME, Volume VI, 384.

[71] Harrison, 'Parliaments, MPs and the Buildings of Westminster', 142.

[72] Harrison, 'Parliaments, MPs and the Buildings of Westminster', 142.

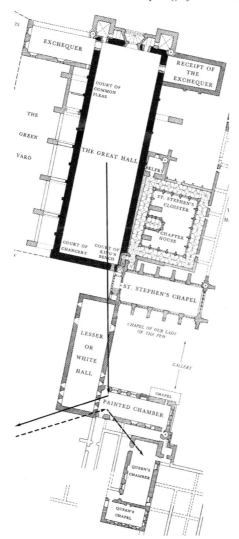

Figure 2: Plan of the Medieval Palace. Detail from *History of the King's Works*, ed. H.M. Colvin (1963), plan III. Crown copyright, reused under OGL Licence. The added lines provide a basic representation of the changes of direction and distance travelled by the Commons (unbroken line) and the Lords (broken line) immediately before and after the opening of the 1485 parliament as there is no information at this time regarding the precise route taken by either during the 15th century.[73]

By the early 14th century, the Palace of Westminster had been split into the privy palace to the south, which included the Painted Chamber, and the great palace to the north which

[73]The lack of clarity in where the king and Lords heard mass prior to the opening of parliament has led to the omission of this information from Fig. 2. The line representing the Commons provides an indication of its movement to Westminster Abbey, which has been omitted from Fig. 2.

housed administrative and legal offices, such as the exchequer, as well as spaces which were kept open to the public.[74] The movement of the Commons crossed this broadly accepted boundary and brings into consideration questions of public and private space in the late medieval period. David Austin has argued that, rather than identifying space as 'private' or 'public', the terms 'privy' and 'open' or 'common' are more useful.[75] By the late medieval period, 'privy' had strong connotations of service which involved contact with the body or person of the lord,[76] but was also used to refer to officers of the state.[77] For the purposes of this article, 'privy' refers to those enclosed spaces within the Palace of Westminster which could be associated with a closeness to the person of the king, and which could only be entered with permission. The terms 'open' or 'common' will then refer to those spaces in the palace where permission was not needed to enter, such as Westminster Hall, unless the definition of the space was altered by the presence of the king.

Using access analysis, Richardson has argued that the Painted Chamber at Westminster evolved from what she defines as a semi-private and semi-public space in the early 14th century, to an 'entirely public venue' in the 1360s.[78] It does not seem accurate, however, to consider the Painted Chamber an 'entirely public venue' in the period 1399 to 1484, nor an open or common space within the definitions utilised in this article. Chronicle evidence suggests that this boundary existed before the 15th century. In May 1357, Londoners congregated in Westminster Hall and waited there without incident, but they were subject to a 'thorough investigation' when they breached the barrier of the privy palace by entering the Lesser Hall.[79] In 1399, when parliament was opened in Westminster Hall, the parliament rolls specifically mention the presence of spectators.[80] From 1401 onwards, in those parliaments opened in the Painted Chamber, there is no mention of anyone other than parliamentary members as being present. Furthermore, petitions were to be received from citizens in open spaces and, although the triers of petitions were always named in the parliament rolls during the openings of parliament, the petitioners themselves would be gathered in Westminster Hall.[81] There was, therefore, a barrier placed, even if only for the duration of parliament, between the Painted Chamber and other areas of the Palace of Westminster through which only particular individuals could pass.

The Painted Chamber was, during the openings of parliament at least, a privy space. Its usage therefore demonstrated the king's authority in two key ways. First, the use of the Painted Chamber showed that the king had the power to define spaces as privy or open and to determine which groups and individuals had access to these spaces. More broadly, the king's power to define spaces can be seen in the displacement of the Commons from the Painted Chamber. The Commons had been allowed to use the Painted Chamber as its own

---

[74] C. Shenton, *The Day Parliament Burned Down* (Oxford, 2012), 12; KW, i, 534.

[75] David Austin, 'Private and Public: An Archaeological Consideration of Things', in *Die Vielfalt der Dinge: Neue Wege zur Analyse mittelalterlicher Sachkultur*, ed. Harry Künnel, Helmut Hundsbichler, Gerhard Jaritz and Thomas Kühtreiber (Vienna, 1998), 184.

[76] Austin, 'Private and Public', 184.

[77] Austin, 'Private and Public', 184.

[78] Richardson, 'Gender and Space in English Royal Palaces', 139–40.

[79] Anon., *Chronicon Anonymi Cantuariensis: The Chronicle of Anonymous of Canterbury, 1346–1365*, ed. and trans. Charity Scott-Stokes and Chris Given-Wilson (Oxford, 2008), 36–7.

[80] 'Parliament of October 1399, Text and Translation', ed. Given-Wilson, 9

[81] Shenton, *The Day Parliament Burned Down*, 8.

chamber for discussions during the 14th century.[82] When communication occurred between the Lords and Commons, delegates from the Lords would often meet the Commons in the latter's chamber.[83] By the 15th century, the Commons was made to communicate with the Lords in the Queen's Chamber,[84] and meetings of the Commons had been moved from the Painted Chamber to Westminster Abbey.[85] The crown had redefined the Painted Chamber, and its ability to manage space can be clearly seen. It was no longer available to the Commons as its own space. Instead, it had become more completely a venue in which the crown, Lords and the selected representatives which comprised the Commons should meet for the opening of parliament.

Second, there is the ability to command the movement of individuals. As Figure 2 shows, there was greater inconvenience to the Commons in its movements especially when considering the requirement for the Commons to move to meet with the Lords in the Queen's Chamber.[86] Even if the Lords is assumed to have heard mass in Westminster Abbey throughout this period, as it did in 1485, it would remain the case that once it was inside the Palace of Westminster that is where it would remain. The movements of the Commons through the Palace of Westminster more broadly echoed the authority which the king extended across the polity when he summoned a parliament. The Lords would be summoned directly through a writ of summons, whereas the Commons would be elected. However, they would all be required to move from separate parts of the country to the place which the crown had decided upon for parliament, showing the king's ability to demand investments of time, money, and energy from any of his subjects. During the openings of parliament the Commons was made, through this same means, to move into the Painted Chamber before being dismissed from the Palace of Westminster entirely. Thus, the king's control of the Commons' movements through the palace reflected his authority, as he was able to summon and dismiss members from his own presence, define which spaces they could enter and impose conditions upon this access.

This is not to suggest that these movements could not also be a means of fostering dialogue between the crown and Commons. Certainly, there was a definite societal hierarchy reflected in the differing levels of convenience in the movements of the Commons, Lords, and king. As part of undertaking this movement, however, the Commons was socially elevated. In being made to move from the common space in the north of the palace to the privy palace, the Commons was raised, even if only temporarily, above those whom it was meant to represent. The example of the 1399 opening of parliament in Westminster Hall has already been noted for its inclusion of spectators. It has also been observed that the move to the Painted Chamber massively decreased this accessibility. The Commons' ability to enter the space of the Painted Chamber denoted its political influence as a group of elected individuals. Unlike the wider commons whom they were elected to represent, the parliamentary Commons was able to communicate through the Speaker directly to the king. This access to the crown and to the Lords as a collective, albeit to a lesser

---

[82]Alasdair Hawkyard, 'From Painted Chamber to St Stephen's Chapel: The Meeting Places of the House of Commons at Westminster until 1603', *Parliamentary History*, xxi (2002), 62–4.

[83]J.G. Edwards, *The Commons in Medieval English Parliaments* (1958), 4–7.

[84]Edwards, *The Commons in Medieval English Parliaments*, 4–7.

[85]Harrison, 'Parliaments, MPs and the Buildings of Westminster', 142.

[86]Edwards, *The Commons in Medieval English Parliaments*, 4–7.

extent, provided a means of forming dialogues. It is plausible then that the command for the Commons to move into the Painted Chamber also behaved as an invitation to enter a parliamentary dialogue with the crown. A necessary part of this invitation was the elevation of the Commons above those whom it broadly represented.

Once all members were gathered, the opening of parliament was dominated by the Speaker for the Lords. The Lords' Speaker was also the mouthpiece for the crown and would be selected by the king in advance of parliament's opening.[87] In most cases the Speaker was the lord chancellor and occupied the position of bishop or archbishop. There were only seven occasions between 1399 and 1484 when the lord chancellor was not the Lords' Speaker,[88] and only in 1401 and 1411 was the Lords' Speaker a layman. By contrast, the election of the Commons' Speaker and his presentation to the king were not part of the opening of parliament. The Commons was directed to move into the chapter house or refectory of Westminster Abbey, returning later to present its Speaker to the king. By the 16th century, the crown nominated the Commons' Speaker.[89] For this earlier period there is insufficient evidence that the crown actively participated in selecting a Commons' Speaker,[90] although the Speaker did require the agreement of the crown to assume the role.[91] Speakers, if not agreed to by the crown or lord chancellor, could be pressured into stepping down. For example, in 1399 John Cheyne was nominated and assented to as Speaker on 14 October but pleaded to be excused on 15 October for sudden infirmity,[92] possibly following pressure from Archbishop Arundel.[93]

The differing roles of the Speakers for the Lords and Commons certainly emphasized royal authority as the Speaker chosen by the king, the individual most likely to behave as the crown's mouthpiece, dominated the opening of parliament. This dominance was curbed, however, by the placement of the election of the Commons' Speaker within the broader proceedings of parliament. In the order of parliament, the election of the Commons' Speaker occurred immediately after the opening of parliament.[94] Legislation was not passed, and taxation could not be granted, until the Commons' Speaker had been elected. It cannot be assumed that the crown intended its dialogue with the Commons to ever occur on equal terms. A necessary part of its formation was that the king would remain the key authority, and it is this which can be seen in the differences between the Commons' and Lords' Speakers as opposed to a lack of dialogue entirely. The Lords' Speaker took on the leading role in the opening, which would set up the forthcoming parliament, but parliament was fundamentally incomplete without at least the potential of input from the Commons.

---

[87] Philip Laundy, *The Office of the Speaker* (1964), 4.

[88] These were Oct. 1399, Jan. 1401, Jan. 1410, Nov. 1422, June 1467, and Oct. 1472.

[89] Alasdair Hawkyard, 'The Tudor Speakers 1485–1601: Choosing, Status, Work', in *Speakers and the Speakership: Presiding Officers and the Management of Business from the Middle Ages to the 21st Century*, ed. Paul Seaward (Chichester, 2010), 22–4.

[90] J.S. Roskell, *Parliament and Politics in Late Medieval England* (1981), 37–9.

[91] 'Introduction', in *Speakers and the Speakership*, ed. Seaward, 3.

[92] See 'Parliament of October 1399, Text and Translation', ed. Given-Wilson, 29: 'although he had been appointed … such an infirmity and illness had come to him just now … that he could not undertake the work'.

[93] Laundy, *The Office of the Speaker*, 144–5.

[94] E.g., see the election and presentation of the speaker in 'Richard III: Parliament of January 1484, Text and Translation', ed. Rosemary Horrox, in PROME, Volume XV, 9–10.

The Speaker for the Lords, once all members were gathered in the Painted Chamber, would deliver an opening address. These addresses could cover a wide variety of topics, but a main theme was often recorded in the rolls of parliament on those occasions when an opening address included the delivery of a sermon. The inclusion of a sermon was common during this period. Of the 50 parliaments held between 1399 and 1484, there are no enrolled records of sermons on only seven occasions.[95] The content of these sermons, upon initial examination, appear to reflect the king's authority without any sense of fostering a political dialogue. Much as the individual parliaments themselves, the opening addresses were meant to reflect the crown's response to contemporary circumstances. Like the images which adorned the walls of the Painted Chamber, however, the themes presented during the opening of parliament belied the expectations placed on those gathered for parliament, including the king. For example, in 1427, parliament gathered in the Painted Chamber and heard a sermon based on 2 Maccabees 4.6 in which the archbishop of York and chancellor of England spoke of the 'obligation of rulers to the subjects [and] … the obligation of subjects to their rulers'.[96] This invoked ideas of service which may have aided the facilitation of a dialogue between king and Commons, who were also surrounded by the Maccabees images featured on the walls of the Painted Chamber. Of those parliaments which were held in the Painted Chamber, four were opened under the main theme of the need for counsel,[97] two under the theme of the requirements for rule,[98] and two under the theme of justice.[99] In 1420, Henry V, at that time occupied with leading English campaigns in France, requested through the Lords' Speaker that those gathered in parliament should work to increase the 'common benefit of the realm'.[100] In this example the king has commanded the Commons as well as the Lords, but has also essentially requested aid in providing good governance while he is away from England. It is this element of requesting aid which best exemplifies the sort of co-operative dynamic between the crown and Commons which kings attempted to present throughout the 15th century. A rhetoric of shared responsibility for ensuring the common good of the realm underpinned the image of a co-operative dynamic between the crown and members of parliament. Overall, the theme presented within the sermon acted as a reminder of the duty of both parliamentarians and the king to serve the realm, prompting dialogue and lessening friction within parliament. The ideals and characteristics depicted by the images of the Painted Chamber were afforded authority through their connections to past kings. Similarly, the themes presented during

[95] There is very little extant information for the Nov. 1470 parliament, so it is unknown if a sermon was included in the opening address.

[96] 'Henry VI: Parliament of October 1427, Text and Translation', ed. Anne Curry, in PROME, Volume X, 326.

[97] 'Henry IV: Parliament of January 1404, Text and Translation', ed. Chris Given-Wilson, in PROME, Volume VIII, 227; 'Henry IV: Parliament of March 1406, Part 1: Text and Translation', ed. Chris Given-Wilson, in PROME, Volume VIII, 326; 'Henry V: Parliament of May 1413, Text and Translation', ed. Chris Given-Wilson, in PROME, Volume IX, 5; 'Henry V: Parliament of December 1420, Text and Translation', ed. Chris Given-Wilson, in PROME, Volume IX, 249.

[98] 'Parliament of September 1429, Text and Translation', ed. Curry, 376; 'Henry VI: Parliament of January 1431, Text and Translation', ed. Anne Curry, in PROME, Volume X, 444.

[99] 'Henry VI: Parliament of July 1433, Text and Translation', ed. Anne Curry, in PROME, Volume XI, 75; 'Edward IV: Parliament of April 1463, Text and Translation', ed. Anne Curry and Rosemary Horrox, in PROME, Volume XIII, 92.

[100] 'Parliament of December 1420, Text and Translation', ed. Given-Wilson, 249.

the openings of parliament were imbued with authority as they were presented as part of a sermon.

The importance of the use of sermons in forging this dialogue cannot be underestimated. In 15th-century parliaments, speeches and sermons were considered distinct from one another. The parliament rolls used the key phrases 'the reasons for summons' and 'taking as his theme' to emphasize the distinction between the two, with the latter always followed by a scripturally-based theme.[101] Furthermore, the phrase 'taking as his theme' is not used in the parliaments of 1401 or 1411 when the Speakers were laymen and so unable to present a sermon.[102] Evidently parliament could be opened without a sermon featured in the opening address, yet the 'taking as his theme' phrase is recorded in 42 of the 49 extant rolls available for this period.[103] The sermon not only added authority and an additional element of formality to proceedings overall, but also aided in the creation of a greater sense of equality. Discussion could be fostered because the delivery of the chosen theme also served as a reminder of the religious authority which all the members of parliament, including the king, were bound to obey.

5. *Conclusion*

Dialogue was undoubtedly integral to the functioning of late medieval parliaments on numerous levels. This article has attempted to provide a glimpse into just one very particular element of parliament, but there remains more work to be undertaken to improve collective understanding of the nuances of 15th-century political culture and its impact upon political realities. That the Painted Chamber at Westminster was a key parliamentary building during the late medieval period is shown by its continued usage for the openings of parliament, as well as its earlier function as the Commons chamber and a meeting place between both the Lords and the Commons. Part of the Painted Chamber's significance, and a reason for its continued usage, was its usefulness as a tool in presenting a fundamentally cooperative, albeit uneven, dynamic and maintaining a political dialogue between the crown and the Commons which crossed social strata and extended outwards from the centre of the polity, through the Commons, and to the localities. Evidence of conscious efforts by the crown to construct this dynamic can be seen in a number of the material and historical features of the Painted Chamber, echoed in the proceedings of the opening of parliament in terms of the movements of the Commons, the role of the two Speakers, and the content

[101] For examples of this phrasing, see 'Parliament of January 1404, Text and Translation', ed. Given-Wilson, 227; and 'Henry IV: Parliament of October 1407, Text and Translation', ed. Chris Given-Wilson, in PROME, Volume VIII, 419.

[102] 'Parliament of January 1401, Text and Translation', ed. Given-Wilson, 98; 'Henry IV: Parliament of November 1411, Text and Translation', ed. Chris Given-Wilson, in PROME, Volume VIII, 515–6.

[103] This phrase is not seen in 'Parliament of January 1401, Text and Translation', ed. Given-Wilson, 98; 'Parliament of November 1411, Text and Translation', ed. Given-Wilson, 515–6; 'Henry VI: Parliament of February 1449, Text and Translation', ed. Anne Curry and Rosemary Horrox, in PROME, Volume XII, 41; 'Parliament of November 1449, Text and Translation', ed. Curry and Horrox, 81; 'Henry VI: Parliament of November 1450, Text and Translation', ed. Anne Curry and Rosemary Horrox, in PROME, Volume XII, 172; 'Henry VI: Parliament of March 1453, Text and Translation', ed. Anne Curry and Rosemary Horrox, in PROME, Volume XII, 229. There is no extant parliament roll for the 1470 parliament held during Henry VI's readeption period. 'Edward IV: Parliament of November 1470, Introduction', ed. Rosemary Horrox, in PROME, Volume XIII, 391.

of the opening sermons presented within the Painted Chamber. The increasing political influence of the Commons, and its willingness to exercise this influence to challenge the authority of the king, ensured the continuing need for this dialogue throughout the 15th century.

The Elizabethan House of Commons and St Stephen's Chapel Westminster

J.P.D. COOPER

This essay explores the significance of the Elizabethan house of commons meeting in a converted royal chapel within the Palace of Westminster. In 1548 the dissolved collegiate chapel of St Stephen at Westminster was given over to the exclusive use of the Commons, providing MPs with a dedicated meeting space for the first time. Although a great deal has been written about Elizabethan parliaments, little attention has been paid to the physical spaces within which MPs gathered, debated and legislated. Drawing on parliamentary diaries and exchequer records and informed by digital reconstructions of the Commons chamber modelled by the St Stephen's Chapel project at the University of York, this essay argues for the enduring influence of the architecture and decoration of the medieval chapel on the procedure, culture, ritual, and self-awareness of the Elizabethan house of commons. Famously likened to a theatre by the MP and writer on parliamentary procedure, John Hooker, the Commons chamber is analysed as a space in which parliamentary speeches were performed and disrupted. The sound of debate is contrasted with other kinds of noise including scoffing and laughter, disruptive coughing, and prayers led by the clerk and the Speaker of the Commons. The iconography of the chamber, including the royal arms above the Speaker's chair and the mace carried by the serjeant-at-arms, is interpreted as enabling a culture of counsel and debate as much as an assertion of monarchical power. Evidence is also presented for the Commons chamber as a site of political memory.

Keywords: debate; house of commons; memory; Palace of Westminster; prayer; royal arms; serjeant-at-arms; Speaker of the Commons; St Stephen's Chapel; voting

1

The parliaments of Elizabeth I's reign have long been identified as a key moment in the development of the house of commons. Lively debates about the religious settlement and the succession to the throne brought the mysteries of state into the public domain, sparking the queen to complain that 'Parlyment matters was the common table talk at ordinaryes, which was a thing against the dignitie of the Howse.'[1] Petitions from MPs pointing out Elizabeth's responsibility to marry, or demanding the execution of Mary Stuart, seemed to cut into the royal prerogative. The Elizabethan Commons heard some remarkable speeches, whether Sir Walter Mildmay on the 'swarming hither of popish priests and monkish Jesuites', or

---

[1] *Proceedings in the Parliaments of Elizabeth I*, ed. T.E. Hartley (3 vols, 1981–5), ii, 118; David Dean, 'Public Space, Private Affairs: Committees, Petitions and Lobbies in the Early Modern English Parliament', in *Parliament at Work: Parliamentary Committees, Political Power and Public Access in Early Modern England*, ed. Chris R. Kyle and Jason Peacey (Woodbridge, 2002), 174; Norman L. Jones, 'Parliament and the Political Society of Elizabethan England', in *Tudor Political Culture*, ed. Dale Hoak (Cambridge, 1995), 236.

member for Barnstaple, Richard Martin, condemning monopoly suppliers as 'these blood-suckers of the commonwealth'.[2] By any measure this was a remarkable generation of MPs: noisy and articulate, challenging traditional boundaries of the acceptable in politics, balancing their loyalty to God, crown and nation with their responsibilities to their local communities. The queen might exchange conventional courtesies with the Speaker at the opening of parliament, but she also harangued the Commons as 'unbrydelyd parsons whose hedes were nevere snaffled by the rydere' when her blood was up.[3]

The Elizabethan Commons has been the subject of intense scrutiny from some of the best-known historians who work on this period, with much attendant controversy and counter-argument. And yet this formidable array of scholarship has had surprisingly little to say about the Commons as a place, namely the former royal and collegiate chapel of St Stephen acquired in 1548 and adapted for the exclusive use of MPs, as distinct from a legislative powerhouse or 'the premier point of contact between rulers and ruled'.[4] Certainly, Edward VI's modification of the former royal chapel at Westminster as a home for the Commons has been noted by parliamentary historians, indeed elevated into a turning point: David Dean describes the move into St Stephen's Chapel as 'one of the most significant developments in the history of parliament'.[5] However, the reasons why this should be the case have not been fully thought through. Claims that St Stephen's 'immediately gave a distinctive tone to the Commons' proceedings and determined much of how the House did its business', as one recent study of parliament puts it, need to be substantiated.[6]

In pursuing this theme, innovation must be balanced with continuity. The Commons had a long history of meeting at Westminster, albeit in borrowed, rather than dedicated, space: the Painted Chamber within the palace in the 14th century, and more recently in the refectory of the abbey.[7] The proceedings of the Commons were also of some antiquity, documented in texts including the 14th-century *Modus Tenendi Parliamentum*, as glossed and printed by the Elizabethan antiquary and MP, John Hooker, in 1572.[8] Attributing procedural development to the move into St Stephen's is not straightforward, and cannot simply be assumed. For instance, the custom of voting by division, sometimes associated with the new chamber, was first recorded in the 1523 parliament meeting at Blackfriars; it could be older than that.[9]

And yet there can be no doubt that meeting in a converted royal chapel, at the junction between the public and 'privy' spaces of the Palace of Westminster, gave a distinct architectural context to the political culture of the elected house of parliament. New practices

---

[2] *Proceedings in the Parliaments of Elizabeth I*, ed. Hartley, i, 505; iii, 375.

[3] *Proceedings in the Parliaments of Elizabeth I*, ed. Hartley, i, 146.

[4] G.R. Elton, 'Tudor Government: The Points of Contact', in G.R. Elton, *Studies in Tudor and Stuart Politics and Government* (Cambridge, 1982), iii, 21.

[5] David Dean, 'Image and Ritual in the Tudor Parliaments', in *Tudor Political Culture*, ed. Hoak, 246. Dean dates the move to 1549.

[6] Chris Bryant, *Parliament the Biography: Ancestral Voices* (2014), 157.

[7] On the Painted Chamber, see Jennifer Caddick's essay in this volume.

[8] David Harrison, 'Parliaments, MPs and the Buildings of Westminster in the Middle Ages', in *Westminster II: The Art, Architecture and Archaeology of the Royal Palace*, ed. Warwick Rodwell and Tim Tatton-Brown (Leeds, 2015), 134–6, 142–6; S. Mendyk, 'Hooker, John (*c.*1527–1601)', *ODNB*.

[9] Alasdair Hawkyard, *The House of Commons 1509–1558: Personnel, Procedure, Precedent and Change* (Chichester, 2016), 5–6, 332–3. I am grateful for Paul Seaward's advice on this point.

developed, and existing trends were accelerated or given greater solidity by the inherited space of St Stephen's. The identity of being a member of the Commons was likewise inflected by the new meeting place. Its function may have changed, but St Stephen's remained royal space. MPs had acquired their own premises more as tenants than owner-occupiers. The iconography and ceremony which surrounded them made it clear that Westminster remained a palace, even if no longer habitually inhabited by the sovereign. The famous conflicts (if conflicts they were) between Elizabeth and her parliaments took place within one of the queen's houses. That did not mean that MPs were quiescent; there is much evidence to the contrary. But it did supply an architectural backdrop to the relationship between crown and Commons, of which MPs would have been acutely aware and which needs to be factored into our understanding of Elizabethan politics.

This essay considers themes of space and sound in the Elizabethan house of commons, informed by the research and digital modelling conducted by the St Stephen's Chapel AHRC-funded project at the University of York.[10] How much did it matter that, unlike the parliaments of Henry VIII's reign, the elected knights and burgesses now had a home of their own? In what ways did the converted space of St Stephen's Chapel influence the development of parliamentary procedure, or the ritual which regulated the rhythm of the Commons, or the experience of being a member of parliament? Do the architecture and geography of the Palace of Westminster have any significant bearing on the vexed question of the institutional maturity and self-awareness of the Elizabethan Commons? Analysed in project meetings and study days with the History of Parliament Trust, these questions have been further refined by the Virtual St Stephen's 3D modelling of the chapel and Commons chamber which has run in parallel with the archival work of the project. This essay represents an attempt to distil the results of a collaborative set of research processes, and to bring them into conversation with a historical debate on Elizabethan parliaments which has lost some of its impetus in recent years. In short, it seeks to restore both space and sound to the Elizabethan house of commons, be that formal debate, laughter and scoffing, or prayer.

The following discussion is divided into three sections. The historiography of later 16th-century parliaments is full and contested, offering sometimes diametrically opposed interpretations of essentially similar sources. Having introduced St Stephen's Chapel itself, the next section of the essay identifies key features of these debates in order to make a case for closer scrutiny of the architectural environment in which Elizabethan MPs came together. The spaces of St Stephen's Chapel, their modification for use as a chamber and lobby for the Commons and the influence of the building upon parliamentary procedure and the culture of debate, form the subject of the following section. John Hooker's description of the Commons as 'made like a Theater' is well known among parliamentary historians, but until now it has been difficult to visualise owing to the absence of any depictions of the interior of the chamber before the 1620s (and even this evidence needs to be questioned). The digital reconstruction of a Commons chamber which Hooker might have recognized, modelled by the St Stephen's project team from a range of manuscript, architectural and visual data, offers a new tool to historians seeking to understand the lower House as a

---

[10] 'St Stephen's Chapel Westminster: Visual and Political Culture 1292–1941', AH/K006991/1 (2013–17), funded by the Arts and Humanities Research Council and the University of York in partnership with the UK parliament; principal investigator, Dr John Cooper.

functioning institution and place of assembly as distinct from a collective biography of MPs. The St Stephen's visualisations are freely available on the web, underpinning and complementing the argument of this essay.[11]

By highlighting key features of the chamber, including the Speaker's chair and the royal arms, the digital model can also inform discussion of symbolism and ceremony in the Commons. Influenced by art history and textual studies, historians of Tudor political culture have become ever more alert to the importance of ritual and representations of power. Efforts to apply this methodology to parliament, however, have been sporadic and focused more on the upper than the lower House. The final section of the essay reflects on symbol and ritual in the Elizabethan Commons, the prominence of royal iconography and the practice of prayer within the chamber, in order to cast light on the common life and collective identity of Elizabethan members of parliament. Most importantly, evidence will be presented in support of the contention, present in the existing scholarly literature but hitherto not fully explored, that the relocation of the Commons to St Stephen's Chapel had profound political consequences which played out during Elizabeth I's reign. St Stephen's was no longer sacred space, but visual traces of its former use could still be seen. Just as important were the royal connotations of the building, both the former chapel itself and the wider Palace of Westminster. Exploring space and sound in the Elizabethan house of commons enables a subtler understanding of the parliamentary politics of a period often seen as crucial in its constitutional significance.

2. *Locating Elizabethan Parliaments*

Founded by Edward I in 1292 but not fully furnished until late in Edward III's reign, St Stephen's Westminster was the most splendid royal chapel in the king's principal residence in the capital.[12] Built at a right angle to Westminster Hall at its south-east corner and facing east across the river, St Stephen's Chapel was made up of five richly-decorated bays, surmounted by a clerestory and topped with a timber vault. A sequence of exceptional wall paintings mingled biblical scenes from the books of Job and Tobit with royal and noble heraldry. A depiction of St George presenting King Edward III to the Virgin and Child appeared next to the altar. In 1348 a college of dean, canons, vicars and lay clerks was endowed to serve the chapel, requiring the insertion of choir stalls and a substantial pulpitum or screen to divide the space reserved for the college and royal family from the more public western part of St Stephen's; the second of these features would be an important influence on the post-dissolution use of the chapel as the Commons chamber. Stonework in the royal colours of red and blue was complemented by Purbeck marble which had been highly polished to reflect candlelight. The precise relationship between the two buildings is disputed by art historians, but St Stephen's Chapel has often been seen as a response to

---

[11] Visualisations of St Stephen's Chapel, the Commons chamber and the palace environment can be seen at *https://www.virtualststephens.org.uk/explore* (accessed 19 Sept. 2018).

[12] The following two paragraphs draw freely on research conducted by the medieval section of the St Stephen's project and the digital modelling team at the Centre for the Study of Christianity and Culture at York, notably the work of Tim Ayers, Elizabeth Biggs, Anthony Masinton, and Maureen Jurkowski. I have benefited greatly from their guidance on the pre-1548 chapel and college of St Stephen. This essay also utilises transcriptions of manuscript records made by project research assistant, Simon Neal.

the Sainte-Chapelle in Paris, a 'life-sized reliquary' for the Crown of Thorns relic owned by Louis XI. Within England it became widely recognized as 'a benchmark of architectural grandeur', closely associated with royal power.[13] As a choral foundation, St Stephen's shared responsibility with the Chapel Royal for the liturgical cycle of masses and prayers for the royal dead maintained by the Plantagenet and early Tudor monarchy.[14] That the acoustics of St Stephen's Chapel were designed for sacred polyphony more than speech-making is a factor which needs to be taken into account in our understanding of space and sound in the Elizabethan Commons.[15]

Like the Sainte-Chapelle, St Stephen's was a two-storey structure: a loftily magnificent upper chapel dedicated to St Stephen protomartyr (where the royal family and elite visitors had worshipped, converted to become the house of commons in 1548 and destroyed in the fire which consumed the old Palace of Westminster in 1834), and a lower chapel dedicated to the Virgin Mary (which partially survived the 1834 fire and was restored as a chapel by Edward Barry, now known as St Mary Undercroft). The distinctive double height of St Stephen's Chapel is captured in two near-contemporary views across the river: one by the Flemish topographical artist, Anthonis van den Wyngaerde, dating from c.1544, the other provisionally attributed to Lucas Cornelis de Kock and currently split into two sections owned by the Victoria & Albert Museum and the Louvre.[16] These drawings show St Stephen's to be a landmark on the Westminster skyline, instantly identifiable and particularly impressive from the river. At around 116ft (35.35m) to the parapet of the east gable, it stood a good 15ft higher than the roof of Westminster Hall.[17] Its painted windows were replaced with clear glass on the dissolution of the college, further modified by a 'penthouse' or awning in 1621 to reduce the glare of the morning sun (the Commons met mainly in the mornings), but otherwise the exterior of St Stephen's was not very significantly altered until the clerestory was removed by Christopher Wren in 1692. To Elizabethan MPs approaching across Old Palace Yard or disembarking at one of the landing stages along the river, the Commons would have presented itself as an obviously medieval building, symbolic of the antiquity of the lower House even if its occupation of this space dated only from Edward VI's reign.

If there has been comparatively little discussion of questions of space and sound within the Elizabethan house of commons, then the broader history of the institution hardly qualifies as a neglected topic. The 13 sessions of parliament under Queen Elizabeth have been

[13]John Goodall, 'St Stephen's Chapel, Westminster', in *Westminster: Art, Architecture and Archaeology*, ed. Rodwell and Tatton-Brown, 112–13.

[14]On St Stephen's and the Chapel Royal see Elizabeth Biggs, 'The College and Canons of St Stephen's, Westminster, 1358–1548', University of York PhD, 2017, ch. 6.

[15]On the acoustics of St Stephen's as the Commons chamber, see Catriona Cooper's essay in this volume.

[16]Wyngaerde's drawing of Westminster is in the Ashmolean Museum in Oxford, WA.1950.206.1; see *The Panorama of London circa 1544*, ed. H.M. Colvin and Susan Foister (1996), 17; and H.M. Colvin, R.A. Brown, J.M. Crook, M.H. Port et al., *The History of the King's Works* (6 vols, 1963–82) [hereafter cited as KW], iv, 9. The two sections of the drawing perhaps by Lucas Cornelis de Kock are in the Victoria & Albert Museum (acc. no. E 128–1924) and the Musée du Louvre, Paris (INV 18702, verso); see Mark Collins, 'The Topography of the Old Palace of Westminster, 1510–1834', in *Westminster: Art, Architecture and Archaeology*, ed. Rodwell and Tatton-Brown, 207; and Ann Saunders, 'Westminster Hall: A Sixteenth Century Drawing?', *London Journal*, xii (1986), 29–35.

[17]Estimated dimensions from Anthony Masinton, based on surveys by John Carter and Frederick Mackenzie and the 16th-century drawing of St Stephen's in the Victoria & Albert Museum, see above, note 16. The height of Westminster Hall is 90ft 6ins (27.58m) to the ridge of the roof.

a focus of scholarly interest ever since Sir Simonds D'Ewes borrowed from the clerk of the Commons 'one of the original journal-books of Parliaments of that House in Queen Elizabeth's time' in order to compile his own account, complete by 1637 and published by his nephew, Paul Bowes, in 1682.[18] The modern historiography has gone through several waves of interpretation and revision since John Neale conceptualised the debate about Elizabethan parliaments as a series of encounters between the Commons and the monarchy. Neale's influential book *The Elizabethan House of Commons* appeared in 1949, aiming to analyse the institution at work during what he characterised as a 'crucial stage' in the history of the Commons. Two further studies of Queen Elizabeth and the Commons had followed by 1957, and Neale's research also fed into the biographical survey of Elizabethan MPs published in three volumes by the History of Parliament Trust in 1981. Where is the Commons chamber in all of this?

Aimed at the general, as much as the academic, reader but drawing on deep knowledge of local and national archives, Neale's *The Elizabethan House of Commons* has three pages on St Stephen's Chapel, in chapter 19. The narrative is framed in an interesting way. Interpreting a description of the lower House in John Hooker's *The Order and Usage How to Keepe a Parlement in England*, Neale likened the seating arrangements in the 16th-century house of commons to practice in the modern-day British parliament. Neale described a 'front government bench' on the Speaker's right, a 'front opposition bench' on his left: a 'strikingly familiar' basic setting, 'unchanged through the centuries'.[19] In the seminal modern study of Elizabethan parliaments, we appear to have an informed argument that the move into St Stephen's was a significant step along the way towards modern-day parliamentary practice. The problem is that Neale slightly misquotes his source, John Hooker, who actually describes the privy council and other chief officers of the crown sitting 'Upon the lower rowe on bothe sides [of] the Speaker', thus facing each other rather than sitting together.[20] Proximity to the Speaker's chair was clearly a marker of political and social status, hence the councillors and household officers arranged on either side. Writing in the *Oxford Dictionary of National Biography*, Patrick Collinson noted what he calls Neale's 'instinct … to look for the first shoots of the modern parliamentary constitution'; we see that instinct represented here.[21]

One of John Neale's pupils was Geoffrey Elton, also destined to write a formidable amount on the subject of Tudor parliaments. Elton's own entry in the *Oxford Dictionary of National Biography*, similarly written by Patrick Collinson, describes the 'almost obsessional vendetta' which he conducted against John Neale. Elton moved firmly onto his former tutor's territory in his final book *The Parliament of England 1559–1581*, and he came to a 'drastically different' set of conclusions about a house of commons that Neale had characterised as rising on a wave of puritan opposition to the crown. Elton used the History of Parliament volumes which Neale had inspired to prove that 'the puritan choir is a myth

---

[18] *The Autobiography and Correspondence of Sir Simonds D'Ewes*, ed. J.O. Halliwell (2 vols, 1845), i, 414; J.M. Blatchly, 'D'Ewes, Sir Simonds, First Baronet (1602–1650)', *ODNB*.

[19] J.E. Neale, *The Elizabethan House of Commons* (1949), 364–5.

[20] *Parliament in Elizabethan England: John Hooker's Order and Usage*, ed. V.F. Snow (New Haven, CT, 1977), 164.

[21] Patrick Collinson, 'Neale, Sir John Ernest (1890–1975)', *ODNB*.

and should be removed from the annals of history'.[22] He did not, however, have anything significant to say about the Commons chamber.

Building on the work of both Neale and Elton, Jennifer Loach's monograph on Tudor parliaments observed that 'the layout of [St Stephen's], and, in particular, of its antechamber, was to have an important effect on the way in which procedure developed in the Lower House', notably the way in which voting took place. Loach's opinion is telling, given her expertise on the subject, but regrettably she took the point no further.[23] Considerably richer in architectural detail is Alasdair Hawkyard's exploration of the meeting places of the Commons since the 14th century and the procedures that developed within them. Hawkyard suggests, for instance, that the tiered seating visible in the earliest visual sources for the Commons' interior had a precedent in temporary structures installed in the chapter house of Westminster Abbey when the Commons assembled there for the Good Parliament of 1376.[24] Work by David Dean on the practice of lobbying within the Commons, and Norman Jones on numerous aspects of parliamentary culture, similarly invites questions about the physical spaces of, and patterns of movement within, parliament.[25] The St Stephen's Chapel project offers an opportunity to locate this body of research within a fuller understanding of the topography of the Elizabethan Commons chamber and the wider Palace of Westminster. Bringing together an edited collection on Elizabethan parliaments, Dean and Jones explained how the book arose from their 'conviction that the Elizabethan parliament needed to be located in its context, identifying what it did and how it did it'.[26] To that agenda, we can now add, *where* it did it.

There is another justification for reviving the debate about the Elizabethan house of commons. Early modern political historians have grown steadily more confident about interpreting representations of power, whether the ritual of the royal court, preaching at Paul's Cross and in parish churches, the architecture of great houses and town halls, or civic ceremonial in London and other urban centres. Parliament naturally lends itself to analysis as a theatre. It was in precisely these terms that John Hooker described the house of commons in 1572, and even Elton referred to the Commons as a 'stage for political argument and general debate'.[27] Elizabethan historians can take inspiration from colleagues studying the 17th century who have engaged more directly with this aspect of the political culture of the Commons. For Chris Kyle, parliament in the 1620s was 'an auditorium as vigorous and dynamic as any playhouse', 'preeminently a place of performance'.[28] The Palace of Westminster has been likened to 'a seventeenth century tourist attraction', the Hall in particular drawing large crowds to witness 'spectacles' such as state trials or royal

---

[22] G.R. Elton, *The Parliament of England 1559–1581* (Cambridge, 1986), viii, 351.

[23] Jennifer Loach, *Parliament under the Tudors* (Oxford, 1991), 43, 49.

[24] Alasdair Hawkyard, 'From Painted Chamber to St Stephen's Chapel: The Meeting Places of the House of Commons at Westminster until 1603', *Parliamentary History*, xxi (2002), 64–6, 68, 74.

[25] The recorder of London, William Fleetwood, for instance, was lobbied by a draper and a London alderman 'at the parliament door' in favour of reducing the statutory breadth of woollen cloth: David Dean, *Law-Making and Society in Late Elizabethan England: The Parliament of England, 1584–1601* (Cambridge, 1996), 135.

[26] D.M. Dean and Norman L. Jones, 'Representation, Ideology and Action in the Elizabethan Parliaments', in *The Parliaments of Elizabethan England*, ed. D.M. Dean and N.L. Jones (Oxford, 1990), 1.

[27] *Hooker's Order and Usage*, ed. Snow, 163; Elton, *Parliament of England*, 25.

[28] Chris R. Kyle, *Theater of State: Parliament and Political Culture in Early Modern England* (Stanford, CA, 2012), 1–2.

speeches.[29] If the Elizabethan Commons also qualifies as a stage, then we need more of an understanding of backdrop and props as well as players.

3. *St Stephen's Chapel as the Commons Chamber*

St Stephen's college was dissolved under the provisions of the second Chantries Act in 1547, the speed of its fall implying it may have been a test case for the government of Edward VI.[30] Surveyor of the royal works, Lawrence Bradshaw, was authorised to spend £15 14s. on 'sondry charges made & done in & upon the P[ar]lyament house at Westm[inster] some tyme Saynt Stephens Chappell' in January 1548, before the Easter date when the king was formally empowered to take possession of properties dissolved under the act. Hawkyard concludes that the chapel had been 'designated in advance for the Commons' use' as its 'permanent home', and that MPs moved into St Stephen's in November 1548 for the second session of Edward VI's first parliament.[31] Given the sum spent, the preparation of the chapel for its new role can have been rudimentary at best: perhaps an experiment. If so, then it was clearly successful, because within a year the crown was spending much larger sums to create a chamber that could accommodate several hundred MPs.

Whether St Stephen's was intended to be a 'permanent' new home for the Commons is a moot point. The lord chancellor directed the Commons to choose its Speaker 'at their accustomed Place' when Edward VI's second parliament opened in March 1553, implying that there may already have been a degree of association between the institution and the building.[32] Set against this is the fact that Queen Mary initially planned to summon her own second parliament to Oxford in February 1554, perhaps out of queasiness that her Commons should assemble in a plundered catholic chapel; the substantial sum of £116 17s. 2½d. was spent readying Christ Church 'and other places' before parliament reverted to Westminster.[33] In August 1625, the Commons relocated to Oxford's Divinity School, and Oxford would host the parliament summoned by King Charles I in 1644. Practice did sometimes vary in Elizabeth's reign, for instance the use of the Lesser or White Hall instead of the House for the practical ceremony of taking the roll-call of MPs arriving in November 1584: 'not befor so used', as Thomas Cromwell noted in his journal.[34] But the debating chamber itself remained in St Stephen's, the growing solidity of its fixtures and fittings contrasting with the temporary structures installed in previous meeting places and serving as a reminder of the Commons' existence even when parliament was not in session. Payments to the serjeant imply that the royal arms above the Speaker's chair were removed for safe keeping when parliament was prorogued or dissolved, but other features remained in place: presumably the Speaker's chair and the clerks' table, certainly the distinctive tiers of seating for members.[35] Given its proximity to the public space of Westminster Hall and

[29] Chris R. Kyle and Jason Peacey, ' "Under Cover of So Much Coming and Going": Public Access to Parliament and the Political Process in Early Modern England', in *Parliament at Work*, ed. Kyle and Peacey, 4.

[30] Biggs, 'College and Canons of St Stephen's', 117.

[31] TNA, E 351/3326; Hawkyard, *House of Commons 1509–1558*, 195; KW, iv, 291–2.

[32] *CJ*, i, 27.

[33] Hawkyard, *House of Commons 1509–1558*, 199.

[34] *Proceedings in the Parliaments of Elizabeth I*, ed. Hartley, ii, 66.

[35] For instance, the fee of 40s. claimed by Serjeant Cowyer at the end of the 1589 parliament: TNA, E 351/3223.

the accessibility of the lobby located in the former outer chapel of St Stephen, it is not unlikely that the curious could have gained access to the chamber when parliament was not in session, for a fee to the serjeant or the keeper of the palace. Hooker explains that no one 'beeing not one of the Parlament house: ought to enter or come within the house, as long as the sitting is there', leaving open the possibility of access at other times.[36] Visiting Westminster in 1598, the German traveller, Paul Hentzner, seems to have been describing the Commons rather than the Lords when he refers to seats and wainscot of Irish wood 'in the chamber where the parliament is usually held'.[37]

As a college and chapel closed down by the dissolution of the chantries, St Stephen's fits into a broader pattern of the recycling of monastic and other ecclesiastical buildings made redundant by the religious reformations of Henry VIII and Edward VI. Maurice Howard has estimated that as many as half of the former monastic buildings in England may have been put to new use, even if their collective contribution to architectural development has not been fully appreciated.[38] In the case of St Stephen's, this process of adaptation invites questions about the fate of its sumptuous decoration and fabric. Did any of the furnishings of the former chapel remain in place? The altar coverings of crimson velvet and cloth of gold, devotional images made of silver and elaborate red and blue hangings in the quire were all carefully inventoried before being removed, despite the persistent myth in the modern Palace of Westminster that the altar itself somehow remained in place, hence the culture of MPs bowing as they enter the chamber; inconceivable for a house of commons spearheading the Reformation of Edward VI.[39]

Interest has also focused on the choir stalls of St Stephen's, on the assumption that the antiphonal singing of the medieval chapel was somehow echoed in oppositional debate across the aisle of the Commons. One recent account asserts that the stalls 'were at once used by the opposing sides of Parliament without alteration to the ecclesiastical layout, thus instituting the traditional plan of the Commons' Chamber down to the present time', a claim also upheld on the Living Heritage pages of the UK parliament website.[40] Quite apart from the question about what 'opposing sides of Parliament' might mean in this period, this interpretation of the evidence cannot be correct. At full strength (as it was on the eve of the Reformation) the college of St Stephen numbered 12 canons and 13

[36] *Hooker's Order and Usage*, ed. Snow, 186. By 'Parlement house' Hooker means both the Commons and the Lords ('parliament chamber' referred exclusively to the Lords in this period). Thomas Cromwell's journal distinguishes between 'the Howse' and 'owr Howse': *Proceedings in the Parliaments of Elizabeth I*, ed. Hartley, ii, 102.

[37] Paul Hentzner, *Itinerarium Germaniae, Galliae, Angliae, Italiae* (Nuremberg, 1612), 126, 'In Camera, ubi Parlamentum congregari & haberi solet, *sellae & parietes* [seats and walls] *ex ligno Hybernico* fabricate sunt'. The former St Stephen's Chapel would have been easier for a visitor to access than the house of lords in the privy palace, where the benches were presumably cleared away when not in use and the walls were hung with tapestries: *CSP Ven.*, 1558–80, p. 23. I am grateful to Paul Hunneyball and Robin Eagles for their advice on these points. See also L.L. Ford, 'Hentzner, Paul (1558–1623)', *ODNB*.

[38] Maurice Howard, 'Recycling the Monastic Fabric: Beyond the Act of Dissolution', in *The Archaeology of the Reformation 1480–1580*, ed. David Gaimster and Roberta Gilchrist (Leeds, 2003), 221.

[39] The 1548 inventory of St Stephen's Chapel and the 'nether' or lower chapel (the modern St Mary Undercroft) is TNA, E 117/11/49.

[40] Collins, 'Topography of the Old Palace of Westminster', 215; Living Heritage pages at *http://www.parliament.uk/about/living-heritage/building/palace/estatehistory/reformation-1834/shaping-the-commons/* (accessed 18 Sept. 2018).

vicars, supplemented by four lay clerks and seven choristers.[41] At Elizabeth's accession, the Commons stood at 398, its rapid recent growth attributable to the admission of Welsh MPs and the vigorous enfranchisement of boroughs under Edward and Mary. The disparity in numbers is obvious: the Commons exceeded the canons by a factor of ten. For the former chapel space to function in its new role, the choir stalls must have been replaced with tiered seating as part of the £344 16s. 10½d. spent to convert the upper chapel as summarized in Lawrence Bradshaw's retrospective account for 1549–50. A further £18 12s. 2¼d. was spent on the new house of commons in Edward's reign and £63 15s. 1d. under Philip and Mary, presumably for maintenance and readying of the chamber rather than significant further modification.[42]

Reporting on the opening of Elizabeth's first parliament in January 1559, the Venetian ambassador likened the Commons chamber to a 'theatre'. The same description was expanded by John Hooker, who described the chamber as 'made like a Theater, having foure rowes of seates one aboove an other ro[u]nd about the same'.[43] James Burbage's pioneering theatre in Shoreditch dates from 1576, four years after the publication of the *Order and Usage*; Hooker may, instead, have been thinking of the temporary wooden scaffold known as a *theatrum* constructed in St Mary's in Oxford for the academic disputations held annually in the church.[44] Even with the provision of tiered seating, the new Commons chamber was too small to seat all the elected members at one time – one feature that the first dedicated house of commons arguably has bequeathed to its modern successor.[45] Hawkyard contends that the location of the royal pew in the medieval chapel has a bearing on the location of the government front bench in the modern parliament, to the Speaker's right: 'the original choice of these seats by ministers was determined by their awareness of the exact location occupied by Plantagenet and Tudor kings when worshipping in the chapel'. But this may be too much of an argument for continuity. As we have seen, Hooker described the chief officers of the crown sitting on both sides of the Speaker, and by the time that 'government leaders' developed in anything like the modern sense, the location of the royal stall would long have been forgotten.[46]

The new chamber measured some 62ft 5ins (19.04m) in length and 32ft 2ins (9.8m) in width, according to the most recent calculations, appreciably smaller than the refectory of Westminster Abbey where the Commons had usually met during the 15th and earlier

---

[41] In 1548, the college of St Stephen was one canon short (owing to the recent death of John Crayford) but otherwise had its full stipulated staff of clerks, choristers and chantry priests: Biggs, 'College and Canons of St Stephen's', 163.

[42] TNA, E 351/3326.

[43] *Hooker's Order and Usage*, ed. Snow, 163; *CSP Ven.*, 1558–80, p. 23.

[44] Anthony Geraghty, *The Sheldonian Theatre: Architecture and Learning in Seventeenth-Century Oxford* (New Haven, CT, 2013), 15–18. With its tiered seating, vice chancellor's throne and doorkeepers to raise and lower the bar, St Mary's as configured for the act of disputations shared several key features with the house of commons meeting in St Stephen's Chapel. I am grateful to James Jago for discussion of this point.

[45] The Virtual St Stephen's reconstructions estimate the seating capacity of the Commons chamber at 334, based on 50cm per MP; information courtesy of Anthony Masinton. In 1604 a gallery was constructed at the western end of the chamber, to ease overcrowding: Alasdair Hawkyard, 'Inigo Jones, the Surveyors of the Works and the "Parliament House" ', *Parliamentary History*, xxxii (2013), 17–18.

[46] Hawkyard, 'From Painted Chamber to St Stephen's Chapel', 80–1. The mural of Edward III and St George was on the north side of the chapel, which could be interpreted as an argument for the location of the royal pew. Other authorities place the pew on the south side.

16th centuries.[47] The height is more difficult to estimate, depending on assumptions about the installation of a ceiling below the original vaulting of the chapel. Bradshaw's accounts are insufficiently detailed to determine whether a ceiling was added as part of the initial conversion from 1548, although the sums spent were on such a scale that this is certainly a possibility. A ceiling would have improved the acoustics of the chamber as well as making the space more comfortable to inhabit, in keeping with the secularisation and domestication of equivalent ecclesiastical buildings. It could also have created a convenient space for the storage of the parliamentary papers which were being generated in increasing quantities. In 1552–3, Bradshaw made account of the £39 19s. 6d. spent 'for saffe kepinge the Recordes' in the parliament house, which since 1547 would have included the *Commons Journal*; a reference in 1597–8 indicates that the papers were by then stored high in the structure of the former chapel.[48] By 1585, a ceiling was certainly in place, since it was repaired and whitewashed in that year.[49] The Virtual St Stephen's reconstructions opt for a ceiling from the outset, modelling the chamber at 27ft 5ins (8.37m) in height. The alternative is that the Commons initially remained open to the vault of the roof, in which case MPs would have had a view of a fine timber construction of ribs and bosses, brightly painted and spangled with stars.

How did debate function within the inherited space of St Stephen's Chapel? The journals and diaries kept by Elizabethan MPs are frustratingly thin on specific details of the architecture or acoustics of the chamber, but there is some indicative evidence. Sir Henry Unton's speech on the subsidy in March 1593 was 'farr of[f]' and evidently difficult for the journal writer to hear, while Sir Walter Raleigh's intervention two days earlier regarding a conference with the Lords was repeated by the Speaker 'because it might be the better heard'; whether on genuine grounds of audibility or for political emphasis is unclear.[50] The authority on parliamentary procedure, William Hakewill, describes the clerk straining to hear the names of committee members shouted out through the 'confusion'.[51] A crowd of MPs standing waiting for a seat 'breedes a confused sound', as serjeant-at-law, Thomas Harris, complained in 1601.[52] Members also talked among themselves, earning them a rebuke from Speaker Edward Coke: 'Mr Speaker, perceavinge some men to use private speeches together, said it was not the manner of the Howse that any should whisper or talke secretly, for her[e] only publique speeches are to be used.'[53] Peter Wentworth's readmission to the Commons following his imprisonment for his celebrated 1576 oration on freedom of speech was excused by Sir Walter Mildmay on grounds that his words had been spoken

[47] Calculations made for the Virtual St Stephen's visualisations. These dimensions differ slightly from two different sets given by Hawkyard: see Hawkyard, *House of Commons 1509–1558*, 198, and Hawkyard, 'From Painted Chamber to St Stephen's Chapel', 79. Whether the refectory had itself been able to seat everyone is unclear; Jennifer Loach thought it likely that 'most members had to stand': see Loach, *Parliament under the Tudors*, 44.

[48] TNA, E 351/3326, E 351/3233 ('raising the batlements where the recordes of the Parliament Howse lyeth'). For the *Commons Journal*, see Alasdair Hawkyard, 'The Journals, the Clerks of the Parliaments and the Under-Clerks 1485–1601', *Parliamentary History*, xxxiii (2014), 413.

[49] TNA, E 351/3219. The 'p[ar]ticion … in the lower Howse' mended at the same time as the ceiling may refer to the re-worked pulpitum.

[50] *Proceedings in the Parliaments of Elizabeth I*, ed. Hartley, iii, 100, 106.

[51] Kyle, *Theater of State*, 60–1.

[52] *Proceedings in the Parliaments of Elizabeth I*, ed. Hartley, iii, 453.

[53] *Proceedings in the Parliaments of Elizabeth I*, ed. Hartley, iii, 97.

not 'by any comon person abrode, but by a member of this Howse, and not in any private or secrett place, but openly in this most honorable assembly of the parliament being the highest court and councell of the realme'.[54] Rank, age, and experience were all factors in being granted leave to speak, but others also had their turn: as a younger member 'from the upper end of the Howse' put it, 'It is and hath bene allwaies the manner of this House to allowe a mixture in speaking, and after the grave, honnorable, and wisest to heare the meanest alsoe.'[55]

Discontent with proceedings could be registered with other kinds of noise: 'murmure', theatrical coughing, throat-clearing and laughter. When James Dalton rose to speak against James Morice's attack on the court of high commission in February 1593, arguing that Morice's objective was 'the maynteyning of puritanes in their impure opinions, and breache of all good orders', he was hit with a barrage of sound: 'it was straunge and shamefull to see', wrote the diarist who recorded the event, 'howe a number of the House without all modestie or discretion coughed and hauked, of purpose to putt him out'.[56] Arthur Hall's argument against the death sentence for the Duke of Norfolk in 1572 had similarly been met by 'a great murmor, spitting, and coughing'.[57] The cramped conditions in the chamber, the lack of air and sanitation, the competition for a seat and for space for the table-desks and writing implements which some MPs brought with them to take notes, must all have contributed to the heated atmosphere.[58] Although numbers in the chamber could be thinned by absenteeism, at other times the House was packed. A division called on 3 March 1593 recorded that 434 members were present in the House, not far short of a full complement and too many for everyone to sit.[59] A show of humour could still bring MPs together: when the member for Boston prefaced a speech on subsidies with the declaration that: 'I no more meant to speake in this matter then I did to bidd yow all to breakfast', he was rewarded with a 'generall laughing'.[60] But laughter could also be more aggressive, provoking an irritated reaction from William Fleetwood in 1585: 'Do yow laughte? Laught not at me no more then I do at yow. Yow dele uncivilly with me, it is yow allwayes ther in that corner of the Howse.'[61] Fleetwood's words imply that groups of MPs habitually sat together, in this case presumably at the western end of the chamber furthest from his own privileged position (as recorder of London) near the Speaker; similar complaints about the rowdiness of the gallery would be made in the early 17th century. On occasion the House could be surprised into silence, as when Paul Wentworth cut through

[54] *Proceedings in the Parliaments of Elizabeth I*, ed. Hartley, i, 452.

[55] *Proceedings in the Parliaments of Elizabeth I*, ed. Hartley, iii, 78. The anonymous journal describes the speaker as '*ignotus et obscurus*'.

[56] *Proceedings in the Parliaments of Elizabeth I*, ed. Hartley, iii, 46–7; J.E. Neale, *Elizabeth I and her Parliaments 1584–1601* (1957), ch. 3.

[57] *Proceedings in the Parliaments of Elizabeth I*, ed. Hartley, i, 357.

[58] On note-taking and table desks, see Kyle, *Theater of State*, 67–8.

[59] *Proceedings in the Parliaments of Elizabeth I*, ed. Hartley, iii, 95–6. For absenteeism, see M.A.R. Graves, 'Managing Elizabethan Parliaments', in *Parliaments of Elizabethan England*, ed. Dean and Jones, 52.

[60] *Proceedings in the Parliaments of Elizabeth I*, ed. Hartley, iii, 117.

[61] *Proceedings in the Parliaments of Elizabeth I*, ed. Hartley, ii, 125. When his anecdote about poison and the bishop of Winchester's cook prompted unwelcome laughter in the House, Fleetwood silenced it with a memory of watching a convicted poisoner boiled to death: 'I was a litle boye sitting behind m[y] grandfather apon a horse and was taken away when I cryde for feare, for I tell yow it was a terrible matter to behold' – *Proceedings in the Parliaments of Elizabeth I*, ed. Hartley, ii, 109.

lengthy speeches on the fate of Mary, queen of Scots, in May 1572, by requesting it be put to the question 'whither wee should call for an axe or an acte'.[62] At the opening of the 1593 parliament, the door to the Lords remained closed some way into the lord keeper's oration, at which members of the Commons 'murmured so loude that the noise came to her Majestie's hearing, who presentlie commaunded the dore to be lett openn, which was done'.[63]

There was one particular feature of the former St Stephen's Chapel that survived the building's transformation after 1548, and had an important influence on parliamentary procedure thereafter. When MPs filed into the chamber or divided for a formal vote, they passed through a structure which offers the clearest connection between the topography of the medieval chapel and the post-Reformation house of commons. In 1348, a timber pulpitum was constructed to screen the dean and canons of St Stephen and any elite visitors, from other worshippers in the chapel. This was a substantial architectural feature, 12ft deep (based on Henry VI's stipulations for Eton College, which copied the St Stephen's pulpitum) and incorporating an internal stair to enable access to the rood and presumably to the organ listed in the 1548 inventory. While there is no explicit evidence, the likelihood is that the pulpitum was adapted rather than removed; inner and outer chapel thus becoming Commons chamber and lobby respectively. The distinction between the two spaces is clear in Hooker's account:

> Without this house: is one other in which the under Clarks doo sit, as also such as be Suters and attenda[n]t to that house, and when so ever the house is devided upon any Bil: then the rowme is voided, and the one parte of the house commeth down into this to be numbred.[64]

Working back from architectural plans of the early 19th century, where the dividing line between the Commons chamber and the lobby is clearly marked, the Virtual St Stephen's reconstruction places the west side of the screen on a line with the east wall of the lobby, enabling the pulpitum to fit between the second and third bays of the 14th-century chapel. How it was converted we cannot tell, beyond the removal of the rood and the altars in the former outer chapel, but the fact that it was made of wood rather than stone would have made the pulpitum quicker and cheaper to adapt. The lobby was roofed, logically at the same time that the Commons chamber got its ceiling, creating upstairs spaces for a committee chamber and a room for the serjeant where offending members or unauthorised intruders could be committed to ward until the House decided what to do with them.[65]

Hooker's evidence demonstrates how the inherited space of St Stephen's Chapel confirmed the practice of voting by division. On the third reading of a bill, the Speaker invited members to voice their opinion 'yea' or 'no'. If the outcome proved difficult to determine,

---

[62] *Proceedings in the Parliaments of Elizabeth I*, ed. Hartley, i, 376. Chris Kyle has explained how silence operated as a 'deliberate signifier of shock and protest' in the Commons: Kyle, *Theater of State*, 47.

[63] *Proceedings in the Parliaments of Elizabeth I*, ed. Hartley, iii, 62.

[64] *Hooker's Order and Usage*, ed. Snow, 164.

[65] The committee room is mentioned in two sources dating from Mar. 1576: *CJ*, i, 111, and *Proceedings in the Parliaments of Elizabeth I*, ed. Hartley, i, 458. Hooker's journal for 1571 records two men, Thomas Clerk and his companion from the Inner Temple, 'founde to be yn Howse, being none of that company', committed to the serjeant's ward for two days: *Proceedings in the Parliaments of Elizabeth I*, ed. Hartley, i, 245.

as it did in 1581 when the motion to hold a sermon every morning and a public fast was finely balanced:

> the[n] must a devision be made of the house, and the affirmative parte must arise, & departe into the utter rowme, which (by the Sergeant) is voided before hand of all persons that were there, and then the Speaker must assigne two or foure to number them first which sit within, & then the other which be without, as they doo come in, one by one.[66]

Anyone familiar with the modern British parliament will recognize similarities with the practice that Hooker describes, albeit with a single door in the pulpitum rather than the two division lobbies in the current houses of parliament.[67] The principle of those in favour of a change in the law being required to leave the chamber was explained by an anonymous commentator: 'they must sitt still that hold the old law still, that as they would kepe the possession of the law, so, their places'.[68] The sense of uncertainty that a member entering the lobby would be able to regain his seat seems to have acted as a disincentive to voting in the affirmative when divisions were called, and, indeed, the question whether supporters or opponents of a bill should rise from their seats was itself a subject for debate.[69] Social rank also played a role in the practice of voting. The privy councillors, members of the royal household and citizens of London and York whom Hooker describes as occupying the 'lower rowe' enjoyed their seats by privilege of their position, but others had to shift for themselves. Peter Wentworth, meanwhile, criticized his colleagues who stayed seated in spite of their earnest speeches because 'it was comon policy in this Howse to marke the best sorte of the same and either to sitt or arise with them'. Wentworth wanted this craven practice banished: members should 'rise or sitt as the matter giveth cause, for the eyes of the Lord behold all the earth'.[70]

The reordered pulpitum was not the only visual reminder of the medieval past in the Elizabethan Commons. The statues of the 12 Apostles in the image brackets on the main piers survived until 1641, albeit in defaced form: a lasting symbol of the Reformation in a chamber so often focused on questions of religion. The medieval chapel had been an extraordinarily opulent display of colour and heraldry, including tens of thousands of foils of gold leaf. According to the antiquary, Frederick Mackenzie, who saw the shell of St Stephen's after it was gutted in the fire of 1834, almost every part of it had once been painted. The architect, George Gilbert Scott, had a similar recollection, describing St Stephen's 'glowing with the scorched but quite intelligible remnants of its gorgeous decorative colouring'.[71] John Carter's watercolours of the chapel, commissioned by the Society of Antiquaries in the 1790s, demonstrate how much more paint had survived until the destructive renovations of James Wyatt to make way for Irish members in 1800. Much of this

---

[66] *Hooker's Order and Usage*, ed. Snow, 169; *Proceedings in the Parliaments of Elizabeth I*, ed. Hartley, i, 434.

[67] The Living Heritage pages of the UK parliament website incorrectly state that there were two doors in the pulpitum: *http://www.parliament.uk/about/living-heritage/building/palace/estatehistory/reformation-1834/shaping-the-commons-/* (accessed 19 Sept. 2018).

[68] *Proceedings in the Parliaments of Elizabeth I*, ed. Hartley, ii, 113.

[69] Dean, *Law-Making and Society in Late Elizabethan England*, 22.

[70] *Hooker's Order and Usage*, ed. Snow, 164; *Proceedings in the Parliaments of Elizabeth I*, ed. Hartley, i, 434.

[71] George Gilbert Scott, *Personal and Professional Recollections* (1879), 76.

decoration had probably been hidden by wainscot panelling (hence its preservation), and tapestries may also have hung in the Commons as they did in the Lords. But some imagery evidently did remain visible to Elizabethan MPs. On 12 December 1601, the parliamentary diarist, Hayward Townshend, rose to his feet in support of an act 'ffore redresse of certayne abusees and deceiptes used in paynetinge', involving a dispute between the plasterers and the painter-stainers company. Recalling a statute of Edward III's reign (in truth, selectively recalling it), Townshend concluded his speech with an appeal to the heraldry apparently still visible in St Stephen's: 'These walles thus curiouslye paynted in fformer agees, the armes soe arteficyallie drawne, the imagerye soe perfectlye done, doe witnesse our fforeffathers' care in cherisheinge this arte of paynteinge.'[72] Whitewash was purchased at various points; in the exchequer account for 1565–7, for instance, there is a reference to 'whyting and plaistering both the houses'.[73] However, recent pigment analysis of surviving stonework from St Stephen's in the British Museum has revealed no trace of whitewash.

4. *Symbol and Ritual in the Elizabethan Commons*

In an incidental comment, the parliamentary historian, Michael Graves, proposed that the physical shift into St Stephen's 'in some sense symbolised, belatedly, the arrival of the Commons as a co-equal member of a bicameral Parliament'.[74] Symbolised to whom? Presumably not to the monarch, whose opening and closing speeches (delivered in the 'parliament chamber' or house of lords to the seated nobility and bishops, representatives of the Commons standing at the back) remained strongly hierarchical.[75] Perhaps to the upper House – though the Lords was alert to any perceived lack of respect from the Commons, as witnessed in March 1576 when a delegation of MPs was made to wait in the outer part of the parliament chamber before the lords emerged to sit at a table and vent their frustration that 'the comon howse did not use that reverence towardes them as they ought to do'. In the Commons' subtly-crafted response to the Lords, however, the spirit that Graves is describing can, indeed, be detected. Acknowledging 'with all humbleness' the social superiority of the Lords, MPs countered that 'they would yeild unto their lordshipps all duetifull reverence so farr as the same were not preiudiciall to the libertyes of their Howse, which yt behoved them to leave to their posterity in the same freedome they received them'.[76] The message was clear: in its privileges and powers, the 'nether house' (as often termed in documents originating in the Commons, as distinct from 'common' or 'lower') was a court of equal standing to the upper House.[77]

---

[72] *Proceedings in the Parliaments of Elizabeth I*, ed. Hartley, iii, 470. By his own account, Townshend's intervention did the trick: the bill passed.

[73] TNA, E 351/3203.

[74] M.A.R. Graves, *The Tudor Parliaments: Crown, Lords and Commons, 1485–1603* (1985), 21.

[75] Ventriloquising for the queen at the closing session of the 1584–5 parliament session, Lord Chancellor Sir Thomas Bromley rebuked that element of the Commons which had 'contemteously and disdaynfullye reiectid such matters as cam from their betters, the lordes of the Higher House': *Proceedings in the Parliaments of Elizabeth I*, ed. Hartley, ii, 192.

[76] *Proceedings in the Parliaments of Elizabeth I*, ed. Hartley, i, 459–60.

[77] E.g., 'this Court of the Nether House': *CJ*, i, 59.

The same claim was at work in Hooker's *Order and Usage*. Putting his case that in parliament 'the oppinion, censure and judgement of a mean Burgesse: is of as great avail: as is the best Lords', Hooker cited historical precedent and some inventive etymology in support of his position:

> The Lords and Commons (in times past) did sit all in one house, but for the advoiding of confusion: they be now devided into twoo severall houses, and yet nevertheles they are of like and equall authoritie, every perso[n] of either of the said houses beeing named, reputed, & cou[n]ted a peer of the Realme, for the time of the Parlement, that is to say, equall, for Par, is equall.[78]

Notwithstanding Hooker's optimistic reading, whether the Commons occupied its position as of right or by grace of the monarch was never fully put to the test during Elizabeth's reign, even if numerous speeches circled around the issue. Parliaments were irregular, summoned at the monarch's will and sometimes of short duration. Yet the Commons was also an ancient institution, peopled by lawyers and antiquaries like William Lambarde, William Hakewill (who probably knew John Hooker through Exeter connections) and Hooker himself, whose sense of past precedent was an active influence on their understanding of parliament. Whether an *esprit de corps* had developed among earlier generations of MPs is difficult to analyse with any precision given the nature of the surviving evidence, but it certainly existed by the second half of the 16th century. To quote from a collection of essays on Elizabethan parliaments: 'Drawn from every county and enfranchised borough, parliament gave its members a sense of collective identity, a unity of purpose and a sense of shared experience, of nation.'[79] Having a permanent home since 1548 can only have nurtured that sense of belonging, reinforced through parliamentary ritual and affirmed by an accumulating collective memory of rights and conventions.

Privy councillors and other servants of the crown carried additional heft in the Commons, but a kind of equality was also believed to operate within the confines of the chamber. In the words of one member, speaking in mitigation of William Parry's bizarre outburst against the 1585 bill criminalising Jesuit priests, it was:

> not agreable to the liberties and ffreedome of the House that anie member therof for shewinge his opinion in a bill redd amonge them selves should be taken from his seate and sequestred from the socyetie … ffor that the onelie waye to have matters perfectlie understoode and rightlie digested was to suffer men freelie to utter their conseites of both sides. Besides he thought, it was iniustice that seeinge all men in that place had like authoritie one as muche as an other anie member there should be punished by his fellowe member.[80]

This sense of being part of a 'society' or corporate body, equivalent to the university colleges or inns of court where many of them had spent time, was strong among Elizabethan

---

[78] *Hooker's Order and Usage*, ed. Snow, 183.

[79] D.M. Dean and Norman L. Jones, 'Representation, Ideology and Action in the Elizabethan Parliaments', in *Parliaments of Elizabethan England*, ed. Dean and Jones, 5.

[80] *Proceedings in the Parliaments of Elizabeth I*, ed. Hartley, ii, 159.

MPs.[81] Between the four walls of St Stephen's, things could be said that would lead to claims of libel, disloyalty or worse if voiced outside. The aspiration to amity in the chamber is well described in Hooker's journal covering the final days of the 1571 parliament, when Sir Walter Mildmay put it to the House 'that as all they there mett together yn peax and love, so dyd wyshe they sholde so depart and that no advantage sholde be taken of any words there past, but all to be best'. The old soldier, Edward Grimston, concurred, suggesting that a collection should be made for the French protestant church in London (raising £30), and – apparently no more contentious an issue – that the queen should be encouraged towards 'the recoverye of Ireland yn to good order'. Speaker Sir Christopher Wray summed up the mood of the House by craving the goodwill of every person there, 'that if he hadd slypped yn any thinge they shold impute it to his ignoraunce and not to any wyllfullnes'.[82]

MPs also remembered stories associated with the building. One parliamentary diary explained the holes in the walls above some of the seats in the chamber as dating from the early sessions of the Elizabethan parliament, when posts were installed to support a scaffold running around the house 'for them to sitt on which used the wearing of great Breeches stuffed with haire like woolsacks … This all the old Parliament men affirmed talking one day together in the house before the Speaker came.'[83] Approving references to the 'grave old Parlyment man', as authority figure and upholder of the collective memory of the House, are scattered throughout the journals and diaries which help us to reconstruct the political culture of the Elizabethan Commons. The reassuring presence of old members was missed by William Fleetwood in November 1584, who pictured the new knights and burgesses assembling in the parliament house 'owt of all order, in troops, standing upon the fflowre making strange noises, there being not past vij or viij of the old parliamentes'.[84] On another occasion Fleetwood, characterised by Paul Seaward as a 'prolific rememberer', reminded the House of John Story's challenging paraphrase of scripture in 1549: 'Woe unto thee England when the king is a child'; words that had landed Story in the Tower, and one of the earliest recorded speeches in the new Commons chamber.[85] Referring to a time even before the move into St Stephen's, Peter Wentworth said he had 'divers times heard of auntient Parlament men' that Henry VIII 'would never seeme to punish, nay, that which is much lesse, not once to shew him selfe agreved or offended with any Parlament man for any speeche used in that Parlament House'.[86] The Commons chamber functioned as a site and a stimulus of political recollection, complementing the other repositories of memory – written records, ancient and recent history, members themselves – identified by Seaward as helping to make parliament 'much more concrete' in this period.[87]

---

[81] In 1576, Peter Wentworth reminded the Commons, 'wee are incorporated into this place to serve God and all England': *Proceedings in the Parliaments of Elizabeth I*, ed. Hartley, i, 432–3.

[82] *Proceedings in the Parliaments of Elizabeth I*, ed. Hartley, i, 256.

[83] Huntington Library, San Marino, CA, EL MS 2578, f. 49r. I am grateful to Elizabeth Biggs for this reference; see also *Proceedings in the Parliaments of Elizabeth I*, ed. Hartley, iii, 493.

[84] *Proceedings in the Parliaments of Elizabeth I*, ed. Hartley, ii, 65.

[85] *CJ*, i, 9; *Proceedings in the Parliaments of Elizabeth I*, ed. Hartley, i, 327, 360; 'Story, John (c.1504–71)', in *The History of Parliament: The House of Commons, 1509–1558*, ed. S.T. Bindoff (3 vols, Woodbridge, 1982); Paul Seaward, 'Institutional Memory and Contemporary History in the House of Commons, 1547–1640', in *Writing the History of Parliament in Tudor and Early Stuart England*, ed. Paul Cavill and Alexandra Gajda (Manchester, 2018).

[86] *Proceedings in the Parliaments of Elizabeth I*, ed. Hartley, ii, 328.

[87] Seaward, 'Institutional Memory and Contemporary History', 223.

To whom did the Commons chamber belong? As late as 1674, Sir John Birkenhead asserted that 'the House is the King's chapel, and the Surveyor has orders from the King's own mouth to repair, or make alterations', although this was a technical intervention in a tussle over the door of the gallery into the Speaker's chamber rather than a point of high constitutional theory.[88] The material culture of the Elizabethan Commons chamber was threaded through with royal iconography, starting with the Speaker's chair. Speaker Richard Onslow emphasized his election by the 'plaine commons' and Speaker Coke made a rhetorical play that 'I am a servant to the House', but as they both knew the reality was more complicated.[89] Sir Thomas Smith tells us that the Speaker sat 'somewhat higher' in the Commons chamber, 'that he may see and be seen of them all'.[90] Above the Speaker's head was a 'table' or representation of the royal arms.[91] The exchequer accounts for 1586–7 refer to 'Makinge a chaier for Speaker of the Lower House', evidently a more elaborate replacement of the seat 'at the higher end in the midle of the lower rowe' recorded by John Hooker. William Lambarde's 'Notes' on the procedures of the Commons, datable to the early 1580s, explain that 'The fittest seat for him is the lowest row and the middest thereof, for so he may be best heard when he shall speak'; the implication seems to be that the Speaker sat with his fellow MPs until provided with a chair reserved for his use.[92] In 1584–5, serjeant painter, George Gower, was paid 40s. 'for an Arms of England guilded w[i]th fine golde and wrought in oile collo[ur]s'. Subsequent accounts describe 'a paire of Armes which hangeth over the Speaker', with gilded supporters. The arms were renewed by Gower's successor, Leonard Fryer, for the 1597 parliament, and again in 1601–2, when we have our fullest description of 'the Quenes Armes moulded in a table and a frame with a p[er]tinent over it and guilded knobbs standing upon the topp of the Armes all fyne goulde and bice in oyle Collors'.[93] Hooker describes MPs making 'dutiful and humble obeysaunce' on entering the chamber, before taking their seats.[94] This is surely the explanation of MPs bowing when they come into the Commons: acknowledging the virtual presence of the monarch, in accordance with etiquette in other royal palaces or courts of law and consistent with the three 'obeysaunces' made by the Speaker himself before addressing the queen at the opening of parliament.[95]

Theoretically elected by members of the Commons, the occupant of the Speaker's chair was, in practice, a royal nominee. One modern commentator goes further, arguing that the

[88] *Grey's Debates of the House of Commons* (13 vols, 1769), ii, 363. I owe this reference to James Jago.

[89] *Proceedings in the Parliaments of Elizabeth I*, ed. Hartley, i, 168; iii, 89.

[90] *De Republica Anglorum, by Sir Thomas Smith*, ed. Mary Dewar (Cambridge, 1982), 82.

[91] A payment of 40s. to 'Paynters for paynting the Kinges [*sic*] Armes embossed w[i]t[h] the garter w[i]th fyne oyle colours' was noted in 1565–7, although it is not clear where in the palace these were located: TNA, E 351/3203. The equivalent account for 1576 specifies 20s. for 'armes to hang in the lower p[ar]liamente Howse': TNA, E 351/3211.

[92] TNA, E 351/3221; *William Lambarde's Notes on the Procedures and Privileges of the House of Commons (1584)*, ed. Paul L. Ward (House of Commons Library Document no. 10, 1977), 56. The cost of the new Speaker's chair was included among stools, forms and other joinery work coming to £3 11s. 8d.

[93] TNA, E 351/3219; E 351/3223; E 351/3233; E 351/3237; *Hooker's Order and Usage*, ed. Snow, 164. Bice was a deep blue pigment obtained from smalt, finely pulverised glass coloured by cobalt oxide.

[94] *Hooker's Order and Usage*, ed. Snow, 188.

[95] For instance, in 1563, when Speaker Thomas Williams was brought to the bar of the Lords by comptroller of the household, Sir Edward Rogers, and principal secretary, Sir William Cecil: *Proceedings in the Parliaments of Elizabeth I*, ed. Hartley, i, 73; see also *William Lambarde's Notes*, ed. Ward, 57.

royal arms identified the Speaker as 'the personification in the house of commons of the authority of the crown, without which the House lacked any *raison d'être*'.[96] Certainly the Speaker had to remain in place for the Commons to be in session, hence the infamous incident when Speaker John Finch was held down in his chair in 1629. Whether this gave him complete control over debate was among Peter Wentworth's questions 'towching the libertie of the Parleament Howse' in March 1587, when he asked: 'Whether the Speaker maye rise when he will, anie matter beinge propounded without consent of the House or nott.[97] The Speaker was paid a handsome official salary (in fact the second highest in crown service), wore black clothing marking him out from other members, and enjoyed privileged personal access to the monarch.[98] At the same time, however, the Speaker was 'officially the creation and mouthpiece of the Commons', required to convey often unwelcome messages from the House.[99] In Elizabeth's reign this translated into petitions about marriage, religion, and freedom of speech which the queen found unpalatable at best, and not infrequently interpreted as an outrageous challenge to her prerogative. Through noise and through silence, Elizabethan MPs kept up a degree of commentary over the choice of Speaker. In 1584 the nomination of John Puckering was not well received, some members remaining stubbornly silent when invited to join in his acclamation.[100] MPs were even more restive in 1597, when Hayward Townshend recorded that they 'hawked and spat' during the announcement of Christopher Yelverton.[101] When a conventionally unwilling new Speaker had made his speech of acceptance to the queen, he was escorted to the Commons and 'set in his place by them': a reminder that he was their man as well as the crown's.[102]

One of the most potent appeals to history in the modern Westminster parliament is the Speaker's procession, led by the serjeant-at-arms. As Paul Seaward has pointed out, we actually know very little about the origins of some of the customs and ceremonies cited to justify the long continuity in the British way of doing politics.[103] In a 'thick description' of the opening and closing days of parliament in the Tudor period, David Dean has highlighted the exclusion of the Commons from the royal procession through the streets and the sacred rituals in the abbey, in contrast to the more inclusive 'riding' to parliament in Scotland. The English nobility and senior clergy, privy councillors and members of the royal household took part in this public exercise of royal magnificence, but not the main body of MPs.[104] It needs to be recognized, however, that the 16th-century Commons had a ritual life of its own: less visible than that of the Lords, located more in the daily rhythms of government than the formalised splendour of state occasions, but, none the less, crucial in maintaining the political identity and institutional memory of the lower House.

---

[96] Alasdair Hawkyard, 'The Tudor Speakers 1485–1601: Choosing, Status, Work', in *Speakers and the Speakership: Presiding Officers and the Management of Business from the Middle Ages to the 21st Century*, ed. Paul Seaward (Chichester, 2010), 48.

[97] *Proceedings in the Parliaments of Elizabeth I*, ed. Hartley, ii, 321.

[98] *William Lambarde's Notes*, ed. Ward, 70; Hawkyard, *House of Commons 1509–1558*, 210–11.

[99] *Speakers and the Speakership*, ed. Seaward, 3.

[100] *Proceedings in the Parliaments of Elizabeth I*, ed. Hartley, i, 524.

[101] *Proceedings in the Parliaments of Elizabeth I*, ed. Hartley, iii, 227.

[102] *William Lambarde's Notes*, ed. Ward, 58.

[103] Seaward, 'Institutional Memory and Contemporary History', 214

[104] Dean, 'Image and Ritual', 246, 262–3.

Other than the Speaker himself, the key figure in the ceremonial life of the Commons was the serjeant-at-arms. Describing the office of 'the Sergeant or porter of the lower house', Hooker explained that 'He must alwaies attend the Speaker, and go before him, carying his mace upon his shoulder.'[105] The serjeant was a royal appointee, the mace at this time not a unique object but one of several ceremonial maces kept in the jewel house. His salary derived both from the crown (12*s.* per day) and from members (4*s.* per session from knights of the shire, 2*s.*6*d.* from citizens like Hooker, and 2*s.* from the burgesses), making the serjeant at once a liveried royal retainer and a paid officer of the Commons.[106] As the senior doorkeeper of the House, he wielded the keys to the chamber and the authority to exclude unruly members as well as undesirable petitioners. The mace symbolising his authority was a weighty ceremonial staff topped with an imperial crown, hence the need to carry it on his shoulder.[107] As an illustration of its symbolic value, in 1543 the mace was damaged in a fracas with city of London officials when the serjeant attempted to use it as a warrant to secure the release of an MP imprisoned for debt.[108]

The royal imagery surrounding both the Speaker and the serjeant needs to be understood within a symbolic register of overlapping meanings. Recent work on portraits and other Tudor royal iconography has steered us away from making straightforward assumptions about fixed interpretations of visual culture. Images of Queen Elizabeth could be perceived in diverse ways by different audiences, an insight into contemporary readings of material culture which can also be extended to the Commons chamber. As a visual language of power, the royal arms and the mace could be read as encompassing crown and nation as well as monarch: the realm of England that Peter Wentworth invoked in his appeal to the Commons 'not to be timeservers and humour feeders'.[109] This interpretation of the royal iconography of the Commons would help to explain the refurbishment of the Speaker's chair with a new set of royal arms in 1645, when parliament and Charles I were actually at war.

The prominence of royal symbolism within the Elizabethan Commons, far from cowing members with a sense of monarchical authority, instead functioned to legitimate counsel and even loyal criticism of the sovereign. Without this protecting veil, it is difficult to see how the Commons could openly have debated William Strickland's assertion in 1571 that parliament possessed 'such fullnes of power as even the right of the crowne was to bee determined … it was fitt princes to have their prerogative but yet the same to bee straytned within reasonable limittes'.[110] That a symbol of royal authority could be read in different ways is affirmed by modern discussion of the current Commons' mace dating from 1660,

[105] *Hooker's Order and Usage*, ed. Snow, 173. Snow draws a distinction between the serjeant in the Lords, 'who served the lord keeper rather than the House', and the serjeant in the Commons, 'who served the House not the Speaker', although it is not clear on what evidence this is based: Snow, n. 71.

[106] Fees from *Hooker's Order and Usage*, ed. Snow, 173, and *William Lambarde's Notes*, ed. Ward, 70. The serjeant theoretically received his livery from the great wardrobe, although the payments have not yet been traced: Hawkyard, *House of Commons 1509–1558*, 216.

[107] Peter Thorne, *The Mace in the House of Commons* (House of Commons Library Document no. 3, 1957); T. Wilson, *Historical Note on Maces, with Special Reference to the Mace in the House of Commons, Westminster* (1922).

[108] Peter Thorne, *The Royal Mace in the House of Commons* (House of Commons Library Document no. 18, 1990), 36–7.

[109] *Proceedings in the Parliaments of Elizabeth I*, ed. Hartley, i, 432–3.

[110] Strickland's words as explained and justified by Christopher Yelverton: *Proceedings in the Parliaments of Elizabeth I*, ed. Hartley, i, 238–9. Strickland had been sequestered from the House and questioned by the council, but

explained variously as 'the emblem of the King's authority' (according to one 20th-century clerk of works) and 'a symbol of the authority of the House' (quoting a deputy serjeant-at-arms).[111] A similar point could be made about house of commons' green: the dominant colour for the upholstery and fabrics of the lower House by the 17th century and a defining feature of Pugin's decorative scheme for the post-1834 house of commons, but in Elizabeth's reign carrying associations of the green adopted by Henry VII for his family heraldry. In 1584–5, six 'longe grene quishinges [cushions]' were purchased for the chamber at 3s. 4d. the piece, presumably for the benefit of the privy councillors and prominent citizens sitting on the 'lower rowe'.[112]

Other customs and rituals regulated the working life of the Elizabethan Commons. Admission of members to the chamber following their election required the swearing of an oath, a long-standing practice given additional meaning by the context of the Reformation (in which oaths of loyalty had featured since the 1530s), and in Elizabeth's reign by concerns for the queen's safety from conspiracy and assassination. Hooker's account of the opening of the 1571 parliament describes how every MP 'was sworne to the Quene' while Elizabeth and the Lords attended the sermon in Westminster Abbey, 'as also order taken that [n]one shoulde enter yn to that Howse being of that companye oneles he were sworne upon payne'. An anonymous journal for the same session specifies that members of the lower House were 'sworne to the supremacie' before a panel of privy councillors sitting in the Commons chamber, thus demanding their subscription to one of the central tenets of the Elizabethan religious settlement.[113]

If they missed out on the dean of Westminster's preaching at the opening of parliament, then members of the Commons were drawn together by the orations of the Speaker and the highly-charged speeches justifying supply in which Sir Walter Mildmay specialised. In 1571, Speaker Wray elaborated on the maxim that 'Of religion the prynce was the cheffe protector and governore yn his owne realme and no foreyn potentate', echoing the Act in Restraint of Appeals which had launched Henry VIII's break from Rome.[114] In 1581, and again six years later, Mildmay whipped up the House with his vision of 'England our native countrey one of the most renowned monarchies in the world', protected by the sea and the love of her majesty's subjects but in deadly peril from the Holy League: 'a plott longe agoe prepared by the Pope and his confederates to overthrowe the gospell in all places where the same is professed'. The equivalent speech in 1589 exulted in the recent defeat of the Spanish enterprise against England, but warned that a wise mariner knew that a second and yet more dangerous storm commonly followed the first: 'our enemyes so greate, so

[110] (continued) not arrested; he returned the day after Yelverton's speech: see 'Strickland, William (d. 1598)', in *The History of Parliament: The House of Commons, 1558–1603*, ed. P.W. Hasler (3 vols, 1981).

[111] Wilson, *Historical Note on Maces*, 6; Thorne, *Mace in the House of Commons*, 6–7.

[112] TNA, E 351/3219. One of the battle standards presented by the victorious Henry VII to St Paul's in 1485 depicted a red dragon painted on green and white sarsenet: Sydney Anglo, *Spectacle, Pageantry and Early Tudor Policy* (Oxford, 1969), 10. The image of Henry VIII in parliament in the 1523 Wriothesley Garter Book imagines a green and white chequerboard floor, in homage to the Tudor royal colours: reproduced in Christopher Lloyd and Simon Thurley, *Henry VIII: Images of a Tudor King* (Oxford, 1990), 42. When the Elizabethan privy council sat as the court of Star Chamber, a green cloth replaced the usual red on the council table; the choice of green for the councillors' cushions in the Commons was thus consistent with its own status as a court.

[113] *Proceedings in the Parliaments of Elizabeth I*, ed. Hartley, i, 194, 243.

[114] *Proceedings in the Parliaments of Elizabeth I*, ed. Hartley, i, 244.

malitious, so covetous, so cruel, so prowde as they will seeke to repaire the credyt they have lost'.[115] Secular sermons such as these complemented the patriotically protestant preaching which had galvanised the nation to resist the Armada and continued to keep England on a war footing throughout the 1590s.

David Dean describes Tudor parliaments as 'surrounded in liturgical ceremony'.[116] His subject is the sovereign and the Lords, but the point can be extended to encompass the third estate of knights, citizens and burgesses. Prayer was essential to the common life of Elizabethan MPs, preceding every day's business in the chamber and cited as a rhetorical point in debate. When the House was considering the election of a new Speaker in 1581, Edward Lewknor moved 'that we might all ioyne in prayer to God to directe us in our doyngs' and offered a prayer suitable for the occasion which he conveniently had with him. This was duly read out by the clerk, the whole House then reciting the Lord's Prayer.[117] According to William Lambarde, one of the first tasks of a new Speaker was to exhort members 'that for the better order of the House they will frequent the common prayer'. He should also ask their opinion 'concerning prayers that shall be usually said every morning', implying that the format of morning prayer in the Commons was chosen by common consent of the House rather than necessarily following the same rubric in every session.[118] There is ample evidence in parliamentary diaries and the *Commons Journal* that prayers were, indeed, read out before the start of each morning's business, as they were in the chapels of the two universities and the inns of court.[119] Since there was no Speaker's chaplain in this period, and no Church of England ministers sat in the Commons, prayers were led by the clerk or the Speaker himself. The replacement of catholic modes of worship in a royal chapel with godly prayer in a secularised debating chamber cannot have escaped the notice of members of the Commons; indeed, it was emblematic of the English Reformation. On occasion, the juxtaposition of common prayer and parliamentary business must have been particularly significant, as on the morning of 28 February 1593 when 'imediatlie after praiers the bill against [Catholic] recusantes was redd'.[120] For some members, an act of spoken morning prayer was insufficient: in 1571 'order was taken that too of the Howse shold[e] be there apoynted to go to the byshop of London for a precher, who on everie mornynge at vii of the clocke sholde rede a lecture of iii quarters of an howre yn the parlament howse'.[121]

The experience of praying together bound Elizabethan MPs to each other and to the act of governance. Within a political context moulded by the rule of a woman, internal and external threats to stability and the ever-present pressure for further religious reform, the texts of those prayers assume particular significance. John Hooker describes his working day beginning early with 'the Common prayer, and Letanye which are openly red in the house'. The reading of the litany was also 'the first thinge done when the Speaker is sett'.[122] In the

[115] *Proceedings in the Parliaments of Elizabeth I*, ed. Hartley, i, 502–8; ii, 272–6, 434–8.

[116] Dean, 'Image and Ritual', 270.

[117] *Proceedings in the Parliaments of Elizabeth I*, ed. Hartley, i, 524.

[118] *William Lambarde's Notes*, ed. Ward, 59.

[119] E.g., *Proceedings in the Parliaments of Elizabeth I*, ed. Hartley, iii, 85, 88, 94, 103.

[120] *Proceedings in the Parliaments of Elizabeth I*, ed. Hartley, iii, 80.

[121] *Proceedings in the Parliaments of Elizabeth I*, ed. Hartley, i, 245–6.

[122] *Hooker's Order and Usage*, ed. Snow, 178; *Proceedings in the Parliaments of Elizabeth I*, ed. Hartley, iii, 69. The practice of the Commons' clerk reading the litany had apparently begun in Elizabeth's first parliament in 1559: Norman L. Jones, *Faith by Statute: Parliament and the Settlement of Religion 1559* (1982), 89.

prayer book as revised in 1559, the litany consisted of a series of responsory intercessions for divine protection from perils including the wrath of God, lightning and tempest, hypocrisy and vainglory, and 'the craftes and assaultes of the Devil'. The language had a strongly penitential tone, offering petition for the forgiveness of the sins of the people and the avoiding of God's judgment. The service was participatory rather than passive, requiring members to respond to the clerk after every verse, 'Good Lorde delyver us' and 'We beseche thee to heare us good Lorde'.[123] The *Commons Journal* describes the clerk kneeling to recite the litany, 'answered by the whole House, of [sic] their Knees, with divers Prayers'.[124] The psychological impact in the intimate surroundings of the former St Stephen's Chapel, in the half-light of an early morning in winter or spring, can be imagined. At the very least, its collective stillness must have contrasted with the noise and movement of the day's business to come.

In common with other parts of the English liturgy as revised for the Book of Common Prayer, the 1559 litany put prayer for the monarchy centre stage.[125] Three successive petitions focused on the person of the queen, for her preservation, her faith in God and true religion, and her triumph over her enemies:

> That it may please thee, to kepe and strengthen in the true worshipping of thee in righteousness and holynes of lyfe, thy servaunt Elizabeth our most gracious Quene and governour … to rule her harte in thy faith, feare, and love, that she may evermore have affiaunce in thee, and ever seke thy honoure and glory … to be her defender and keper, geving her the victory over al her enemyes.[126]

Members offered an affirmation of their own after each verse. The litany also included a separate 'prayer of the Quenes majesty', different in details but similar in tone to the collect for the queen in the prayer book communion service, beseeching God to bless and strengthen Elizabeth 'that she may alway incline to thy wil, and walcke in thy waye'.[127] Given the emphasis placed by godly MPs on ensuring that Elizabeth did, indeed, incline to the will of God (by allowing further reform in the Church) and wake up to the threat posed by her catholic enemies, it is tempting to speculate that they would have taken additional inspiration from such prayers. In 1563, prayers for the monarchy themselves became a reference point in a speech on the succession, when members were rhetorically invited to 'pray for the Queene's Majestie and her magistrates that they may governe in such sort / that the people committed to their charge may leade a quiet, not a quarrelous, and peaceable, not a bloudy, life' – blessings that only a settled succession could bring.[128]

---

[123] *The Book of Common Prayer: The Texts of 1549, 1559, and 1662*, ed. Brian Cummings (Oxford, 2011), 117–23.

[124] *CJ*, i, 54.

[125] On the subject of prayers for the monarchy in the reformed English liturgy, see J.P.D. Cooper, ' "O Lorde Save the Kyng": Tudor Royal Propaganda and the Power of Prayer', in *Authority and Consent in Tudor England*, ed. G.W. Bernard and S.J. Gunn (Aldershot, 2002), 179–96.

[126] *Book of Common Prayer 1559*, ed. Cummings, 118.

[127] *Book of Common Prayer 1559*, ed. Cummings, 121.

[128] *Proceedings in the Parliaments of Elizabeth I*, ed. Hartley, i, 134. The editor notes that there is some doubt whether this 'speech' was delivered in the chamber as we have it.

The petition specifically 'for the high court of parliament' in modern versions of the prayer book litany did not appear in either the 1559 or 1662 texts, which limited it-self to praying for the 'Lordes of the Counsayle', nobility and magistrates.[129] Thanks to the careful transcriptions of Hayward Townshend, however, we know that a prayer for parliament was in use in the Elizabethan house of commons, and it is worth quoting here at length. On the morning of 5 November 1597, 'according to the usuall course the Speaker brought in a prayer, which I w[r]ott word for word out of the Clerke of the Parliamentes' booke'. Referring to the Commons as 'this honarable senate' in the mode of classical Rome, the Speaker's prayer moved from a confession of sins and appeal for wisdom to an act of collective dedication to the good governance of the nation:

> most mercifull Father since by thy providence wee are called from all partes of the land to this famous councell of Parliament to advise of those thinges that concerne thy / glorie, the good of thy Church, the prosperitie of our prince and the weale of all her people, wee most intirelie beseech thee ... expell darknesse and vanitie from our myndes and partiallitie from our speeches and graunt unto us such wisdome and integritie of heart as become the servantes of Jesus Christ, the subjectes of a gratious prince, and members of his honorable Howse. Lett us not, O Lord, whoe are mett togather for the publique good of the whole land be more carelesse and remisse then wee use to bee in our owne private causes. Give grace wee beseech thee that everie one of us may laboure to shewe a good conscience to thy majestie, a good zeale to thy word, a loyall hart to our prince and a Christian love to our countrie and common wealth.[130]

Our principal sources for the political culture of the Elizabethan Commons, treatises by Hooker and Lambarde and the various journals and diaries kept by MPs, of their nature focus more on matters of legislation and debate and parliamentary procedure than on the self-perception of being a member of the lower House. In the Speaker's prayer for parlia-ment, however, we are offered a window in the soul of the house of commons gathered together in the ancient chapel of St Stephen. Members were reminded that they were servants of Christ as well as subjects of a gracious queen, drawn from across the king-dom to counsel the monarch for the good of the Church and the commonwealth. The prayer concluded with an image of parliament as a 'threefold cord not easilie broken', ensuring that existing godly laws were properly executed and new ones enacted 'for the bridling of the wicked and the encouragement of the godlie and well-affected subiectes'.[131] Queen Elizabeth might sometimes resent its implications, but the members of her lower House were in no doubt about their God-given authority within the government of England.

[129] *Book of Common Prayer 1559*, ed. Cummings, 118, 261. A prayer for parliament was printed in 1625: G.J. Cuming, *A History of Anglican Liturgy* (1982), 126.

[130] *Proceedings in the Parliaments of Elizabeth I*, ed. Hartley, iii, 230.

[131] *Proceedings in the Parliaments of Elizabeth I*, ed. Hartley, iii, 230, and nn. 44, 46, following the alternative readings of 'cord' for 'boorde' and 'godlie' for 'ungodlie'.

5. *Conclusion*

So far as we know, Elizabeth I never stepped inside the royal chapel refurbished by her brother as the first dedicated house of commons. This was her own decision: Henry VIII had personally brought the bill suppressing the lesser monasteries into the Commons chamber in March 1536, and John Hooker was clear that the sovereign 'is at his choice and libertie to come, or not to come to the Parlament' (though he was probably thinking about its formal opening and closing rather than the daily deliberations of the two Houses).[132] The image of the queen in parliament popularised by the 1682 edition of Simonds D' Ewes's *Journals* depicts Elizabeth as she appeared in person in the Palace of Westminster, presiding from her chair of estate in the house of lords. In the lower House her presence was represented by the royal arms above the Speaker's chair, the mace borne by the serjeant, and the prayers for her welfare which preceded every morning's business in the chamber. Sworn to uphold the supremacy of the queen and surrounded by visual reminders of her authority, members of the Commons transacted their business within the broader culture of professed devotion which defined the rule of Elizabeth. The symbolism through which that loyalty was expressed, however, could have more than one layer of meaning. If portraits of the queen commissioned by her courtiers aimed at counselling Elizabeth through praising her, so the iconography and ritual of the Commons chamber served to sanction a dialogue about the proper exercise of royal power. The Speaker and the serjeant served two masters: the Commons as well as the crown. The acquisition of a settled meeting-place added a sense of location to the political memory of the Commons, even as it provided new space for the storage of its physical records.

The culture of debate in the early modern house of commons derived from many sources. Networks of patronage and clientage, religious faith, codes of social deference, and understandings of history and the law all played their part besides the impulse to serve monarchy and state. But the architecture of the former St Stephen's Chapel was also crucial in framing how the Commons functioned as a place of meeting and debate. The layout of that chamber, its size and furniture and acoustics, could have different consequences in different political contexts. Chris Kyle has commented on the 'tonal, even auditory, difference in speech between Elizabethan and Jacobean Parliaments', as the leisured rhetoric characteristic of the later 16th century gave way to a sharper and adversarial debating style reflective of a more challenging relationship between crown and commons.[133] The search for the first shoots of the modern British parliament in the Elizabethan period, the origins of oppositional debate or a government front bench, is based on a false assumption as well as a selective reading of the evidence. That said, the relationship between space, sound and politics in the parliaments of Elizabeth I remains worthy of the closest attention. Procedure in the Commons, contemporary understanding of the institution, and the self-perception of MPs were all moulded by the move into St Stephen's. Elizabethan members of parliament did not openly conceptualise the links between architecture and politics, as modern politicians at Westminster and Holyrood and the Welsh Assembly are wont to do. But the sources they have left us enable those connections to be explored, revealing the converted St Stephen's Chapel as a site of ceremony, of memory, and of prayer as well as a place of debate.

[132] BL, Cotton MS, Cleopatra E IV, f 131v; *Hooker's Order and Usage*, ed. Snow, 180.
[133] Kyle, *Theater of State*, 30.

In the preface to what would be his final monograph, Sir Geoffrey Elton was in reflective, maybe even mischievous, mood. 'The completion of a book is always a relief, but I am perhaps exceptionally relieved to be done with the Parliaments of Elizabeth', he wrote. The Victorians – and their 'obedient successors' – have misled us by reading the modern parliament back into history. Elton even wondered aloud whether parliament 'ever really mattered all that much in the politics of the nation, except perhaps as a stage sometimes used by the real contenders over government and policy'.[134] While applauding some of what Elton says, we may turn it around by turning back to Hooker's 1572 reference to parliament as a kind of theatre. The Elizabethan Commons did, indeed, constitute a theatre: for affairs of state and individual political careers, but also for representations of power, for negotiating the boundaries between crown and commonwealth, and for the assertion of the equality of MPs with their social betters in the Lords. We might fairly conclude that, by moving into St Stephen's Chapel, 'the common house' became, in a new sense, the house of commons.

[134] Elton, *Parliament of England 1559–1581*, ix.

The Sound of Debate in Georgian England: Auralising the House of Commons

CATRIONA COOPER

St Stephen's Chapel, Westminster became the first permanent home of the house of commons in 1548. The building had to be adapted to conform to its new use. Visual and architectural adaptations to the space have been discussed in detail, but the building's new role also required improvements to the working use of the space as a forum for public debate. In this essay, acoustic techniques are used to explore how speeches and debate would have sounded during the Georgian period and consider how St Stephen's was adapted for this new use. The results demonstrate that, despite these alterations, the 18th-century house of commons was not ideally suited to speaking or listening to debate. The listening experience was not uniform across the chamber, and its former use as a medieval chapel may have influenced how well certain positions in the chamber would have experienced speech.

Keywords: acoustics; auralisation; debate; house of commons; oratory; sound; space; Speaker's chair; speeches; St Stephen's Chapel

1

'We shape our buildings and afterwards our buildings shape us'[1]

Following the destruction of the house of commons in 1941, Winston Churchill insisted that the rebuilt chamber should retain its original layout. A similar design had also been followed by Charles Barry in his rebuilding of Westminster Palace following the fire of 1834. Unlike the semicircular layouts developed from classical architecture, Britain has retained a rectangular space for its elected house of parliament.[2] The layout of the first dedicated house of commons chamber derived from the re-use of the medieval royal chapel of St Stephen at Westminster, converted to its new role in 1548. To this day, members sit in stalls facing one another within a space that is too small to seat all MPs at once.[3] Churchill described the architecture of British politics as intimate and conversational. The sense of two opposing sides confronting each other across the room became more clearly established in Georgian

---

[1] Quoted on UK parliament's Living Heritage webpage 'Churchill and the Commons Chamber', available at *http://www.parliament.uk/about/living-heritage/building/palace/architecture/palacestructure/churchill/* (accessed 5 Mar. 2018).

[2] Gavin Stamp, ' "We Shape Our Buildings and Afterwards Our Buildings Shape Us": Sir Giles Gilbert Scott and the Rebuilding of the House of Commons', in *The Houses of Parliament: History, Art, Architecture*, ed. Christine Riding and Jacqueline Riding (2000).

[3] *The Oxford Handbook of Later Medieval Archaeology in Britain*, ed. Christopher Gerrard and Alejandra Gutierrez (Oxford, 2018), 379.

England as two parties came to dominate the Commons chamber.[4] It was this theme of free and impassioned debate that Churchill intended to replicate in the building of the current house of commons chamber. In preserving the layout he also preserved elements of the acoustical character of the room.

Oratorical skills, rhetoric, and performance were valued and celebrated attributes of members of parliament in the later 18th century.[5] A well-presented speech could sway an audience and define policy change. A speech could also be made more challenging for other members by exploiting the acoustics of the space.[6] How easy was it to understand speeches in the Commons, and did it make a difference where you were speaking from?

This essay uses acoustic techniques to explore how speeches and debate would have sounded during the Georgian period. These techniques allow us to reconstruct the lost space of the 18th-century house of commons, and to compare written evidence of the experience of debate with the acoustic experience of the space. The results show that the Commons chamber was not ideally suited to speaking or listening to public speeches. We can also see that audience position had an effect on the experience of listening; some seats are better suited than others to enabling the occupant to hear clearly. Further, the better seats for clarity of hearing are not necessarily those considered to be of higher status. The research for this essay was undertaken as part of the Arts and Humanities Research Council funded project 'Listening to the Commons' at the University of York, following on from the AHRC-funded 'St Stephen's Chapel, Westminster' research project.[7] The Listening to the Commons team draws together experts from the department of history, the AudioLab in the department of electronic engineering and Digital Creativity Labs at York, in collaboration with staff from the UK parliament.

2. Background

Westminster Palace has been at the centre of British politics since its construction. In 1548 Edward VI granted the Commons the use of the former St Stephen's Chapel, where MPs would remain until the great fire of 1834.[8]

We conceive of buildings both as spaces constructed for particular (social) purposes, and as spaces that define the purposes (social actions) that occur within them. At its creation a building orders and divides space for a specific purpose or a range of purposes (Figure 1).[9]

---

[4]Tim Harris, *Politics under the Later Stuarts: Party Conflict in a Divided Society, 1660–1715* (1993).

[5]Christopher Reid, *Imprison'd Wranglers: The Rhetorical Culture of the House of Commons 1760–1800* (Oxford, 2012).

[6]Clare Wilkinson, 'Politics and Topography in the Old House of Commons, 1783–1834', in *Housing Parliament: Dublin, Edinburgh and Westminster*, ed. Clyve Jones and Sean Kelsey (Edinburgh, 2002), 141–65; Jason Peacey, 'Disorderly Debates: Noise and Gesture in the 17th-Century House of Commons', *Parliamentary History*, xxxii (2013), 60–78.

[7]'Listening to the Commons: The Sounds of Debate and the Experience of Women in Parliament c. 1800', AH/P012094/1 (2017–18), principal investigator, Dr John Cooper, co-investigator, Prof. Damian Murphy, post-doctoral research assistant, Dr Catriona Cooper; 'St Stephen's Chapel Westminster: Visual and Political Culture 1292–1941', AH/K006991/1 (2013–17), principal investigator, Dr John Cooper.

[8]Alasdair Hawkyard, 'From Painted Chamber to St Stephen's Chapel: The Meeting Places of the House of Commons at Westminster until 1603', *Parliamentary History*, xxi (2002), 62–84.

[9]Bill Hillier and Julienne Hanson, *The Social Logic of Space* (Cambridge, 1984).

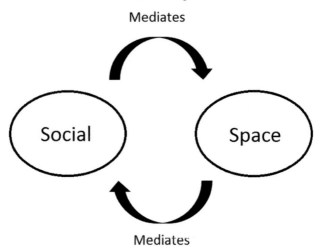

Figure 1: The Relationship between Social Action and the Use of Space.

During and after construction, this intended purpose can change and in doing so the use of the space will change, as with St Stephen's Chapel. Begun in the 1290s and completed by Edward III, St Stephen's was originally constructed as an ecclesiastical space and it evolved to fulfil this purpose. When it was adopted for use as the house of commons, the chapel acquired a new purpose and so had to be adapted for political debate. Since St Stephen's Chapel had not been consciously created for this purpose, the space had to evolve. At the same time, the existing space also influenced how the Commons functioned socially and for political debate.

Thinking about intentionality of construction in this way allows us to consider the changing social identity of the building and how it defines social interactions, and therefore can be considered as an agent that produces an effect in us.[10] We can consider buildings as agents which stage social interactions and use of space. Focusing on these elements of the creation of the building and how it has been adapted for changing uses can allow the exploration of the social context within which these buildings were used.[11]

Until recently, it was believed that the house of commons occupied the choir stalls of the former chapel; this has been disproved by the St Stephen's Chapel project. However, the layout of the building remained influenced by its origins. MPs occupied benches facing each other and gave speeches opposite the divide with proceedings governed by the Speaker, seated at the eastern end of the room close to where the altar had once stood. The practice of bowing to the Speaker is sometimes likened to the medieval liturgy, although this is based on a misunderstanding.[12] By the 18th century, the building had been through a number of alterations and restorations to improve its use as a space for political speech and debate. Some of these were visual: for instance the covering of medieval wall paintings, no longer

---

[10] J. Hoskins, 'Agency, Biography and Objects', in *Handbook of Material Culture*, ed. C. Tilley (2006), 76.

[11] B. Olsen, 'Material Culture after Text: Re-Membering Things', *Norwegian Archaeological Review*, xxxvi (2003), 100.

[12] See J.P.D. Cooper's essay in this volume.

considered appropriate in post-Reformation England. Others were practical: the addition of galleries and extra benches following the Act of Union of 1707, and then the Union of Great Britain and Ireland in 1801, which made space for the new MPs to be seated.[13] However, some changes were specifically introduced to improve the acoustic experience of the room.

Medieval liturgy made use of the architectural properties of the spaces within which it was performed: for example, the western European musical polyphony that developed during the medieval period worked in tandem with the architecture of the high-ceilinged buildings in which it was performed to sustain notes to extend the length and breadth of these buildings. However, the use of St Stephen's for public speaking required a space which did not extend musical notes or syllables, in order for what was being said to be understood.[14] A ceiling had been introduced to the chamber by the end of the Elizabethan period, subsequently restored by Christopher Wren. The introduction of the ceiling was presumably intended to improve the acoustics of the space. Other changes would also have had an effect on the quality of sound in the chamber, whether intended or not.

Research papers and projects have considered various aspects of the spatial layout and appearance of politics in the pre-1834 period.[15] This body of work references the large number of images of the Commons in session, considers the historical records indicating building materials used to complete repairs, and analyses personal accounts. These discussions largely focus on the visual experience of the house of commons. This is not surprising: preserved material from the past is visually engaging, whereas smells, sounds, and tastes are lost.[16] We are conditioned to think about the experience of the past in a visual way.[17] However, the world is not normally experienced in a visual way alone. Our understanding is based on all of the senses in combination, not just one in isolation.[18] When we try to separate these experiences we generally perceive them differently: 'an object is perceived differently by eye and by ear. So the object of the eye is a different object than that of the ear'.[19] So when we consider visual material, we need also to consider ephemeral experiences. Although there are some accounts of sound within the house of commons, they largely draw on complaints of noise during debates, indicating how the building could be manipulated to alter individuals' experiences.[20]

---

[13] Wilkinson, 'Politics and Topography'; see Elizabeth Hallam Smith's essay in this volume.

[14] D. Howard and L. Moretti, *Sound and Space in Renaissance Venice: Architecture, Music, Acoustics* (New Haven, CT, 2009).

[15] Wilkinson, 'Politics and Topography'; St Stephen's Chapel project, available at *https://www.virtualststephens. org.uk/* (accessed 29 Oct. 2018).

[16] P. Dawson, R. Levy, D. Gardner and M. Walls, 'Simulating the Behaviour of Light Inside Arctic Dwellings: Implications for Assessing the Role of Vision in Task Performance', *World Archaeology*, xxxix (2007), 17–35.

[17] K. Ray, 'Transcending an Archaeology of the Visual: Some Spheres of Implicated Discourse in Past Material Culture', in *Archaeology and the Politics of Vision in a Post-Modern Context*, ed. J. Thomas and V.O. Jorge (Cambridge, 2008), 13–30.

[18] A. Chalmers and E. Zanyi, 'Multi-Sensory Virtual Environments for Investigating the Past', *Virtual Archaeology Review*, i (2010), 13–16.

[19] Marx, cited in J. Goldhahn, 'Roaring Rocks: An Audio-Visual Perspective on Hunter-Gatherer Engravings in Northern Sweden and Scandinavia', *Norwegian Archaeological Review*, xxxv (2002), 29–61.

[20] Wilkinson, 'Politics and Topography'; *The Correspondence of John Campbell MP, with His Family, Henry Fox, Sir Robert Walpole and the Duke of Newcastle, 1734–71*, ed. J.E. Davies (Parliamentary History: Texts & Studies, 8, Chichester, 2013), ch. 4.

Table 1: *Terminology*

Impulse response or room impulse response	The acoustic fingerprint of an enclosed space. It is generated from how sound decays within a real or digital space, and is used to characterise their properties.
Reverberation time	The duration required for the space-averaged sound energy density in an enclosure to decrease by a specified number of decibels (usually 60 decibels, or 60dB) after the source emission has stopped. This value is used to characterise a room's acoustics allowing it to be compared with other spaces. Shorter reverberation times are spaces with high levels of absorption or smaller volumes, whereas more reverberant spaces have longer reverberation times and typically larger volumes.
Clarity (C50)	Can be measured from the impulse response. It is the balance between early and late arriving energy and gives an objective measure to how clearly we can understand sound.
CAD	Computer Aided Design. Software used by architects, engineers, drafters, artists, and others to create precision drawings or technical illustrations.
CATT Acoustic	Widely adopted acoustic modelling software.
Anechoic	Free from reverberation or 'without-echoes'; a 'dead space'.

3. *Architectural Acoustics*

The study of building acoustics originates with the work of Professor Wallace Clement Sabine. In the late 19th century he was asked to approve the acoustics of the lecture hall at the Fogg Art Museum at Harvard University. Over several years he explored how sound worked within the space and his work resulted in the discovery of the link between the volume of a space, absorbing area of the surfaces, and how reverberant the space was as a consequence.[21] Sabine's research was fundamental to describing the acoustical character of a room, how well suited it is to its purpose and how we can formally define it. Specifically, he formally defined numerical values (for example reverberation time, see properties of a room, Table 1) which are still used to characterise the sonic properties of a room.

While the techniques employed by Sabine were very basic, in principle they remain the same today; only the sophistication of the equipment has changed. The characteristics of rooms can now be captured and preserved as digital information, or 'impulse response' data.[22] By recording this information, the features of the space can be interacted with via a number of quantitative measures, as well as preserving elements of the multisensory experience of the space.

[21] A. Chodos, 'January 10, 1919: Death of Wallace Sabine, Pioneer of Architectural Acoustics', *American Physical Society News*, xx (2011), 2.

[22] D. Murphy, S. Shelley, A. Foteinou, J. Brereton and H. Daffern, 'Acoustic Heritage and Audio Creativity: The Creative Application of Sound in the Representation, Understanding and Experience of Past Environments', *Internet Archaeology*, xxxxiv (2017), available at *https://doi.org/10.11141/ia.44.12* (accessed 29 Oct. 2018).

In the 1980s, acousticians began to predict this impulse response data digitally.[23] Primarily this technique has been used to help design new rooms and buildings, or to improve or adapt the acoustics within existing buildings. In more recent years, however, archaeologists have adopted the techniques to reconstruct the acoustics of spaces that no longer exist. The subdiscipline of *archaeoacoustics* has emerged, bringing together acoustic technique with experimental archaeology, reconstruction and music history to study both the propagation and experience of sound. These explorations combine practical, theoretical, and digital approaches towards a multisensory understanding of the past. From an archaeological background, prehistoric monumental architecture[24] and Palaeolithic rock art[25] have tended to take centre stage in these explorations. These studies incline towards big questions such as site selection and the experience of ritual events. For their part, acousticians have tended to focus on case studies form the Graeco-Roman world[26] and later religious spaces.[27]

From archaeoacoustics the field of acoustic heritage has emerged, which focuses more on quantifiable acoustic properties and has seen a shift towards the more recent past.[28] Medieval and post-medieval sites offer a rich body of evidence, and often more complete or comparative buildings can be explored. In another context, I have used these processes to engage with the bodily experience of the medieval great hall and how the space was used,[29] while Damian Murphy and others have created interactive auralisations to allow an audience to hear a choir sing in a reconstruction of the medieval St Mary's Abbey, York, while seated in its ruins.[30]

Being able to record and explore past spaces has provided us with tangible ways to discuss the acoustical properties of a space. However, technology is now allowing us to move beyond numerical data to explore the intangible experience of a space through

[23] B.-I. Dalenbäck, CATT-Acoustic v.9.0 (2011), available at *http://www.catt.se/* (accessed 29 Oct. 2018).

[24] P. Devereux and R.G. Jahn, 'Preliminary Investigations and Cognitive Considerations of the Acoustical Resonances of Selected Archaeological Sites', *Antiquity*, lxx (1996), 665–6; R. Till, *Sounds of Stonehenge: Experimental Multimedia Archaeology* (2011), available at *http://soundsofstonehenge.wordpress.com/* (accessed 29 Oct. 2018); A. Watson, '(Un)intentional Sound? Acoustics and Neolithic Monuments', in *Archaeoacoustics*, ed. C. Scarre and G. Lawson (Cambridge, 2006), 11–23.

[25] S.J. Waller, 'Intentionality of Rock-Art Placement Deduced from Acoustical Measurements', in *Archaeoacoustics*, ed. Scarre and Lawson, 31–41; R. Till, 'Sound Archaeology: Terminology, Palaeolithic Cave Art and the Soundscape', *World Archaeology*, xxxxvi (2014), 292–304; I. Reznikoff, 'Sound Resonance in Prehistoric Times: A Study of Paleolithic Painted Caves and Rocks', *Journal of the Acoustical Society of America*, cxxiii (2008), 4137–41; Bruno Fazenda, 'Cave Acoustics in Prehistory: Exploring the Association of Palaeolithic Visual Motifs and Acoustic Response', *Journal of the Acoustical Society of America*, cxlii (2017), 1332.

[26] E. Rocconi, 'Theatres and Theatre Design in the Graeco-Roman World: Theoretical and Empirical Approaches', in *Archaeoacoustics*, ed. Scarre and Lawson, 71–7; A. Farnetani, N. Prodi and R. Pompoli, 'On the Acoustics of Ancient Greek and Roman Theaters', *Journal of the Acoustical Society of America*, cxxiv (2008), 1557–67.

[27] M. Galindo, T. Zamarreño and S. Girón, 'Acoustic Simulations of Mudejar Gothic Churches', *Journal of the Acoustical Society of America*, cxxvi (2009), 1207–18; F. Martellotta, 'Identifying Acoustical Coupling by Measurements and Prediction-Models for St Peter's Basilica in Rome', *Journal of the Acoustical Society of America*, cxxvi (2009), 1175–86.

[28] Catriona Cooper, 'The Exploration of Lived Experience in Medieval Buildings through the Use of Digital Technologies', University of Southampton PhD, 2015; Murphy *et al.*, 'Acoustic Heritage and Audio Creativity'; M.J. Lopez, 'The York Mystery Plays: Exploring Sound and Hearing in Medieval Vernacular Drama', in *Sensory Perception in the Medieval West*, ed. S. Thomson and M. Bintley (Turnhout, Belgium, 2016), 53–73.

[29] Cooper, 'Exploration of Lived Experience'.

[30] Murphy *et al.*, 'Acoustic Heritage and Audio Creativity'.

reconstruction.[31] Digital visualisation has been a technique championed as a method for creating interpretations of the past.[32] These interpretations are generated for a variety of reasons; to inform, educate, and explore. Critically they are largely ocularcentric in approach.[33] We can now move towards auralisation: the reconstruction of sound in the past. We take the same process applied to digital visualisation and interpret the same body of evidence. Combining recordings produced under anechoic conditions (a space free from reverberation) with the impulse response of a modelled or measured space will allow the resulting sound to be heard as if it were played in that space at the position of a programmed source from the perspective of the listener.

These processes will allow us to move beyond the interpretations of the Georgian era house of commons that currently exist; those generated from traditional historical discourse, and the visualisation produced as part of the St Stephen's project. These acoustic techniques will be used to discuss how sound was experienced within the chamber: whether it was easy or hard to follow the proceedings, and the ability to hear clearly, or not, from different seats.

4. *Methodology*

For this exercise, a single moment in political history will be focused upon: a debate on the slave trade on 12 May 1789.[34] On this date, William Wilberforce MP spoke to support the abolition of the slave trade following the presentation of petitions from those supporting the movement. This moment has been selected as it is widely considered to be the beginning of a parliamentary campaign that eventually, after 18 years, led to successful abolition. In this speech, which lasted in excess of three hours, Wilberforce presented evidence describing the conditions faced by transported slaves during their passage, how the abolition would affect trade in Africa, and the economic arguments of his opponents.[35] The whole debate was recorded in the newspapers including interruptions, for example:

> Mr. Burke declared, that in his opinion not merely the British nation, but all Europe were under very great and furious obligations to the honourable gentleman, for having brought the subject forward in a manner the most masterly, impressive, and eloquent.

[31] The word 'reconstruction' is difficult. Although frequently the visualisation or simulation process is referred to as digital reconstruction, in fact the past can never be reconstructed; we are limited to constructing models and simulations of the past. In that process, it is important not to forget that what we are doing is interpreting the evidence or material remains that are available to us, and that our results are just one perceived reality of the past. The term is used here for simplicity to discuss the shift from 'visualisation' to 'auralisation'.

[32] A. Chalmers, 'Very Realistic Graphics for Visualising Archaeological Site Reconstructions', in *Proceedings of the 18th Spring Conference on Computer Graphics* (New York, 2002), 7; K. Devlin and A. Chalmers, 'Realistic Visualisation of the Pompeii Frescoes', in *Proceedings of the 1st International Conference on Computer Graphics, Virtual Reality and Visualisation* (New York, 2001), 43; S. Hermon and P. Fabian, 'Virtual Reconstruction of Archaeological Sites: Avdat Roman Military Camp as a Case-Study', in *Virtual Archaeology: Proceedings of the VAST Euroconference, Arezzo 24–25 November 2000* (Oxford, 2000), 103–8.

[33] *Archaeology and the Politics of Vision in a Post-Modern Context*, ed. Thomas and Jorge.

[34] John Wolffe, 'Wilberforce, William (1759–1833)', *ODNB*.

[35] Brycchan Carey, 'William Wilberforce's Sentimental Rhetoric: Parliamentary Reportage and the Abolition Speech of 1789', *The Age of Johnson: A Scholarly Annual*, xiv (2003), 281–305.

Principles so admirably laid down, with so much order and force, were equal to any thing he had ever heard of in modern oratory …[36]

The implication is that the speech was presented well, even if its subject matter was not well received by all.

To recover an understanding of the experience of being within the chamber, we must recover the impulse response of the house of commons that stood in 1789 and use this to assess how different individuals would have experienced those moments. The acoustic research projects discussed above largely consider the recovery of the impulse response by undertaking measurements within a space as it stands today. Unfortunately, St Stephen's Chapel, where the house of commons had found its home, burnt down in 1834, so we must rely on a digital model.

There are two elements to the creation of these models: the technical and the interpretative. The technical steps involve the creation of a digital model, for which we used the acoustic modelling software CATT Acoustic. The interpretative steps follow the same methodology as that used to generate a visual reconstruction: the examination of the physical and documentary remains and contemporary images. The creation of models in this way has undergone heavy theoretical critique since methodologies started to emerge in the 1990s; while this literature is important in the development of these techniques, it has been discussed elsewhere.[37] More relevant to this essay is the question of how we can negotiate the uncertainty of our interpretations in this context. While both elements require different skill sets, they need to be undertaken as a collaborative exercise.

The University of York St Stephen's Chapel project generated a series of digital models of the house of commons including one which presented the chamber as it appeared in 1707 following a series of renovations by Christopher Wren (Figure 2). The digital models were produced and evolved over the course of the four-year project as more evidence became available, and expert understanding of that evidence developed. These models provided a starting point for the creation of our acoustic models. Visual source material was also drawn together, including later drawings, paintings, cartoons and architectural drawings (Figure 3). These allowed the Listening to the Commons team to observe the changes that were necessary to implement in the 1707 digital model, including boarding up windows which were shut, accounting for the fabric and layout of the benches, and considering the changing level of occupation of the space.

The creation of such a model is informed by interpretative decisions. That decision making is ongoing throughout the modelling process, as new questions arise during the building of the digital space. We started with a basic model of the Commons chamber generated

---

[36] *Parliament 1789. The Parliamentary Register: Or, History of the Proceedings and Debates of the House of Commons [and of the House of Lords] Containing an Account of the Interesting Speeches and Motions … During the 1st Session of the 14th [-18th] Parliament of Great Britain*, available at https://books.google.co.uk/books?id=kpQwAAAAMAAJ&pg=PA130&dq=12th+may+1789&hl=en&sa=X&ved=0ahUKEwj8xsbAk7nYAhXQ16QKHff3AMg4ChDoAQgmMAA#v=onepage&q=12th%20may%201789&f=false (accessed 29 Oct. 2018).

[37] J. Kantner, 'Realism vs Reality: Creating Virtual Reconstructions of Prehistoric Architecture', in *Virtual Reality in Archaeology*, ed. J.A. Barceló, M. Forte and D.H. Sanders (Oxford, 2000), 47–52; S. Moser, 'Archaeological Representation: The Visual Conventions for Construction of Knowledge about the Past', in *Archaeological Theory Today*, ed. I. Hodder (Cambridge, 2001), 262–83; J. Bateman, 'Immediate Realities: An Anthropology of Computer Visualisation in Archaeology', *Internet Archaeology*, viii (2000), available at http://intarch.ac.uk/journal/issue8/bateman_index.html (accessed 29 Oct. 2018).

Figure 2: Model of the 1707 House of Commons Produced as Part of the 'St Stephen's Chapel, Westminster' Project by Dr Anthony Masinton, Centre for the Study of Christianity and Culture, University of York.

from the visualisations in a Computer Aided Design (CAD) format (see properties of a room, Table 1). CAD models are used to create architectural drawings from vector-based graphics, meaning that they are created at full scale in a digital 3-D Cartesian space which is visualised through points, lines, and polygons. These points, lines, and polygons represent exact dimensions and are produced in three dimensions, offering a different method of exploring a space. CATT Acoustic can work with models based in CAD, although the conversion process is not straightforward. CATT requires fully sealed models – that is, having no gaps in their geometric construction from which sound energy might otherwise leak – and the conversion process from CAD usually generates very complex models involving thousands of polygons that are difficult to identify. Instead, we built a simplified model directly in CATT using the CAD model as a source for the size of different parts of the space. The model is generated by first specifying the locations of points in Cartesian space (x,y,z), then using these points to define polygons. The model can then be observed and altered easily as each polygon can be marked up for reference. Being able to alter the space as we build it allows us constantly to reflect on our interpretation of the space. In order to create realistic visualisations, one has to consider how each polygon appears; what textures and fabrics make it up. In the acoustic model the process is similar, but instead of considering how light interacts with the polygons we must, instead, consider how the surfaces of these polygons would absorb or scatter sound. These elements must also be written into the model, generated from a library of materials within the CATT Acoustic program. That library has itself been generated by acousticians working largely with modern or designed buildings, and therefore for use in historic spaces these have to be selected for the best match or occasionally altered to fit.

    The house of commons is, and was, a space in regular use by people. These bodies also need to be considered as part of the modelling process. We know that the chamber was

Figure 3: Unknown Artist, after Sir James Thornhill & William Hogarth. 'The House of Commons; Sir Robert Walpole's Administration', c.1800. Parliamentary Art Collection, WOA 3067, *www.parliament.uk/art*.

considered to be full, its galleries packed, during the Wilberforce debate[38] and we must therefore incorporate this into our model. One of the tools included in the software allows us to model seating as occupied or unoccupied, including height of the audience; hence the chamber can be modelled as full, part full or empty.

The process of digital modelling is reflective and allows for alterations in a way that is not possible in the creation of physical models. At any point during the process the model can, and should, be examined, critiqued and altered until the modellers (in this

---

[38] *General Evening Post* (Tuesday–Thursday, 12–14 May 1789), quoted in Cary, 'William Wilberforce's Sentimental Rhetoric'.

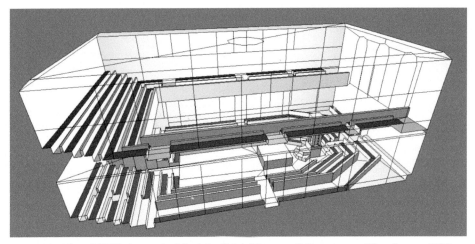

Figure 4: The CATT Acoustic Model of the House of Commons Chamber, c.1789, as Developed for, and Used as, Part of this Study.

case the Listening to the Commons team) are happy that it is the best interpretation of the data available. These decisions must be agreed before moving on to the next stage.

The final stage in model production is to define source and receiver positions. Wilberforce was an independent MP, suggesting that he would have sat on the back benches. We have not uncovered any direct evidence to suggest exactly where he would have sat, but a position towards the Speaker's chair has been selected. We have chosen the following positions to allow us to discuss the experience of sound within the chamber (see Figure 5 for locations):

- Wilberforce (A0)
- The Speaker (01)
- A front bencher opposition (02)
- A back bencher government (03)
- A back bencher opposition (04)
- Entrance (05)
- Public galleries (06, 07 & 08)
- Behind Speaker's chair (09)

The room impulse response is then calculated and generated by CATT Acoustic for each of these positions.

5. *Results*

In processing the model, the room impulse response (see properties of a room, Table 1) was generated for each listener position. From this we can explore a series of numerical

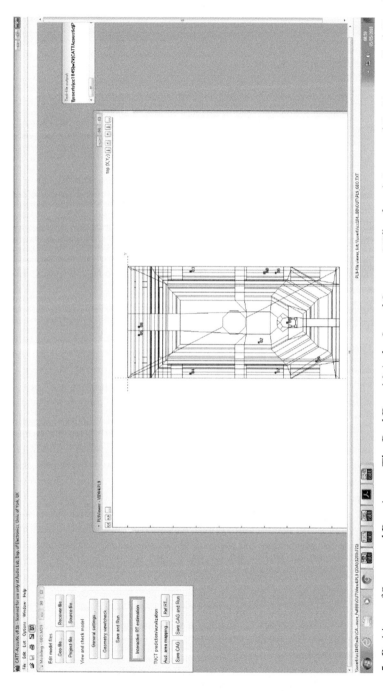

Figure 5: Positions of Source and Receivers – The Red Dot, A0, is the Sound Source – Wilberforce's Suggested Position as a Back Bencher. The Blue Dots are the Positions of our Various Listeners as Outlined in the Main Body of the Text.

Table 2: *Recommended Reverberation Times for an Occupied Room for Different Musical Performances*

Type of music	Reverberation time (seconds)
Organ	≥ 2.5
Romantic classical	1.8–2.2
Early classical	1.6–1.8
Opera	1.3–1.8
Chamber	1.4–1.7
Drama	0.7–1.0

Source: M. Barron, *Auditorium Acoustics and Architectural Design* (2nd edn, 2009), 30.

parameters which can be associated with how sound was experienced in the Commons chamber.

The reverberation time measured across all listener positions gives an average result of 1.56 seconds. Table 2 indicates the recommended reverberation times for an occupied room for different types of musical and dramatic performance. A result of 1.56 suggests that the space has a longer reverberation time than would be recommended for public speaking (paralleled here by drama). Instead, the space appears to be much better suited to musical performance such as opera or early classical. This suggests that, despite the alterations to St Stephen's Chapel, specifically the lowering of the ceiling, the space had not been completely adapted from a building designed for polyphony (and, perhaps, for organ music) to its new function as a forum for public speaking and debate.

To explore the difference in listener position we use the measure of objective Clarity (C50). This explores the balance between sound arriving at the listener from around the space earlier, rather than later (with a threshold between the two of 50 milliseconds). Earlier arriving sound in this context contains more of the 'direct' and non-reflected sound, as opposed to the more reflected reverberant sound that arrives slightly later. A visual analogy would be to consider whether there is line-of-sight between sound source and listener – if the listener can see the sound source, sufficiently early, sound should arrive to increase the Clarity (C50) measure. If the space is very large, the reverberant energy may overwhelm the direct sound, even with good line-of-sight, reducing the Clarity (C50) measure. It would be expected that a lecture room, designed for speech, would have higher values of Clarity (C50) than a very large and reverberant church. Optimal listening conditions for speech would indicate larger, positive values of Clarity (C50). A value close to 0 indicates a balance between early and late parts of the sound, with a value of -2dB (decibels) often being considered as the minimum acceptable for speech clarity for a listener. This comparison of objective clarity is illustrated in Table 3.

The results show that, although certainly acceptable, none of the listening positions are ideal. The optimal positions appear to have been at the entrance to the Commons chamber, and behind the Speaker's chair; positions which would, interestingly, not have offered a particularly good view, which we note as being an indicator of potentially higher Clarity (C50) results, nor placed an MP in direct view of those directly involved with the debate. From these measures it is of interest to note that the Speaker's chair and the front benches do not appear to have had a privileged listening position.

Table 3: *Results Comparing the Objective Clarity (C50) Measure for the Different Listener Positions being Considered*

Position	Objective clarity (C50) in decibels (dB)
01	1.3
02	1.63
03	2.08
04	2.32
05	0.61
06	2.64
07	0.99
08	3.24
09	1.06

6. Conclusion

While the past was not a silent unengaged world, the exploration of places in the past largely struggles to associate with the less tangible parts of experience. This essay has demonstrated one of the ways we can start to consider historic spaces beyond their visual experience, through examination of the wider sensory experience of the pre-1834 house of commons. The results of our modelling indicate some of the measures which we can use to track the acoustical properties of a space. First, we can see that, despite alterations, St Stephen's had not been adapted to function as a good venue for public speaking. Second, we can see that some seats in the House would have been able to hear more clearly the speakers in Commons debates. Third, the seats with a better listening experience were not those which visually and politically would have been considered at a premium. Some back benchers would have been able to listen more clearly to the speeches being given. Based on the measures presented in this work, as obtained from the model we have developed, the Speaker's chair and front benchers have a distinctly poorer experience of speech than those with a restricted view.

Some of these results support conclusions drawn by historians, specifically the poor experience of sound within the Commons chamber.[39] However, other conclusions, such as the lack of parity in the experience of debate, offer new ways of exploring the space. The potentially poor experience of speech at the Speaker's chair is particularly intriguing, possibly linked to its positioning close to where the altar had stood when the space was a medieval chapel. If the medieval liturgy was designed to create the best experience of that worship at the altar,[40] then some of those properties might have been preserved despite subsequent alterations to the building. A poor experience of the spoken word may be consistent with a good experience of the sung liturgy. The perception of sound at the Speaker's chair is less surprising, therefore, than would be expected if the building had been designed for speech in the first instance.

[39] Wilkinson, 'Politics and Topography'.

[40] Howard and Moretti, *Sound and Space in Renaissance Venice*.

Ventilating the Commons, Heating the Lords, 1701–1834[*]

ELIZABETH HALLAM SMITH

In 1833, the Commons chamber was described as a 'noxious vapour-bath', while the Lords deemed the insufferable heat and toxic smoke in its House as injurious to health. This situation was not new, as for more than a century both Houses had been battling with officialdom and technology to improve their working conditions. In their continuing quest for effective heating and ventilation they had drawn in many respected men of science and commerce as well as entrepreneurs and showmen of varying abilities, to little avail. Many machines were tried, Desaguliers's ventilating wheel alone achieving modest success. A notable institution arising from all these experiments was the ventilator in the Commons' roof, enabling ladies, barred from the chamber, to witness debates, albeit in considerable discomfort. After the 1834 fire, parliamentarians renewed their ventilating mission in their temporary chambers, before projecting their cumulative experience and opinions onto the far larger canvas of the new Victorian Palace of Westminster.

Keywords: Commons chamber; history of heating; history of ventilation; house of commons' ladies gallery; house of commons' ventilator; Jean-Frédérique, marquis de Chabannes; John Theophilus Desaguliers; Lords chamber; Sir Humphry Davy; St Stephen's Chapel, Westminster

1

When in 1692, following a major programme of reconstruction, members of the house of commons returned to their chamber in the former St Stephen's Chapel, they found it transformed. At a cost of some £4,600, almost double the sum he had quoted for the work, Sir Christopher Wren had secured the crumbling fabric, removed the medieval clerestory and installed a new roof. He had provided for the House an elegant and far more comfortable wainscoted meeting-place with new galleries, supported in part by elegant and innovative iron columns by Jean Tijou.

Further changes were made in 1707 after the Act of Union, to accommodate the Scottish members, including extending the galleries: the finest craftsmen of the day were deployed, including Grinling Gibbons who carved the capitals of the extended gallery supports.[1] At

[*]Research for this essay was stimulated by the 'Listening to the Commons' project workshop, led by the University of York and held in October 2017, and by discussions with colleagues in the Houses of Parliament Architecture and Heritage Team and Vote 100 Project. The author would particularly like to thank Dr Mark Collins, Adam Watrobski, Tessa Blundy, Dr Mari Takayanagi, Melanie Unwin, Professor Sarah Richardson, Amy Galvin-Elliott, Dr Caroline Shenton, Paul Seaward, and from the University of York, Dr John Cooper, and Professor Tim Ayers. Further thanks are recorded below in the appropriate notes.

[1]For Wren's design for the House, see A. Geraghty, *The Architectural Drawings of Sir Christopher Wren at All Souls College, Oxford* (Aldershot, 2007), 224; H.M. Colvin, R. A. Brown, J.M. Crook, M.H. Port *et al.*, *The History of the King's Works* (6 vols, 1963–82) [hereafter cited as *KW*], v, 402–4.

last, MPs seemed to have gained a modern and fitting setting for conducting their business, created within, and concealing, the formerly echoing gothic shell of their chamber.[2] If the House needed to be warmed, this could readily be achieved by bringing in braziers.[3] But, within a few years of the initial changes, a problem had emerged that would bedevil the Commons chamber until its destruction by fire in 1834: how to prevent intolerable heat from building up when the House was full.

The house of lords, too, had significant heating and ventilation problems. The peers' original chamber, the medieval former Queen's Hall, where they sat from c.1259 to 1801, was afflicted by cold and draughts. But, after their relocation to the former White Hall or Court of Requests nearby, their lordships suffered from wildly fluctuating temperatures and toxic smoke. The response of both Houses was to hold numerous inquiries into their working conditions, seeking advice from a wide range of experts, both real and perceived: leading men of science, philosophers, entrepreneurs, showmen, and crackpots.

Neither these men nor the office of works, responsible for maintaining the old Palace of Westminster, succeeded in making either chamber more commodious. Instead, through sheer neglect, they created conditions which enabled the fire which broke out in the Lords' heating system on 16 October 1834 to rage unchecked for several hours. This might suggest that – apart from providing posterity with visions of eccentric contraptions, cautionary tales of the consequences of neglect, and entertaining moments of high farce – the parliamentary heating and ventilation saga is of little importance. Indeed, recent studies of the building of the new palace after 1834 portray a brand-new chapter in member engagement with the building process and in parliament's drawing upon the talents of many of the leading scientists of the day.[4]

However, as this essay will show, this was not the case. In advising on Charles Barry's new Palace of Westminster as it rose from the ashes, members built on more than a century of active interest and involvement in the heating and ventilation systems of their chambers, a process which had reached a crescendo in the 1830s.[5] In this, the two Houses had consistently deployed the expertise of leading men of science and entrepreneurs – even if the advice was at times ignored or, in its implementation, altered beyond recognition. The opportunities presented by the new palace, built according to rigorous and progressive scientific principles and clothed in a new national style of gothic re-imagined for the age of machines, gave these ingrained habits enormous impetus and members a far wider canvas to work upon. Thus, in proactively seeking to influence the nature and deployment of the vitally-important heating and ventilation systems in the new palace, members would be able to build upon well-established traditions and take them further.

---

[2]Parliamentary Art Collection, WOA 2737.

[3]C.J. Richardson, *A Popular Treatise on the Warming and Ventilation of Buildings* (2nd edn, 1838), 98–9.

[4]E.J. Gillin, *The Victorian Palace of Science: Scientific Knowledge and the Building of the Houses of Parliament* (Cambridge, 2017); H. Schoenefeldt, 'The Temporary Houses of Parliament and David Boswell Reid's Architecture of Experimentation', *Architectural History*, lvii (2014), 175–215; H. Schoenefeldt, 'Architectural and Scientific Principles in the Design of the Palace of Westminster', in *A.N.W. Pugin's Global Influence: Gothic Revival Worldwide*, ed. T. Brittain-Catlin, J. de Maeyer and M. Bressani (Leuven, Belgium, 2016), 174–99.

[5]C. Shenton, *The Day Parliament Burned Down* (Oxford, 2012), 16–21; C. Shenton, *Mr Barry's War: Rebuilding the Houses of Parliament After the Great Fire of 1834* (Oxford, 2016), 9–10.

The story also brings into sharp relief the rebarbative conditions often suffered by the members in the two pre-1834 chambers, especially when there was a full house.[6] In the confined conditions of the Commons, the heat, the fumes and smoke from the candles, the noise of the machines intended to remedy these ills, combined with the variable and challenging acoustics and often rowdy member behaviour, cannot have fostered civilized debate or enhanced comprehension of the proceedings. While the post-1801 upper House had far more space, this was often heated to insufferable levels, and the fumes rising through the floor from the coal fires below were clearly hazardous to health as well as to comfort. The impact of these often-hostile environments on the substance of parliamentary business, highlighted below, would repay fuller investigation.

The pre-1834 Commons' ventilator has, moreover, acquired both fame and infamy in its unlikely guise of a prototype ladies gallery for the Commons. The chaotic arrangements in the roof of the old House allowed a few women, barred from the chamber itself, to listen to debates from here, above its ceiling. This gave them a toehold – albeit of considerable discomfort – and even the ability to report on Commons' proceedings in the press. Whereas it would take until 1852 for the ladies officially to access their own dedicated, if still cloistered and incommodious, gallery in the Victorian chamber, the ventilator would provide an important precedent in their continuing goal to listen to the Commons – if not yet to participate.[7]

2. *Ventilating the Commons, 1701–69*

In 1701, not long after his remodelling work in the Commons was complete, a committee of the House called in Sir Christopher Wren to consider 'what may be done for the letting in the Air into the House, for the conveniency of the Members'.[8] Four pyramidal ventilating shafts were inserted into the wainscot ceiling, one at each corner of the chamber, described by a contemporary as 'four funnels on the top of the House'. These were intended to draw up the foul air and candle smoke.[9] But when the House was packed with MPs, they served only to blow the heat and smoke down onto the heads of the men sitting beneath them.

In 1715, distinguished inventor, Dr John Theophilus Desaguliers, was called by the Speaker, Sir Thomas Hanmer, to attend the board of works to propose 'a method to evaporate the unhealthfull breathing in the House of Commons'.[10] A protégé of Isaac Newton, a prolific and gifted experimenter, a fellow of the Royal Society and later chaplain to Frederick, prince of Wales, he had, in 1714, presented an experiment to the Royal Society about vitiating foul air, and was the author of a treatise on the construction of chimneys to minimise smoke.[11] In 1719, he was summoned by the house of lords to advise on how the

---

[6]Shenton, *The Day Parliament Burned Down*, 16–18.

[7]See *https://www.york.ac.uk/history/listening-to-the-commons/* (accessed 29 Oct. 2018).

[8]*CJ*, xiii, 413, 416.

[9]N. Luttrell, *A Brief Historical Relation of State Affairs from September 1678 to April 1714* (6 vols, Oxford, 1857), v, 36; J.T. Desaguliers, *A Course of Experimental Philosophy* (2 vols, 1733–44), ii, 560–1.

[10]TNA, WORK 4/1: 26, 28 Jan. 1715; *KW*, v, 404.

[11]P. Fara, Desaguliers, 'John Theophilus (1683–1744), natural philosopher and engineer', *ODNB*; A.T. Carpenter, *John Theophilus Desaguliers: A Natural Philosopher, Engineer and Freemason in Newtonian England* (2011), esp. 143; R. Buchanan, *A Treatise on the Economy of Fuel and Management of Heat* (Glasgow, 1815), 310; Royal Society

chimney in its chamber might be made 'more useful'.[12] His more substantial work for the Commons in 1723 was, in contrast, intended to remedy 'the inconvenience arising by the hot steam and want of fresh air in the House … when sitting late and a full House'.[13] Desaguliers believed that the answer was to place two fireplaces in the roof of the Commons, one at each end. When the fires were lit, these would suck the foul air up from the tops of Wren's pyramidal shafts via trunking, and then dispatch it onwards up their chimneys.[14]

Desaguliers installed this system, of which he was hugely proud, at the cost of £105, on the directions of the treasury. As long as the fires were burning and the air circulating before the House sat, this system, according to his own report, worked well. But he had the house of commons' housekeeper, Mrs Sarah Smith, to contend with, whose duties included not just attending committees but supervising the management and flushing out of the house of commons' lavatory, known as the stool room.[15] Occupying compact but comfortable quarters in the loft above the Commons chamber, Mrs Smith frustrated the operation of the ventilation system by refusing to light the fires in advance, as they would make her rooms too hot. The result was that the chamber became even hotter.[16]

This state of affairs continued until 1736. Even while William Kent was engaged with his visionary and strategic plans to remodel Westminster,[17] MPs were focused on more immediate concerns, asking Desaguliers to come up with a replacement system which would circumvent Mrs Smith. Perhaps they already had in mind the fanning wheel which the inventor had described in lectures to the Royal Society in 1734 and 1735 and shown as a scale model, and which was already proving its worth in confined spaces such as sick rooms (see Figure 1).[18] Without more ado, Desaguliers was paid £90 for his 'Centrifugal Wheel or new invented Air Machine', installed over the Commons in order to 'draw away the hot Steam arising from the Candles, and the Breath of the company in the house when it is very full'.[19]

It was a simple but powerful device. A square trunk, or sucking pipe, drew foul air up through an octagonal grille in the centre of the chamber's ceiling into the wheel and then out through an aperture in its front, the blowing pipe, into the internal roof space. From here it could escape outside, probably through the many gaps in the structure rather than louvres. The process could be reversed to suck fresh air into the chamber. Placed most probably over the clerk's room, closely abutting the north side of the chapel's loft at the

---

[11] *(continued)* Archives, C1.P/18ii: Desaguliers Papers, no. 2. My thanks to Rupert Baker, library manager at the Royal Society, for his help and advice.

[12] *LJ*, xxi, 38.

[13] TNA, AO 1/2451/157. Simon Neal's transcripts of building accounts for the old Palace of Westminster, held at TNA, have proved an invaluable resource for the period up to 1780.

[14] Desaguliers, *A Course of Experimental Philosophy*, ii, 560–1.

[15] Sarah Smith took over this role in 1722–3 in succession to her late husband, Thomas Smith, and exercised its duties until 1740–1: TNA, AO 1/2451/157; AO 1/2457/176; Westminster City Archives wills DCW/0120, no. 1483 (12 Aug. 1723), and no. 2356 (15 Apr. 1741); J.C. Sainty, 'The Subordinate Staff of the Serjeant at Arms, 1660–1850', *Parliamentary History*, xxv (2006), 398.

[16] Desaguliers, *A Course of Experimental Philosophy*, ii, 560–1.

[17] F. Salmon, 'Public Commissions', in *William Kent: Designing Georgian Britain*, ed. S. Weber (New Haven, CT, 2013), esp. 328–34.

[18] Royal Society Archives, EL/D2, nos 71–2; RBO/19, p. 91; C1.P/18ii: Desaguliers Papers no. 38. I am grateful to the Royal Society for permission to reproduce the original sketch by Desaguliers (here at Figure 1).

[19] TNA, AO 1/2455/170; Royal Society Archives, RBO/19, p. 288.

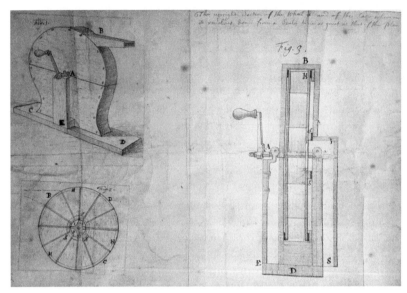

Figure 1: 'Account of an instrument or machine for changing the air of the room of sick people in a little time by either drawing out the foul air, or forcing in the fresh air, or doing both successively without opening doors or windows.' Royal Society Cl.P/18ii/38 Classified Papers series, scientific papers sent to the Royal Society by J.T. Desaguliers, 1734.

junction of the chamber and lobby, the wheel was in easy reach of the chamber but here its sound would, perhaps, not disturb the members.[20] A person known as a 'ventilator' was paid for turning it by hand: although it was 7ft tall, its inventor maintained that 'a Man can keep [it] in Motion with very little Labour, at the rate of two Revolutions in one Second'.[21]

There were clearly some teething troubles with this new system, as the wheel and tubes had to be dismantled and mended in 1737–8, and Desaguliers superintended his wheel in person until 1743.[22] But, successfully demonstrated to the lords of the admiralty in 1740, this 'classical machine' was well received, and widely adopted in ships as well as mines, hospitals and prisons.[23] From 1743 to 1769, Kemble Whatley, an associate of Desaguliers with a burgeoning carpentry business which would, in time, give him a leading role at Kew Gardens, was paid 3s. a day for overseeing and working the centrifugal wheel and air trunks at the house of commons when the house was sitting.[24] Much admired by historians of

[20]Richardson, *Popular Treatise*, 100, and fig. 1, plate 16; Sir John Soane's Museum, London, SM 37/1/25: 1793 copy of a 1718 plan. I am grateful to Dr Susan Palmer, archivist at the Soane Museum, for her helpful advice.

[21]TNA, AO 1/2455/171; Desaguliers, *A Course of Experimental Philosophy*, ii, 563–5; Royal Society, *Philosophical Transactions*, xxix (1735–6), 41–9. The Science Museum holds a 20th-century quarter-size working model of this wheel (ref. 1961-239): my thanks to Dr Oliver Carpenter, curator of infrastructure and built environment at the Science Museum, for his advice on, and demonstration of it.

[22]TNA, AO 1/2456/173; AO 1/2457/176–7; AO 1/2458/173.

[23]Carpenter, *Desaguliers*, 143–5; W. Bernan, *On the History and Art of Warming and Ventilating Rooms and Buildings* (2 vols, 1845), ii, 84–5.

[24]TNA, AO 1/2458/179 AO 1/2466/204; *https://kirbyandhisworld.wordpress.com/2017/10/19/kemble-whatley-carpenter/* (accessed 29 Oct. 2018).

ventilation, at Westminster, Desaguliers's wind machine would prove robust and long-lived: with only a short break in 1819, it and its successors would be used as a key part of the Commons' ventilation system until 1834.

3. *Heating the Lords, 1739–1801*

By contrast with the house of commons, the somewhat ramshackle house of lords, heated by a fireplace on its east wall,[25] had far too much ventilation and suffered from cold draughts. A 1735–6 plan by William Kent to extend and remodel it having come to naught, in 1739, the lords spiritual and temporal ordered the board of works to provide a layer of insulation below the floor of the chamber to prevent 'air and wind issuing through'.[26] Ventilating pipes, a funnel and vane were installed in 1762–3 and an iron range, previously displaced for a while by a stove, put back in 1766.[27]

The House was condemned in 1789 by the eminent architects called in to report on the condition of the palace as 'incapable of useful repair and improvement', and in June 1792, a committee was appointed to advise on making it more commodious.[28] Sir William Chambers was asked to advise if its air could be 'tempered' and, if it could not, whether peers should move to the adjoining former Court of Requests building. The first option was adopted as being cheap and easy, but the estimate of £150 was considerably exceeded: peers insisted on the installation of four stoves and ventilation tubes, with some £435 being paid out in 1793 for the upgrade.[29]

In 1794, their lordships returned to the topic and, having taken advice from John Soane, architect and clerk of the works at the Palace of Westminster, agreed his plan to improve both the heating and ventilation at a cost of £250.[30] Meanwhile, also at the Lords' behest, Soane was working on wide-ranging plans to remodel the Palace of Westminster, to the chagrin of Sir William Chambers, royal favourite and Soane's former superior and now rival.[31] Soane's ideas were both visionary and practical: they included a scheme for a hot air stove adjoining the Lords chamber to improve the temperature, a reflection of his interest in this technology.[32] Yet, to his mounting frustration, all this work went unimplemented and – until 1804 – unpaid for.[33]

---

[25] *KW*, v, 391.

[26] Salmon, 'Public Commissions', 337–8, including a delightful sketch of George II's appearance in the house of lords; *LJ*, xxv, 445: 20 Dec. 1739; Parliamentary Archives [hereafter cited as PA], WLS/2/2.

[27] TNA, AO 1/2464/198; *LJ*, xxxi, 254.

[28] *Report from the Committee Appointed to Inspect the Several Houses and Buildings Adjoining Westminster Hall, 22 July 1789*, esp. 5: in *Reports from Committees of the House of Commons, 1790*, 261–9; *LJ*, xxxix, 488; *KW*, vi, 512.

[29] *LJ*, xxxix, 507, 508, 509; TNA, WORK 4/17, 9 Nov., 7, 28 Dec. 1792; WORK 4/18, ff. 20, 31.

[30] *LJ*, xl, 250–1, 254; *KW*, vi, 513.

[31] *KW*, vi, 513.

[32] PA, HL/PO/JO/10/7/980; HL/PO/LB/1/14; RIBA SC82/12 (RIBA67087), a diagram of pipework, 1800; see also T. Willmer, 'Heating Methods and their Impact on Soane's Work: Lincoln's Inn Fields and Dulwich Picture Gallery', *Journal of the Society of Architectural Historians*, lii (1993), 26–58; S. Sawyer, 'Delusions of National Grandeur: Reflections on the Intersection of Architecture and History at the Palace of Westminster, 1789–1834', *Transactions of the Royal Historical Society*, 6th ser., xiii (2003), 237–50.

[33] *LJ*, xliii, 84, 137, 295; TNA, HO 42/67/10, ff. 27–8; Hansard, *Commons Debates*, 1st ser., i, col. 1131: 29 Mar. 1804; *KW*, vi, 513–14.

Soane would, in turn, be ousted by a rival, for it was James Wyatt, as Chambers's successor and architect to King George III, who took up the task of transforming the houses of parliament from 1798. In 1801, Wyatt moved the peers to the former Court of Requests as a temporary measure that, in the event, lasted until 1834.

4. *The Commons: Regulating the Air, 1769–1818*

Back at St Stephen's,[34] in 1769, MPs, led by the influential Sir George Savile, once again required relief from the 'great inconvenience from the heat of the House of Commons when it is full, and from the cold when it is thin'. John Cust, the ineffectual and ailing Speaker, called in Dr Franklin, Dr Knight, and other 'learned mathematicians' – leading men of science – to advise. The first of these experts was evidently Benjamin Franklin, at this time pursuing the interests of the American colonies in London, and hugely admired for his contributions to scientific discourse: among the numerous accomplishments for which he would later justly be celebrated was his improvement to the design of heating stoves. The second expert was, it seems, Dr Gowin Knight, entrepreneur, librarian at the British Museum and an authority on magnetism, who had served with Franklin on the council of the Royal Society and, like him, had been awarded the Copley Medal.[35]

With the assistance of these scientific titans, a scheme for new ventilators and stoves was devised, priced at £300, but, in the event, costing £220. The centrepiece was a great stove in the lobby with new machinery and piping, while above the chamber, two ventilating shafts were built through the roof to draw in the fresh air. It was almost certainly now that a flue was placed in the space around the central grille and louvres added to the side walls of the loft space to allow the foul air to escape more easily.[36] Yet, because the new equipment was not connected with the existing machinery – most of which, including the Desaguliers wheel, was retained – it proved largely ineffective.[37] Extant accounts from 1772 until 1782 show that the duty of 'working the centrifugal wheel' for the Commons needed two men – including a certain John Stone – to fulfil it. As earlier, their combined fee was 3s. a day, and there was further expenditure in 1773, 1776, and 1782, when the ventilator required minor repairs, cleaning and maintenance.[38]

The Commons returned to the fray in March 1791. A committee was appointed to consider the best way of regulating the air, for 'the members were annoyed with cold which did not depend on the ventilator, and with an accumulation of heat, which did'.[39] By 15

---

[34] For useful background, see Clare Wilkinson, 'Politics and Topography in the Old House of Commons, 1783–1834', in *Housing Parliament: Dublin, Edinburgh and Westminster,* ed. Clyve Jones and Sean Kelsey (Edinburgh, 2002), 141–65.

[35] B. Franklin, *Observations on Smoky Chimneys, their Causes and Cure with Considerations on Fuel and Stoves* (1793); [T. Tredgold], *The Theory and Practice of Warming and Ventilating Public Buildings* (1825), 223, 226–31, plates 5–6; e.g., Royal Society Archives, CMO/5/99: 14 Dec. 1767. For background, see G. Goodwin, *Benjamin Franklin in London, The British Life of America's Founding Father* (2016).

[36] TNA, WORK 29/34: cross section of the roof Section A, (undated).

[37] TNA, WORK 4/14: 23, 30 June, 14 July, 27 Oct. 1769; WORK 6/18, pp. 212–13; AO 1/2466/204; Bernan, *On the History*, 85; *KW*, v, 405.

[38] TNA, AO 1/2468/208; AO 1/2468/210; AO 1/2470/215; AO 1/2468/208; AO 1/2469/211; AO 1/2471/217.

[39] *CJ*, xlvi, 250; Bernan, *On the History*, 85.

April, they had undertaken a comprehensive inquiry, again calling in a range of experts to suggest options for enhancements.

Society architect, Henry Holland, was charged with improving the ventilation arrangements overall. For him, this was evidently a minor and routine piece of work, albeit costing a substantial £1,350,[40] but it played to his interests in new building technologies.[41] He had scant co-operation from Sir William Chambers who, as surveyor-general of the King's Works, was responsible for executing the scheme, but was clearly offended that the committee had gone straight to Holland, his former pupil and now rival. Moreover, Holland, assisted by John Soane, clerk of the works at Westminster, faced the thankless task of combining the disparate elements which the members themselves had selected.[42]

Joseph Bramah, prolific inventor and civil engineer, who was later credited by Samuel Smiles as the leading mechanical genius of his age, had his plans agreed at a cost of £467, although what these comprised is not clear.[43] The most striking known innovation was a huge stove manufactured at a cost of more than £120 and installed, with its pipework, by Messrs Jackson and Moser, ironmongers and braziers.[44] This was to the specification of Adam Walker, philosopher, inventor, and charismatic lecturer in experimental philosophy, famed for dramatic demonstrations of his transparent orrery and, more prosaically, the holder of a patent for a successful 'empyreal air-stove for purifying the air of churches, theatres, gaols, sick and other rooms, and enclosed buildings'.[45]

Walker's stove for the Commons was 6ft square and 14ft high, and filled with earthen pipes and retorts.[46] Placed in the undercroft crypt below the floor of the Commons' lobby, in the former courtroom of the City of Westminster's Burgess Court, its clay pipes carrying hot air pierced through the medieval vaults of the ceiling.[47] The warmth emerged through a floor grate 3ft 6ins in diameter and into the chamber, within 2ft of the clerks' table. Two thermometers were hung in the House to measure the temperature, supplied by David Jones at a cost of £14 14s.[48]

Members also ordered several changes to be made up above in the roof, but it is not known if, and how, all the elements either combined together or contributed to enhancing air quality. The existing air machine – Desaguliers's wheel – formerly above the clerk's room, was moved directly over the chamber by William White and improved for £179: this seemingly involved incorporating a driving wheel and a flue. White added an air machine

---

[40] TNA, T 29/65, pp. 113, 290; WORK 4/17: 22 June 1792; *Kentish Gazette*, 6 May 1791.

[41] This work does not feature in the principal biography of Holland: D. Stroud, *Henry Holland, his Life and Architecture* (1966), or in D. Watkin, 'Holland, Henry (1745–1806)', *ODNB*.

[42] *CJ*, xlvi, 415, 652; TNA, T 29/65, p. 113; WORK 1/5: 29 Mar., 8 Apr. 1781, 20, 22 Apr. 1791; WORK 4/17: 29 Apr., 27 May 1791; *KW vi*, 525.

[43] *CJ*, xlvi, 415; S. Smiles, *Industrial Biography, Iron Workers and Tool Makers*, ed. L.T.C. Rolt (Newton Abbot, 1967 edn), 183–97.

[44] Sir John Soane's Museum, London, Bill Book 4, pp. 188–210 (1791); *Boyles's New London Guide*, 1795.

[45] Adam Walker, *Walker's Method of Purifying the Air of Churches, etc.*: Patent 1533, 21 Feb. 1786; A. Walker, *A Philosophical Estimate of the Causes, Effects and Cure of Unwholesome Air in Large Cities* (1777); TNA, PROB 11/1642/55 (1821); *Manchester Mercury*, 17 Nov. 1789; *Nottingham Universal Advertiser*, 8 Oct. 1790.

[46] Richardson, *Popular Treatise*, 99; Bernan, *On the History*, 85.

[47] *Kentish Gazette*, 6 May 1791: the boiler was in 'a room formerly known by the name of "the Burgesses Court," through the ceiling of which the pipes are carried'; see E. Hallam Smith, ' "The Most Beautiful Specimen of Gothic Architecture which this Country has to Boast of": St Stephen's Cloister and Undercroft, 1548–1834' (forthcoming, 2019).

[48] *CJ*, xlvi, 415; Richardson, *Popular Treatise*, 99; *Kentish Gazette*, 6 May 1791.

of his own, at a cost of £84, supposedly to suck the rancid air directly through into the loft space.[49] These arrangements were experimental, lest the air machines should disturb the members below, and they appear not to have lasted for long, the wheel, once more hand-cranked, long outliving the not dissimilar, but more complex, air machine.

The new configuration necessitated fully opening up the octagonal ornament in the centre of the chamber's ceiling into the wide flue situated just above, which had a room constructed around it. Directly above the new opening, a large new louvre was built, extending through the top of the roof into a rectangular shed, and – probably until 1819 – joining on the skyline of Westminster the two earlier ventilating chimneys with their angled cowls. All these contraptions gave the exterior of the former chapel a distinctive and rather raffish appearance, as vividly shown in an 1805 engraving (see Figures 2 and 3).[50]

While members did not see their conditions as ideal, these arrangements would last for more than 20 years, with only a few modifications.[51] As earlier, the people responsible for 'working the ventilator at the Honourable House of Commons' appear in surviving accounts: between 1812 and 1818, these are John Stone, perhaps the earlier incumbent of the same name or, more probably, his son, and prosperous widow, Martha Gudge, of Old Palace Yard.[52] John's presence seems to reflect the widely-found dominance of family connections in transmitting rights to deliver service contracts at Westminster. Martha's appearance exemplifies the often-underestimated role that women – widows, wives or sometimes the daughters of male contractors – assumed in running businesses in Westminster and beyond.[53]

Until the end of the 18th century the fabric of the old Palace of Westminster – bar the hall – had, by and large, been treated with pragmatic disregard. But now the voices of antiquaries such as John Carter and Francis Douce, who considered the former St Stephen's Chapel as an architectural jewel worthy of preservation, were being heard.[54] In his 1790s schemes for improving the palace, John Soane strongly advised the restoration of the chapel to its medieval splendours.[55] James Wyatt, who ousted him in 1798, would go on, two years later, under the instructions of the House, to hack away its medieval side walls, destroying their sublime paintings in order to create extra space for the Irish members.[56] He would

[49] William White, *White's Machine for Expelling Foul Air from Mines, Ships etc.*: Patent 1681, 12 May 1789; *Oracle Bell's New World*, 6 June 1789.

[50] TNA, WORK 29/34: Section B, (undated); *KW*, v, 405; G. Arnald, 'South Side of the House of Commons from the Roof of the Painted Chamber, 1805', Parliamentary Art Collection, WOA 202, printed in J.T. Smith, *Antiquities of Westminster, The Old Palace, St Stephen's Chapel etc.* (1807), 146. For other images of the Commons' roof before 1819, see, e.g., the view from Westminster Bridge, in R. Ackermann, *Microcosm of London* (1808–10), and the 1815 Ackermann print at the Museum of London Prints and Drawings, Collections A 8763 and Z1390.

[51] E.g., in 1816, replacing a fireplace in the lobby with a stove to diffuse the heat more effectively throughout the House but reversing this in 1817: TNA, WORK 1/7, p. 197; WORK 4/22, p. 461; *Morning Post*, 4 Aug. 1818; *KW*, vi, 530.

[52] TNA, WORK 5/101–103; AO 1/2471/218; AO 1/2471/219; AO 1/2472/220; AO 1/2470/221. For Martha Gudge, see Fire Insurance Certificates: London Metropolitan Archives, MS 11936/465/893159 (1814), and MS 11936/488/980112 (1821). In 1810–11, a John Rayner was also rewarded £30 for regulating the ventilators in the Commons: *CJ*, lxvi, 449.

[53] Sainty, 'The Subordinate Staff'; N. Phillips, *Women in Business, 1700–1850* (Woodbridge, 2006), esp. 120–72.

[54] Rosemary Hill, ' "Proceeding like Guy Faux": The Antiquarian Investigation of St Stephen's Chapel, Westminster, 1790–1837', *Architectural History*, lix (2016), 253–79.

[55] TNA, WORK 11/28/10.

[56] *CJ*, lv, 761, 772, 780; Hallam Smith, '*The Most Beautiful Specimen*'.

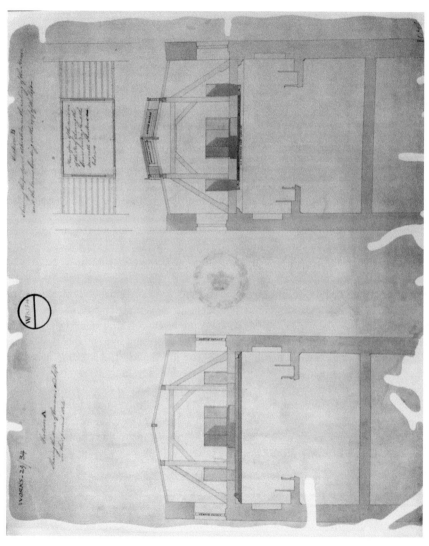

Figure 2: Section through House of Commons and Loft as Existing, and Proposed Alteration in the Ceiling of the House [probably 1791]: TNA, WORK 29/34.

Figure 3: G. Arnald, South Side of the House of Commons from the Roof of the Painted Chamber, 1805, © Parliamentary Art Collection, WOA 202, *www.parliament.uk/art*

subsequently damage much of the late medieval fabric of the adjoining cloister, imposing on it his own faux gothic vision. John Carter could do no more than fulminate, but he did so in the pages of the influential *Gentleman's Magazine*.[57]

Carter's observations, while often emotional in tone, provide valuable evidence about the state of the chapel before and after its remodelling by Wyatt. By contrast, he is not very forthcoming about the arrangements in the undercroft. Visiting it in 1800, Carter excoriated the use of the second bay from the west, the room where the boiler was situated, as 'a store-room for all the rubbish of a low mechanick [*sic*] and his necessary receptacles', with apartments for the same hapless mechanic adjoining in the third bay. In 1807, he describes the second bay simply as a coal-hole, although we know from Rudolf Ackermann that the boiler was still there in 1811.[58] Carter also criticized the misuse of the roof space. 'Who can talk of refinement', he raged in 1800, 'when we behold over the present ceiling, air-engines, … coal holes, maids' garrets, and men's leaking holes … mixing their accommodations with the beauties of art?'[59]

5. *Women in the Commons' Ventilator, 1818–19*

A somewhat more measured description of the arrangements in the space below the roof and above the Commons' ceiling is given by Frances, Lady Shelley, visiting in April 1818 to

---

[57] B. Nurse and J.M. Crook, 'John Carter FSA (1748–1817), "The Ingenious and Very Accurate Draughtsman"', *Antiquaries Journal*, xci (2011), 211–52; J.M. Crook, *John Carter and the Mind of the Gothic Revival* (Society of Antiquaries Occasional Papers, vol. 17, 1995).

[58] *Gentleman's Magazine*, lxx (1800), 725; lxxvii (1807), 735; Ackermann, *Microcosm of London*, 190–1.

[59] *Gentleman's Magazine*, lxx (1800), 838.

hear a debate – despite reports of the cramped and smelly accommodation which awaited her. John Bellamy, Commons' deputy housekeeper and head caterer, ushered her up the stairs directly to the west of the lobby, through the attic, into a dark niche in the wall and through a small door in the loft space. Here, she tells us, 'I found myself in a room about eight feet square, resembling a cabin of a ship. There was a window to admit air, two chairs, a table, and a thing like a chimney in the centre. This was the ventilator, which opens into the body of the House of Commons. Through it the sound ascends so perfectly that, with attention, not a word is lost.' The experience she counted as 'one of the most interesting days of my life'.[60]

Albeit much lacking in dignity and comfort, these arrangements marked a step forward for women who wanted some involvement with the political life of the nation.[61] For, while during the 18th century ladies had been permitted to sit in the strangers' gallery to witness debates, following a disturbance in 1778 when large numbers refused to clear the House, Speaker Fletcher Norton barred them. This was not an absolute ban, but their attendance was thereafter much frowned upon.[62] In 1804, Hester Sheridan had recourse to wearing a man's frock coat and trousers to enable her to sit under the gallery and hear her errant husband's speeches, while in 1810, Speaker Charles Abbott ejected even the princess of Wales and her female attendant from the gallery.[63]

In an innovative way of circumventing this exclusion, Lady Shelley was probably among the earliest women to have been admitted to the ventilator: a press report of 1822 described parties of ladies assembling in the roof as having occurred 'during recent sessions, and particularly during the last session'.[64] Candidates for the trailblazers include Frances, Lady Jersey, cited by Lady Shelley, and, championed in later suffragette writings, Elizabeth Fry, noted prison reformer and, in February 1818, the first woman to give evidence to a house of commons committee.[65] In reality, how and when these arrangements arose is not clear, but certainly they were embraced by women living in the grace and favour houses close to the Commons, such as the daughters of John Rickman, clerk assistant, who would be regular attendees later on.[66]

In 1819, this still fledgling practice must have been interrupted by an extraordinary and enormous – if short lived – ventilation contraption which was fitted into the roof space to remedy a further upsurge in member concerns about the atmosphere in the Commons chamber. In its aftermath, the space allocated to the ladies of the ventilator would

---

[60] *The Diary of Frances, Lady Shelley, 1818–1873*, ed. R. Edgcumbe (2 vols, 1913), ii, 7–8. For the access stairs, see the William Capon plan at Westminster City Archives, E133 (107).

[61] For a fuller account, see Sarah Richardson's essay in this volume.

[62] J. Hatsell, *Precedents of Proceedings in the House of Commons; under separate titles. With observations* (new edn, 4 vols, 1818), ii, 181–2: my thanks to Paul Seaward for this reference; S. Richardson, *The Political Worlds of Women: Gender and Politics in Nineteenth Century Britain* (2013), 129–35; P.D.G. Thomas, *The House of Commons in the Eighteenth Century* (Oxford, 1971), 148–9.

[63] *The Life and Letters of Sir Gilbert Elliot First Earl of Minto from 1751 to 1806*, ed. The Countess of Minto (3 vols, 1806), iii, 348; A. Wright and P. Smith, *Parliament Past and Present* (1902), 88–90; A.I. Dasent, *The Speakers of the House of Commons* (1911), 301–2. For other examples, see Sarah Richardson's essay in this volume, and P. Seaward, 'Parliament Observed' (forthcoming).

[64] *Morning Chronicle*, 12 Oct. 1822.

[65] *Women's Suffrage Journal*, xvi, 1 May 1885; see Sarah Richardson's essay in this volume, esp. n. 17; my thanks to Sarah Richardson for helpful discussions on this.

[66] *Good Company in Old Westminster and the Temple*, ed. C. Hill (1925), 24–5.

undergo some changes, but without either enhancing their comfort or improving their experience.[67]

6. *The Marquis de Chabannes and the Commons' Heating System, 1818–19*

Of all the heating and ventilation systems employed in the houses of parliament between 1701 and 1834, that of swashbuckling and eccentric inventor, Jean-Frédérique, marquis de Chabannes, is the most infamous for its intrusive presence and ineffective performance, and, indeed, for putting the safety of St Stephen's and the members at risk. Born in 1762 and, in his youth, a dashing soldier, Chabannes had started his business enterprises in London while an exile from the French revolutionary régime. Following the end of the Napoleonic wars, he had established business interests on both sides of the channel, in London operating from a showroom at 56 Howland Street, near Fitzroy Square, and a manufactory and foundry at 121 Drury Lane. A valuable modern assessment of his life and work suggests that 'his fugitive commercial career before this point suggests something of the crackpot or charlatan'.[68]

Chabannes had registered two patents for heating and ventilation systems in 1815 and a third in 1817. His approach, using a combination of hot air, hot water and steam, was not particularly original, but Chabannes was more effective than his competitors in promoting it through pamphlets and press coverage. Its most distinctive feature, which was innovative in England, was the 'calorifère fumivore' stove with its flue to carry off the smoke.[69] Although it was judged, in retrospect, as 'one of the worst in its class' as a ventilator,[70] it was initially a considerable commercial success; for example, in 1818, the marquis successfully deployed it at Covent Garden Theatre and Lloyd's Subscription Rooms, with much positive publicity, and the next year it was rolled out at the eye hospital in Marylebone Fields, at the hospital 'for insane patients of the army' at Chatham, and at the Olympic Theatre.[71]

It was to Chabannes that the Commons, led by their new Speaker, Charles Manners-Sutton, turned. In August 1818, the marquis, expressing 'extreme satisfaction in having been consulted', submitted a comprehensive plan to the office of works to upgrade the Commons' heating system.[72] The impurities in the air in the Commons were attributed by

[67] A. Lee, *Description of the Cosmographic Views and Delineations of the Ancient Palace of Westminster and St Stephen's Chapel* (1821), in PA, ARC/VAM/1, p. vi.

[68] Martin Meade and Andrew Saint, 'The Marquis de Chabannes, Pioneer of Central Heating and Inventor', *Transactions of the Newcomen Society*, lxvi (1994), 205. Chabannes died in 1836.

[69] J.F. de Chabannes, *De Chabannes' New Method of Extracting Caloric from Fuel*: Patent 3875, 16 Jan. 1815; *De Chabannes' Improvements in Regulating the Temperature of Houses etc*.: Patent 3963, 5 Dec. 1815; *De Chabannes' Improvements in Warming, Cooling and Conducting Air in Houses*: Patent 4192, 19 Dec. 1817; J.F. de Chabannes, *Explanation of a New Method for Warming and Purifying the Air in Private Houses and Public Buildings* (1815); e.g., *Morning Post*, 31 Oct. 1817, 25 June 1819; Meade and Saint, 'Marquis de Chabannes', 204–8; Bernan, *On the History*, 91.

[70] Bernan, *On the History*, 92.

[71] J.F. de Chabannes, *On Conducting Air by Forced Ventilation and Regulating the Temperature in Dwellings* (1818); J.F. de Chabannes, *Appendix to the Marquis de Chabannes' publication, on conducting air by forced ventilation, and equalizing the temperature of dwellings* (1819); Anon., 'On the ventilation of Covent Garden Theatre', *Journal of Science and the Arts*, v (1818), 300–5, and plates VII–VIII; M. Wyman, *A Practical Treatise on Ventilation* (Cambridge, MA, 1846), 216; Bernan, *On the History*, 92–5.

[72] TNA, WORK 1/9, pp. 247 50; WORK 11/24/11, no 1586· 6 Mar 1819. For Manners-Sutton, see N. Gash, 'Sutton, Charles Manners–, first Viscount Canterbury (1780–1845)', *ODNB*.

Chabannes – not unfairly – to the inadequacies of the openings in the roof, the ineffective functioning of the wind machine (i.e., the ventilating wheel), the insufficiency of fresh air, and its inefficient distribution within the House.

Chabannes proposed a major upgrade to remedy all these points, at a preliminary estimate of £600, but his plans occasioned some concerns from the office of works as to the efficacy and safety of his proposed scheme.[73] Steam pumping was a relatively new technology, used primarily by Boulton and Watt for industrial premises and, in the preceding few years, violent explosions had 'not unfrequently happened' when water had been allowed to collect in the pipework of steam boilers.[74]

Protracted discussions followed. Manners-Sutton, keen to see the scheme progressed, was warned that: 'it was necessary … to ascertain whether its adoption would endanger the safety of the Building, either in its construction, or by any accident from fire'.[75] These fears were allayed by the marquis, a much-increased price of £1,100 plus £200 for bricklayers' labour was agreed and the works were launched in mid-March 1819.[76]

The commission was Chabannes's most prestigious yet, and he describes it with great pride in an illustrated pamphlet published during 1819 (see Figures 4 and 5). To suck air out of the chamber, a huge case or trunk was constructed above it on the site of the previous ventilator in the roof of the Commons. Twenty feet tall, this contained 16 steam cylinders inside, and was attached to vents to suck the foul air from around the House at gallery and floor level and send it up through the roof via a very substantial cowl, 4ft in diameter and topped by a jaunty weathervane.

Air was pumped into the chamber through another set of trunking, much of it being sucked through 12 steam cylinders fitted under the seats and debouching into the chamber. At the turn of a valve, these could be used to raise the temperature. The copper steam boiler which powered the machinery, made by James Lewis, was once again below the Commons' lobby – in the undercroft, in the second bay from the western end – with a supply of fresh air coming in from Cotton Garden to the south.[77]

The board of works had agreed to fund this major project but had specified that Chabannes's own fee was not to be paid until the efficacy of the new arrangements had been demonstrated. This was a wise caveat, for the final cost was almost £1,700, the increase caused by 'the frequent alterations which the marquis de Chabannes made in his original work' during the deployment. Chabannes cannot have assisted his cause by submitting his invoice in May 1819, well before the works were completed, and by again demanding payment in July.[78]

While the marquis asserted initially that his system was 'more than sufficient to keep the house constantly refreshed',[79] once it was up and running it proved wholly unequal

[73]TNA, WORK 4/23, pp. 211, 214, 217, 221–2.

[74]Buchanan, *A Treatise on the Economy of Fuel*, 172.

[75]TNA, WORK 4/23, pp. 361–2; WORK 11/24/11, no. 1586: 6 Mar. 1819; Soane Museum, Priv. Corr. XI, D no. 38; Priv. Corr. XII, J 1.11.

[76]TNA, WORK 4/23, pp. 368, 371, 373, 393; WORK 5/107: 5 July 1819.

[77]Chabannes, *Appendix*; TNA, WORK 11/24/11, no. 1588: 9 Mar. 1819; Richardson, *Popular Treatise*, 101–2.

[78]TNA, WORK 1/9, pp. 247–54; WORK 4/23, p. 472; WORK 5/107: 5 July 1819; WORK 5/108: Tradesmen's Bills, 5 July 1820; WORK 11/24/11, f. 7: 11 May 1819; *KW*, vi, 530–2.

[79]Chabannes, *Appendix*.

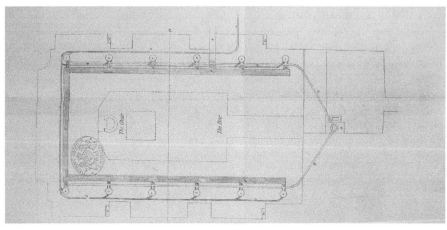

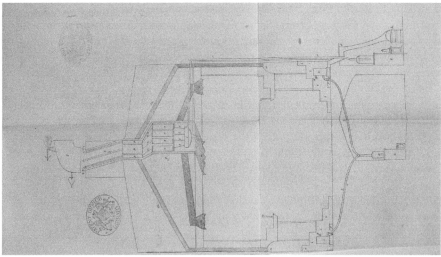

Figures 4 and 5: Plan and Section of the House of Commons' Ventilation System from Appendix to the Marquis de Chabannes's Publication on Conducting Air by Forced Ventilation, pp, 15, 19. © British Library Board.

to the task. On 17 June 1819, the Speaker told the office of works that 'the Marquis de Chabannes has not succeeded in ventilating the House of Commons to his satisfaction or to that of Members of the House'.[80] Below stairs, things were no better: one of the workmen overseeing the boilers attested years later that Adam Lee, labourer-in-trust, was perpetually urging that the fires be kept safe, in case the House should burn down.[81]

Within the chamber, 'the heat was found so excessive', according to an office of works report, 'that resort was had to putting up the old apparatus which was on top of the House of Commons in order to force cold air into the House; but as it was then used, it made such a noise that it disturbed the Members, [so] the marquis undertook to put up a wind machine for the purpose'. This, we are told, he then replaced with a larger wind machine, but that did not serve and was largely demolished. The old machine was brought back, 'which appears now to answer'.[82] It seems that this was none other than the trusty ventilation wheel, hand-cranked, returning at the behest of Adam Lee.[83] As for the marquis, because of these disasters, he was paid a mere £200 for his pains, in July 1820: by this time, his heating business had collapsed in ignominy and debt.[84]

The hasty reinstatement of older arrangements did nothing to improve conditions in the House: on 14 July 1819, Manners-Sutton summoned senior works officials to the House and demanded 'an effectual means for ventilating that building'.[85] By the end of 1819, more elements of the earlier heating and ventilation systems had been brought back into operation in the Commons, although their precise configuration is unclear. But there were some benefits for the antiquaries: so extensive had been the 1819 works in the roof of the Commons that the partitions for the servants' rooms and the wainscot from the walls had all had to be removed, opening up the roof space and exposing the medieval features of St Stephen's Chapel.[86]

A further significant change was the arrival of a large octagonal ventilator, also known as the lantern, hidden from below by the great central chandelier in the chamber. Constructed above the octagonal void in the same place as the earlier large flue, and built perhaps in stages, it was in place possibly in 1819 and certainly by 1821.[87] A distinctive feature in the 1834 plans and sections of Thomas Chawner and Henry Rhodes (see Figure 6), it stood about 14ft high and had 16 rows of apertures designed for the egress of foul air into the roofspace. These also provided limited views of proceedings below.[88]

[80]TNA, WORK 1/9, p. 353: 16 June 1819.

[81]*Report of the Lords of the Council respecting the destruction by fire of the two Houses of Parliament* (HC 1835, Vol. xxxvii [1]), pp. 58–9.

[82]TNA, WORK 1/10, pp. 166–8; Soane Museum, Priv. Corr. XI, D 38: an engineer's report on the performance of the ventilating machine shows it was being turned by hand in 1828.

[83]Soane Museum, Priv. Corr. XI, D 38.

[84]TNA, WORK 5/8: Grant of Parliament Account, 5 July 1820; WORK 1/10, pp. 167–8; WORK 5/108: Tradesmen's Bill, 5 July 1820; Bernan, *On the History*, 94–5; Meade and Saint, 'Marquis de Chabannes', 209.

[85]TNA, WORK 4/23, p. 466.

[86]Lee, *Cosmographic Views*, pp. v–vi.

[87]Lee, *Cosmographic Views*, p. vi. See the comments by Mrs Bankes about the creation of protective barriers in this area to prevent the women above from their previous practice of dropping items through the gap: *Morning Post*, 9 Aug. 1832.

[88]TNA, WORK 29/20–27, with facsimile and commentary in M.H. Port, *The Palace of Westminster Surveyed on the Eve of the Conflagration, 1834* (London Topographical Society Publications no. 171, 2011); TNA, WORK 29/3288: C.J. Richardson's 1835 plan.

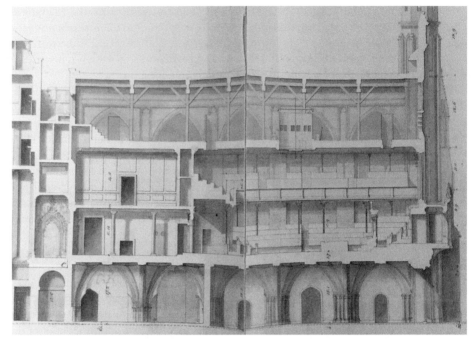

Figure 6: No. 7 Section from West to East … Showing the Different Storeys of the House of Commons Buildings, August 1834: TNA, WORK 29/27.

7. *Women in the Ventilator, 1820–34*

As before 1819, the space around the ventilator was occupied by a select band of women – wives of MPs and officials, high-ranking women and their attendants – to hear debates.[89] A lively watercolour of c.1821 attributed to the young Georgiana Lascelles (later Lady Chatterton) depicts society ladies peering through the apertures at the proceedings going on below, also showing the chandelier and – apparently – some scaffolding in the chamber (see Figure 7).[90] This preceded, or was perhaps connected with, the works initiated by Speaker Manners-Sutton in August 1822 to provide 'some additional ventilation to the House', given that it was 'still in a very defective state'.

By November 1822, the work had been completed: the chandelier had been upgraded and two extra ventilators now flanked it, measuring 7ft by 2ft. One was over the strangers' gallery, and the other over the Speaker's chair, with a further six small openings set at intervals around these three larger apertures.[91] Press reports noted that no extra 'peep holes' for the women observers were added, instead singling out for positive comment the tasteful

---

[89] A. Galvin-Elliott, 'Out of "Site", out of Mind? The Hidden Ladies of the Ventilator', available at *https://ukvote100.org/2017/05/19/out-of-site-out-of-mind/#_ftnref3* (accessed 29 Oct. 2018).

[90] Watercolour attributed to Lady Georgiana Chatterton showing the ventilator above the house of commons chamber, c.1821 (Baddesley Clinton Collection), Shakespeare Birthplace Trust, DR759/4.

[91] TNA, WORK 4/25, p. 350; *Morning Post*, 30 Aug. 1822.

Figure 7: Watercolour attributed to Lady Georgiana Chatterton Showing the Ventilator above the House of Commons Chamber, c.1821, Baddesley Clinton Collection, Shakespeare Birthplace Trust, DR759/4. Image Courtesy of the Shakespeare Birthplace Trust.

embellishment of the gratings in the ceiling with national emblems – the rose, the thistle, and the shamrock – reflecting the design of the gratings in the floor.[92]

The use of the great central ventilator by the ladies was well established by the mid-1820s, and widely reported. The sergeant-at-arms issued 25 tickets each night through a ballot, enabling MPs and senior parliamentary staff to admit their family members and

[92]*Morning Chronicle*, 12 Oct. 1822; *Morning Post*, 28 Nov. 1822; Port, *The Palace of Westminster Surveyed*, no. 6, Attic Story. There are floor gratings of this type in the Great Hall at Penrhyn Castle: see *http://www.hevac-heritage.org/items_of_interest/heating/national_trust_properties/penrhyn_castle/penrhyn_castle.htm* (accessed 29 Oct. 2018).

Figure 8: Sketch by Frances Rickman of a Ventilator in the Ladies Gallery Attic in St Stephen's, 1834. © Parliamentary Art Collection, WOA 26, *www.parliament.uk/art*

distinguished political women. Not all ticketholders could be accommodated at once: for example, the press reported 29 ladies attending in February 1829. Refreshments could be purchased and, at times, with gentlemen present too, a party atmosphere prevailed.[93]

Yet the viewing of proceedings was a most uncomfortable experience, likened by a contemporary MP to a form of martyrdom.[94] Once in place, the ladies endured the smoke and heat rising from the House below. Mrs Georgiana Bankes, wife of George Bankes MP, commented wryly in 1832 that they did their best 'to stifle the voice of the House of Commons, by preventing its members from breathing freely'.[95] Sixteen old chairs were provided around 'what seemed like a sentry-box of deal boards' for the women at first to stand and later to sit on, and peer down through the apertures through the chandelier and into a small area of the House.[96] This arrangement is depicted in a pencil sketch of 1834 by Frances Rickman, daughter of John Rickman, clerk assistant (see Figure 8).[97]

[93] *Brighton Gazette*, 12 Feb. 1829; Dasent, *The Speakers of the House of Commons*, 280; Richardson, *Political Worlds of Women*, 132; K. Gleadle, *Borderline Citizens: Women, Gender and Political Culture in Britain, 1815–67* (Oxford, 2009), 55–9, 183–4; Sarah Richardson's essay in this volume.

[94] J. Grant, *Random Recollections of the House of Commons from the Year 1830 to the Close of 1835* (1836), 11–12.

[95] *Morning Post*, 9 Aug. 1832.

[96] An 1828 inventory of Commons' furniture and fittings itemises material in 'The Roof of the house'. This includes, around the ventilator '16 chairs leather seats, side of enclosure, footmatting round enclosure, 2–4 leaf screens, 2 wainscot tables, 1 back lantern': PA, OOW/51. See also A.J.C. Hare, *The Life and Letters of Maria Edgeworth* (2 vols, 1894), ii, 66–7: letter of 9 Mar. 1822.

[97] Parliamentary Art Collection, WOA 26, see also an anonymous watercolour of the ventilator in 1833: Westminster City Archives, E133.2 (005).

Figure 9: James Scott, View of the Interior of the House of Commons during the sessions of 1821–3 (1836). © Parliamentary Art Collection, WOA 3102, *www.parliament.uk/art*

Nevertheless, the acoustics in the ventilator were far superior to those in the chamber, where contributions from the gallery were often inaudible (see Figure 9).[98] In 1831, architect Benjamin Wyatt told the select committee on improvements to the House that the lantern above it allowed voices to be heard most distinctly.[99] This was echoed by Frederick Trench MP during a debate in the same year: 'the voice was continually, in consequence of the current of air from the eastern windows, carried into the lantern or loft above, and lost to all but the persons, generally females, seated there, whom the gentlest and softest sigh uttered by Gentlemen below never escaped.'[100] Consequently, the women could – and did – report in the press in a most lively fashion on politicians and proceedings in the House.[101]

The Lords allowed the ladies considerably better access to its chamber, for women, mainly the wives of peers, could enter the House and view the proceedings, spilling out from behind the curtains next to the throne into the space behind the throne itself.[102] The practice dated back to the late 17th century but did not command universal respect from the House,[103] and although, during the 1820s, the women were accommodated in one of the temporary galleries designed by Soane upon certain occasions, the arrangement did not persist. By the end of the decade, the attraction of listening to the Lords' proceedings proved so popular

[98] Hansard, *Commons Debates*, 2nd ser., xxiii, col. 916: 25 Mar. 1830; 3rd ser., i, col. 563: 16 Nov. 1830.

[99] Select Committee on House of Commons Buildings, *Report* (HC 1831, 308), p. 6, para. 4.

[100] Hansard, *Commons Debates*, 3rd ser., v, col. 1262: 12 Aug. 1831.

[101] E.g., *Leicester Chronicle*, 18 Aug. 1832; Sarah Richardson's essay in this volume.

[102] Hansard, *Lords Debates*, 1st ser., xxiv, col. 11: 30 Nov. 1812; 1st ser., xli, col. 1279: 17 Dec. 1819; Richardson, *Political Worlds of Women*, 135.

[103] Seaward, 'Parliament Observed'.

Figure 10: Print by Shury and Son of the House of Lords in 1834. © Parliamentary Art Collection, WOA 1331, *www.parliament.uk/art*

that the ladies frequently overflowed from behind the throne onto its steps, eliciting adverse reactions from the peers (see Figure 10).[104]

The position of the ladies gallery in Barry's lavish new Lords chamber in the new houses of parliament would be behind and above the throne, and the wives of peers were permitted to sit on its steps, reflecting to a degree these earlier arrangements.

Back in the Commons, in February 1835, as the House reconvened for the first time since the fire, the women spectators, deprived of their ventilator, found their way to the space behind the Speaker's chair in the temporary House.[105] This had been built in the shell of the pre-1834 house of lords, and their positioning was clearly no coincidence: it was the precise spot which the ladies had occupied in the Lords just a few months earlier. Speaker Manners-Sutton, who would be voted out of office on 19 February, the first sitting day in the temporary chamber, must surely have intimated his acquiescence, perhaps with the encouragement of his wife, Ellen, who had listened to debates from the ventilator.[106]

Yet this arrangement was fleeting, for attempts to provide a gallery for the women in the temporary chamber were overruled in 1837.[107] While by 1842 they had succeeded in covertly establishing themselves in a tiny apartment concealed at gallery level, this held only

[104] Wright and Smith, *Parliament Past and Present*, 89–92; *The Times*, 5 Mar. 1833.

[105] *Athlone Sentinel*, 27 Feb. 1835; *Sussex Advertiser*, 23 Feb. 1835.

[106] Hansard, *Commons Debates*, 3rd ser., xxvi, cols 3–59: 19 Feb. 1835; see the anecdote about Manners-Sutton's positive reaction to a lady straying into the gallery in 1834, in Grant, *Random Recollections*, 17–18; Sarah Richardson's essay in this volume.

[107] Hansard, *Commons Debates*, 3rd ser., xxxviii, cols 1481–4: 15 June 1837; Sarah Richardson's essay in this volume.

12 or 13 ladies.[108] It was not until 1852 that they were officially, if grudgingly, permitted to hear the proceedings of the House. This time, they were confined to Barry's ladies gallery, which, perched high above the new Commons chamber and concealed behind its infamous metal grilles, was, in 1908, admitted by Speaker James Lowther to have been 'a survival of the old ventilating shaft and the fiction that ladies were not in the House at all'.[109]

8. *Ventilating the Lords, 1801–34*

During the first third of the 19th century, the heating and ventilation systems of the house of lords were consistently ineffective, hazardous, and poorly managed. In 1801, the House had been moved into the great Romanesque hall to the south of Westminster Hall, known formerly as the White Hall, and occupied since about 1516 by the Court of Requests. In the early 1720s, it had been modernised by the addition of a clerestory of Diocletian windows, and an undercroft vaulted in brick, which was used for storage, had been created at ground level.[110] Its medieval origins and historical significance almost unrecognizable, unlike St Stephen's Chapel, the Court of Requests occasioned very little interest from the antiquaries.[111] Wyatt fitted it up for the Lords initially as a temporary chamber.[112] In 1816, Soane, as attached architect, would report that this had been done in great haste, and that the buildings surrounding it were crowded together, of poor quality, lacking external staircases and constructed with combustible and perishable material.[113]

This temporary house of lords was heated by two furnaces housed in apartments to the south and feeding warm air into two narrow brick flues under the chamber, 100ft in length.[114] Provisions for the heating, ventilation and lighting of the House had not been made; and peers evidently found their new quarters rather bleak, setting up a committee in 1802 to improve their accommodation. They consulted James Wyatt, who recommended that two fireplaces be added, and when the Lords returned to the fray in 1804, proposed further improvements. Over the next two years, Wyatt, absorbed in his other massive and complex remodelling schemes at Westminster, became erratic in attending the House and sluggish in implementing his plans.[115] In 1808, Adam Lee, his labourer-in-trust, produced a fantastical drawing for the House, of a ventilator with a gothic revival chimney, but it was never executed.[116]

In 1810, peers tried a different approach. Setting up a new committee, they drew on the burgeoning expertise in natural philosophy which London now had to offer, summoning

---

[108] Sarah Richardson's essay in this volume, also citing *Derby Mercury*, 9 Mar. 1842.

[109] Select Committee, 1908, on House of Commons (admission of strangers), *Report* (HC 1908, Vol. ix [371]), p. 33.

[110] E.g., TNA, T1 /252, f. 259.

[111] J. Crook and R. Harris 'Reconstructing the Lesser Hall: An Interim Report from the Medieval Palace of Westminster Research Project', *Parliamentary History*, xxi (2002), 22–61; TNA, T 1/252, f. 259; Shenton, *The Day Parliament Burned Down*, 9; *KW*, vi, 514–19.

[112] *LJ*, xlvii, 636, 639.

[113] TNA, WORK 11/24/12, esp. f. 11.

[114] Museum of London, Prints and Drawings Collection A 15453: plan of the Palace of Westminster by Adam Lee, 1807.

[115] *LJ*, xliv, 16, 43, 482, 502; xlv, 187–8, 209, 212.

[116] Royal Institute of British Architects, London (RIBA) Drawing, SC82/3 (RIBA21591).

one of its leading lights, Sir Humphry Davy, to advise them.[117] At the peak of his career, at the helm of the Royal Institution, and famed for his scientific innovations and brilliant lectures, he was an expert of great standing with skills of considerable relevance. Yet, in mitigating the Lords' ventilation problems, despite at times attending and overseeing the work,[118] he was no more successful than the entrepreneurial chancer Chabannes would be in the Commons: modern biographies do not feature this aspect of his career.[119] However, it was a failure which he much regretted and for which he was much mocked by contemporaries.[120]

Summoned by a committee of the House in February 1810, Davy gave his advice pro bono.[121] He suggested that air flow in the chamber would be greatly improved by introducing cold air from outside into the flues below, heating it when necessary to raise the temperature and adding grates in the floor of the chamber. The foul air would find a ready exit through three copper pipes in the roof, converging in a ventilator. However, peers opted for far more minor modifications to the existing system, and these proved ineffective. Davy was – unjustly – criticized for this failure[122] and, after further consultations in September 1811, went back to his original proposal. In this he had great confidence, exhibiting a model of it during a lecture at the Royal Institution early in 1812.[123]

Davy once more attended a committee of the House in March,[124] and was clearly persuasive: the flues and grates in the floor were accordingly introduced in the chamber to his designs, with two fires above the chamber to warm his newly-installed ventilators in the ceiling and suck the foul air out.[125] All this served only to increase the discomfort of peers, in particular from the draughts from the 'vast number of small holes in the floor'. This was deemed injurious to health by some members,[126] and was satirised in an unkind epigram:

> For boring twenty thousand holes,
> The Lords gave nothing, damn their souls.[127]

In the face of hostility from peers and public ridicule, Davy was defensive about his new system. He stated that it could be readily adjusted since, thanks to the enhancements made, 'it is now practicable to change the whole air of the house in a very few hours'.[128] This was

---

[117] *LJ*, xlvii, 424, 456; I. Morus, S. Schaffer and J. Secord, 'Scientific London', in *London – World City, 1800–1840*, ed. C. Fox (New Haven, CT, 1992), 129–42.

[118] *Fragmentary Remains, Literary and Scientific, of Sir Humphry Davy, Bart.*, ed. J. Davy (1858), 139–40.

[119] D. Knight, *Humphry Davy, Science and Power* (Oxford, 1992); D. Knight, 'Davy, Sir Humphry, baronet', *ODNB*; but *cf* the mention in the *DNB* at *https://doi.org/10.1093/odnb/9780192683120.013.7314* (accessed 29 Oct. 2018).

[120] J.A. Paris, *The Life of Sir Humphry Davy* (2 vols, 1831), i, 347–8.

[121] Bernan, *On the History*, 85.

[122] Richardson, *Popular Treatise*, 102–4.

[123] *Morning Chronicle*, 3 Feb. 1812.

[124] *LJ*, xlviii, 613.

[125] Richardson, *Popular Treatise*, 102–4, and diagram opposite p. 104.

[126] Hansard, *Lords Debates*, 1st ser., xxi, col. 1076: 2 Mar. 1812.

[127] Bernan, *On the History*, 85.

[128] *The Globe*, 3 Mar. 1812. A letter from Davy to Lord Auckland at BL, Add. MS 58926, f. 49, dated 27 January but with no year, is likely to have been written in 1812 rather than in 1810 as the catalogue suggests.

to no avail: further complaints about the heat and atmosphere followed in 1813, the earl of Darnley making it clear that, much as he and the House admired Davy for his scientific talents, he had taken further advice from other experts which left him in no doubt that considerable improvements could be achieved.[129]

The eminent scientist now withdrew from the scene, travelling extensively with his new wife and recuperating from a laboratory accident which had damaged his eyesight. Between 1813 and 1818, the contractors who had to cope with the impact of Davy's heating arrangements were William Hanstock and Martha Gudge (who also held a similar contract in the Commons). They were paid £52 and £22 respectively per session for regulating the ventilators in the house of lords and for supervising its stoves and flues.[130]

After a gap in proceedings, the matter was revived in 1817, when the peers, in desperation, turned for advice to Adam Lee, still labourer-in-trust.[131] He told their committee that Davy's ventilating pipes, at only 1ft in diameter, were not capable of drawing off the heated air when the House was full, with the result that the temperature rose to more than 80 degrees Fahrenheit and the windows had to be opened. At times, these pipes sucked air into the chamber from outside – where the stench from the river Thames was notorious – rather than ejecting it, while the 100ft-long flues beneath the floor were known to expel hot and noxious gases from the coal fires in the furnaces, into the House, instead of trapping them below.

Lee advised enlarging the pipes and dispensing with the fires in the roof, and this was agreed – but these modifications served, if anything, to worsen conditions.[132] Major changes to the chamber were made in 1820 for the proceedings against Queen Caroline, including an extra gallery and an upgrade to its ventilation system at a cost of £582 and which featured a centrifugal wheel. But they were all swept away by the end of the year.[133]

After a lull, in 1828–9, the Lords' committee on the office of the clerk of the parliaments strayed once more into heating and ventilation. An expensive proposal to revamp the whole system – costing £700, although reduced from £1,054 – was put forward to the office of works by W. and M. Feetham of Ludgate Hill. They had recently cleaned and maintained the house of lords' basement flues and were experts in remedying smoky fireplaces. That was followed up with an offer of a patent atmospheric air dispenser for £300 from Robert Howden and Son. While all this was going on, the ever-active Adam Lee went on manœuvres, attempting to take control of the Lords' heating systems and to bring back a ventilating wheel.[134]

In July 1829, the committee decided it wished to proceed with the ventilation plans but not with the scheme to improve the heating. Benjamin Stephenson, surveyor-general of works, who was clearly exasperated with all the machinations, wrote to black rod, Sir

[129] Hansard, *Lords Debates*, 1st ser., xxvi, col. 209: 17 May 1813; 1st ser., xxvi, col. 564: 11 June 1813.

[130] *CJ*, lxx, 956; lxxiii, 518; Select Committee on Income and Expenditure of United Kingdom, 1816–18, *Tenth Report (Civil Contingencies)* (HC 1818, Vol. iii [269]), p. 98.

[131] *LJ*, li, 191, 332.

[132] Bernan, *On the History*, 86–7; TNA, WORK 4/23: 5 Dec. 1817; Hansard, *Lords Debates*, 2nd ser., iii, col. 463: 10 Oct. 1820, contains a comment by the lord chancellor on excess heat in the chamber.

[133] TNA, WORK 5/108: Tradesmen's Bills, 10 Oct. 1820; Soane Museum, Priv. Corr. XI, D 28; Priv. Corr. XI, D 38 no. 28. Richardson, *Popular Treatise*, 100, 102–4; Wyman, *Practical Treatise*, 219; *KW*, vi, 520.

[134] TNA, WORK 4/29, pp. 108, 125, 138, 255; WORK 1/17, p. 25; Soane Museum, Priv. Corr. XI, D no. 38.

Thomas Tyrwhitt, to inform him that he had had the machinery examined: 'It was found quite sufficient if properly managed for ventilating the House of Peers.' He said that he had ordered William Hanstock – who was still, as in 1818, in charge of the air systems – to attend black rod in order to receive his instructions on the matter.[135]

In 1831, the continuing unpleasant conditions in the House prompted the select committee on the library and related matters to call in Robert Smirke, attached architect to the office of works, with the remit of improving the ventilation system. Various works were authorised at a cost of £1,800 but, on the heating and ventilation front, the changes seem to have comprised little more than the removal of a fireplace.[136] So commonplace was extreme heat in the chamber that the housekeeper's deputy, Mrs Elizabeth Wright, who was on duty on 16 October 1834, told the committee investigating the conflagration that, initially, she saw nothing amiss there at the time when the fire was taking hold.[137]

Below the chamber, the hot and toxic smoke from the coal fires continued to surge through the flues directly below, their incremental cracking over two decades gradually allowing more and more heat to escape into the adjoining woodwork. As the years passed by, the risks were compounded by the build-up of clinker in the flues, the narrowness of which made their annual sweeping highly problematic, and by the proximity of much further flammable material – not just wood, but canvas and cloth as well – in the House above.[138] Fires in the matting in this area were a not infrequent occurrence and in c.1829 one had reportedly broken out in another flue nearby, below the Lords' lobby.[139]

In September 1834, black rod, Sir Augustus Clifford, who was particularly aware of the risks, since one of the stoves lay almost directly below his box in the chamber, issued new instructions to his staff, including mandating extra fire patrols.[140] But the tipping point came with the burning of wood in the stoves, rather than the best quality Welsh coal for which they were best suited. The unusually high temperatures which resulted put an exceptional strain on the antiquated heating arrangements, with all too predictable consequences.[141]

9. *Ventilating the Commons, 1822–34*

From 1822 to 1834, MPs continued to grumble about conditions in the House and to pursue their quest for the holy grail of its effective ventilation. But, given lingering official nervousness on this issue, any changes made were incremental and within existing office of works' budgets, rather than constituting any major remodelling.[142] The best visual evidence

[135] Select Committee on Office of Clerk of the Parliaments, *Report* (HL 1828, 181), p. 5; TNA, WORK 4/29, p. 273; WORK 1/17, pp. 150–1; *LJ*, lxi, 303; Soane Museum, Priv. Corr. XI, D no. 38; *Morning Post*, 3 Feb. 1827; *KW*, vi, 524.

[136] *LJ*, lxiii, 932: 22 Aug. 1831; 1091–2: 15 Oct. 1831; 1098–9, 18 Oct. 1831; *LJ*, lxiv, 7; Select Committee on the House of Lords Library, *Report* (HL 1831, Vol. 291 [126]); TNA, WORK 11/24/12; WORK 5/111: Mich. and Xmas Quarters 1831; WORK 4/31, p. 221; *KW*, vi, 524.

[137] (HC 1835, Vol. xxxvii [1]), pp. 5, 43.

[138] Shenton, *The Day Parliament Burned Down*, esp. 62–9; (HC 1835, Vol. xxxvii [1]), pp. 5–6, 37–8.

[139] (HC 1835, Vol. xxxvii [1]), pp. 31, 37–8.

[140] (HC 1835, Vol. xxxvii [1]), pp. 53–4, 62.

[141] (HC 1835, Vol. xxxvii [1]), p. 42.

[142] *Morning Post*, 30 Aug. 1822; TNA, WORK 4/26–31.

of the set-up – the depictions of the ventilator by Frances Rickman and the Chawner and Rhodes plans and section of the Commons[143] – dates from 1834 but is likely to reflect the configuration which obtained after the changes made in 1822.

From 1819, the system was managed by John Riches, reporting to Mr Bellamy, the deputy housekeeper, who was paid £105 per year, and was described in an 1833 select committee report as 'Ventilator Man'.[144] A significant weapon in his armoury was the ventilating wheel above the chamber, cranked by hand, and now micro-managed in person by Adam Lee, self-styled superintendent of the heating of the two Houses, who claimed it as his own invention.[145] Tantalisingly, the very edge of it appears in Frances Rickman's sketch (Figure 8), located near to the lantern. She also depicts a very large inverted umbrella-shaped cover atop the ventilator which is likely to be an acoustic baffle.[146] By now, all the excrescences on the top of the roof had disappeared, so the foul air ascending into the roof space through the nine internal flues must have, once again, been escaping outside through louvres and gaps in the side walls.[147]

Below the chamber there had also been some changes. An inventory of furniture and fixtures in the Commons in 1828 shows that, by this time, a 'large copper boiler and apparatus for warming the House' was located in the 'Ventilating Room (Cotton Garden)', adjoining the southern wall of the Commons' lobby.[148] Marked on the 1834 plan by Chawner and Rhodes as the Furnace Room, it lay directly south of the second bay from the west end of the undercroft, from where the boiler had been moved.[149] The space vacated was used, for a time, as a wine cellar, presumably to serve the Speaker's grand state dining room, which was sited next door beneath the chamber, but in 1834 it lay empty, apart from a few discarded barrels.[150]

By 1831, many MPs, led by the dogged radical, Joseph Hume, had concluded that the problems of lack of space, poor acoustics and defective heating and ventilation in their chamber were insoluble.[151] Henry Hunt suggested that members were at risk from cholera from the noxious air and, during several contributions to the discussions, Colonel Frederick Trench even opined that 'several members had lost their lives on account of the insalubrious atmosphere of the House'.[152] A select committee, set up in August, 'on the possibility of

[143] Parliamentary Art Collection, WOA 26; Westminster City Archives, E133.2 (005); Port, *The Palace of Westminster Surveyed*.

[144] Select Committee on Establishment of House of Commons, *Report* (HC 1833, Vol. xii [648]), pp. 111, 242, 245, 254.

[145] TNA, WORK 4/28, pp. 305; 313 (Lee managed to obtain an allowance of £50 for this in 1827); Soane Museum, Priv. Corr. XI, D 28.

[146] Parliamentary Art Collection, WOA 26.

[147] Port, *The Palace of Westminster Surveyed*, no. 7, Section.

[148] PA, OOW/51: inventory of house of commons furniture and fitting.

[149] Port, *The Palace of Westminster Surveyed*, no. 1, General Ground Plan. There is a depiction of the flue in a drawing of 1845 by Thomas Grissell, made during his restoration of the crypt: see Society of Antiquaries of London Westminster Portfolio, and T. Grissell, 'Observations on a Portion of the Crypt of St Stephen's Chapel, Westminster', *Archaeologia*, xxxi (1846), 323–5.

[150] Parliamentary Art Collection, WOA 1300A, 1300B.

[151] See Paul Seaward's essay in this volume; Shenton, *The Day Parliament Burned Down*, 16–21; *The Houses of Parliament*, ed. M.H. Port (New Haven, CT, 1976), 5–19.

[152] Hansard, *Commons Debates*, 3rd ser., ix, col. 315: 15 Dec. 1831; 3rd ser., v, cols 1261–3: 12 Aug. 1831; *Public Ledger and Daily Advertiser*, 12 Oct. 1831; see also Hansard, *Commons Debates*, 3rd ser., x, cols 270–1: 13 Feb. 1832.

making the House of Commons more commodious and less unwholesome', concluded that this was an impossible task: a new house was needed.[153]

Parliamentary business during the next two years was dominated by the debates on the legislation which became the Great Reform Act 1832, the poor conditions in the chamber doubtless exacerbating the extreme stress of the intensive and lengthy sittings. In March 1833, Hume, calling for further action, declared in exasperation that members were wedged in like herrings in a barrel.[154] A second select committee immediately followed:[155] this examined detailed options for a new chamber, inviting many of the leading architects of the day – including the recently-knighted John Soane – to produce plans, and grilling them on their proposals.

Reporting in May 1833, the committee's consensus was that 'the imperfect Ventilation of the present House is most injurious to the Health of the Members'.[156] While there was no agreement on how this might best be remedied, Hume, despite his reputation for excoriating waste in public spending, strongly pushed for a new House to the east of the existing chamber in St Stephen's Chapel. This, restored to its medieval splendours, could serve as an airy lobby.[157]

Hume's motion for a new House, coming as it did at a time of pressure on public spending, was reviled by numerous members and, in July 1833, was roundly defeated by 154 votes to 70.[158] There was strong criticism of this decision in the press and of the behaviour of members during debates: 'the decencies of civilized society appear to be totally disregarded there'. The first step towards remedying this state of affairs would be to replace the 'noxious vapour-bath' of the chamber and to provide decent accommodation for members: that would encourage attendance by men of good sense.[159]

Hume did not give up, complaining once more in August 1834 of the crowded chamber with its 'pestilential air which prevailed in the neighbourhood where he sat. Indeed, he was almost poisoned by it.'[160] Taunted by fellow MPs once more for his continued championing of a new chamber, at a time of thrift in public spending, Hume failed to gain support, although this seemingly interminable saga continued to be reported in the press.[161]

Two months later, on 16 October 1834, fire made Hume's point for him in a spectacular way. The burning of two large cartloads of tallies in the stoves debouching into the cramped, cracked and unswept flues of the house of lords put these subterranean passages under exceptional stress, but the clear signs – extreme heat and exceptional amounts of smoke

[153] *KW*, vi, 532; *CJ*, lxxxvi, 737; (HC 1831, 308).

[154] Hansard, *Commons Debates*, 3rd ser., xvi, cols 370–9: 7 Mar. 1833; *Dublin Weekly Register*, 16 Mar. 1833; Wright and Smith, *Parliament Past and Present*, 215–22.

[155] Hansard, *Commons Debates*, 3rd ser., xvi, cols 370–9: 7 Mar. 1833.

[156] *CJ*, lxxxviii, 148, 381; Select Committee on House of Commons Buildings, *Report* (HC 1833, 269); (HC 1831, 308), esp. p. 8; *KW*, vi, 532.

[157] Hansard, *Commons Debates*, 3rd ser., xvi, cols 370–9: 7 Mar. 1833; 3rd ser., xix, cols 59–66: 2 July 1833; V.E. Chancellor, 'Hume, Joseph (1777–1855)', *ODNB*.

[158] Hansard, *Commons Debates*, 3rd ser., xix, cols 59–66: 2 July 1833; Shenton, *The Day Parliament Burned Down*, 20–1.

[159] *Bell's New Weekly Messenger*, 7 July 1833.

[160] Hansard, *Commons Debates*, 3rd ser., xxv, cols 1029–31: 7 Aug. 1834.

[161] E.g., *Newcastle Journal*, 16 Aug. 1834; *Dublin Morning Register*, 11 Aug. 1834; see also *Westminster Review*, xxi (1834), 319–34: critique by Henry Cole.

– went ignored through sheer unheeding carelessness. Woodwork, oilcloth and fabric in the chamber above caught fire as it spread, engulfing much of the old palace – including the Commons chamber – in a conflagration.[162] Small wonder that, as parliament blazed, a bystander wryly observed: 'Mr Hume's motion for a new House is carried without a division.'[163]

10. *After 1834*

The press opined that the extraction of the 'aching tooth' at Westminster now allowed a replacement to be created which would save the body politic from 'pain and trouble, and give [it] health, ease and happiness'.[164] The new building clearly needed to confront the political as well as the engineering lessons of combining gimcrack, flimsy construction with poor maintenance and inadequate fire precautions. Thus, while in its substance and style the new Palace of Westminster embodied the Victorian constitution and British identity,[165] key to its successful functioning as a building were architectural and engineering innovations, not least in heating, ventilation, lighting, and acoustics.

These would remain a major preoccupation of parliament as it faced the challenges of sitting in temporary chambers, while at the same time presiding over the planning and building of the Victorian Palace of Westminster. The interim chambers were little more comfortable than their predecessors, and previous patterns of member interventions – with justification – soon reasserted themselves with complaints about noise and heat disturbing debates. In 1836, yet another philosopher-inventor, Dr David Boswell Reid, was summoned to remedy the problems.[166] Convinced that these difficulties could be solved through the application of rational scientific principles, Reid was at the same time very aware of the perennial difficulties in satisfying members on this matter. Their feelings, he wrote, 'necessarily fluctuate with every change of the internal or external atmosphere that is not immediately controlled, independent of the extreme diversity of temperament that may be expected to prevail when so many are assembled in the same apartment'.[167]

Reid deployed his signature heating and ventilation 'stack' system in the temporary house of commons, built in the shell of the pre-1834 house of lords, still standing proud after the fire. This featured a very tall chimney with a ventilation fire at its base[168] and complex arrangements for regulating heat and airflow within the chamber, now under the painstaking supervision of Benjamin Riches. Extended in 1839 to take in the temporary house of lords situated in the Painted Chamber, Reid's system ran until 1851, allowing him to feed his scientific observations into plans for Charles Barry's great new houses of parliament.[169]

---

[162] *Report … on Destruction by Fire of the Two Houses of Parliament*, 5–6, 10; Wyman, *Practical Treatise*, 219.

[163] *The Times*, 18 Oct. 1834.

[164] Shenton, *Mr Barry's War*, 9–10; *Westminster Review*, xliii (1835), 163.

[165] R. Quinault, 'Westminster and the Victorian Constitution', *Transactions of the Royal Historical Society*, 6th ser., ii (1992), 79–104.

[166] Shenton, *Mr Barry's War*, 64–5.

[167] D.B. Reid, *Illustrations of the Theory and Practice of Ventilation* (1844), 294.

[168] See R.H. Nibbs, Westminster Hall and Abbey after the Fire, 1839, showing the chimney of the temporary house of commons: Museum of London Prints and Drawings Collection, 27.18/1.

[169] Schoenefeldt, 'The Temporary Houses of Parliament'; Gillin, *Victorian Palace*, 121–61.

Bitter divisions over plans for the future of the palace which had been seen at the turn of the 19th century were now replayed on a grand scale, with full member involvement. Barry and Reid's epic rivalry over the design of the palace had many causes – not least deep scientific and professional divergences and a complete lack of clarity about responsibilities and processes for the governance and management of the most extensive and expensive building project ever undertaken in Britain. It was further fuelled by political interference and meddling, the glare of publicity, and the huge personal and professional animosity which developed between the two key protagonists.[170]

Yet, for all the resulting dysfunctionalities that bedevilled and delayed the building project, the achievements of both – and of others, including Goldsworthy Gurney who took over Reid's responsibilities in 1854 – were, if greatly flawed, remarkable.[171] Hidden deep beneath the gleaming imperial surfaces of the Palace of Westminster, and today largely unappreciated, except by aficionados and academics, the bones of their heating and ventilation systems still stand as an emblem of member involvement and as an engineering marvel of the Victorian age.

[170] Gillin, *Victorian Palace*, 161–83; Schoenefeldt, 'Architectural and Scientific Principles', 121–61; Shenton, *Mr Barry's War*, 142–5.

[171] Schoenefeldt, 'Architectural and Scientific Principles', 196; Shenton, *Mr Barry's War*, 223–4.

'A Sense of Crowd and Urgency'? Atmosphere and Inconvenience in the Chamber of the Old House of Commons

PAUL SEAWARD

The house of commons before the 1834 fire that destroyed it was small, poky, and uncomfortable. Its effects on the health, audibility, and behaviour of its members were frequently a cause of complaint, and informed the consideration by two select committees in 1831 and 1833 of what could be done to replace the chamber. This article examines the background to the appointment of the committees, and what their discussions reveal about the unsatisfactory nature of the chamber. It considers why there failed to be a consensus on altering the chamber before its destruction.

Keywords: audibility; back benchers; front benchers; heating; house of commons; reporters; speech; ventilation

1. *The Black Hole of Calcutta*

Given its function as a house of assembly, the chamber of the old house of commons was a small, even intimate, room. According to measurements made by William Kent in the 1730s, the internal space was 60ft 8ins long by 32ft 4ins wide, and 26ft 8ins high. The maximum distance between a seat in the chamber and the Speaker's chair was 49ft.[1] The room was shorter than a cricket pitch and not much wider than a tennis court. Many other 18th-century public spaces were much larger. The Banqueting House in Whitehall, often used on occasions when both Houses presented formal addresses to the monarch, was getting on for twice the size, at 110ft by 55ft.[2]

The size, both of the 18th-century chamber and of its successors in the 19th and 20th centuries (for they were built to replicate that basic footprint), has been one of the most distinctive features of the British house of commons, imparting to its debates a drama and

---

[1] The measurements are taken from the Kent drawings for his 1739 house of commons project, in the version in the Victoria and Albert Museum: for the plans, see H.M. Colvin, R.A. Brown, J.M. Crook, M.H. Port *et al.*, *The History of the King's Works* (6 vols, 1963–82) [hereafter cited as KW], v, 420 n. 1. There was often some confusion about the measurements: Hume, for example, in his speech in Mar. 1833, suggests that 49ft was the length of the chamber, rather than the distance from the Speaker to the furthest seat: Hansard, *Commons Debates*, 3rd ser., xvi, col. 371: 7 Mar. 1833. For another description of the chamber, see Clare Wilkinson, 'Politics and Topography in the Old House of Commons, 1783–1834', in *Housing Parliament: Dublin, Edinburgh and Westminster*, ed. Clyve Jones and Sean Kelsey (Edinburgh, 2002), 141–65.

[2] *The Survey of London. Vol. 13: St Margaret, Westminster, Part II: Whitehall I*, ed. Montagu H. Cox and Philip Norman (1930), 121–2.

intensity which its admirers have often felt lacking in the chambers of its continental counterparts. Winston Churchill's speech during the 1943 debate on the replacement of the Commons chamber destroyed by bombing two years before, famously stated the case for the curious intimacy of its politics:

> The essence of good House of Commons speaking is the conversational style, the facility for quick, informal interruptions and interchanges … the conversational style requires a fairly small space, and there should be on great occasions a sense of crowd and urgency. There should be a sense of the importance of much that is said and a sense that great matters are being decided, there and then, by the House.[3]

Not all members in the 18th or early 19th centuries would have agreed that the pokiness of the chamber was an advantage. The remodelling by Christopher Wren in 1692 had enhanced its resemblance to a college chapel, which was entirely appropriate, since it was built inside one.[4] Wren removed the clerestory and roof of the old chapel building and replaced them with a much lower roof and ceiling, lined the chamber with wainscoting, installed galleries on the side walls supported by slender columns (there was already a gallery against the west wall, opposite the Speaker), and created three tall round-headed windows in the eastern wall to replace the old tracery. As the former member, John Wilson Croker, said, giving evidence to a select committee in 1833: 'it would be very surprising if an apartment of the most ancient palace in England, applied accidentally in the lapse of ages to a purpose for which it was not originally intended, should now be found to be, by some strange accident, the most convenient of all possible places'.[5] James Grant (1802–79), the Scottish journalist who worked on the *Standard* from 1833, gave in his *Random Recollections of the House of Commons* (1836) a famous and atmospheric description of what was, by then, the 'old' House, destroyed by fire two years before:

> I shall not soon forget the disappointment which I experienced on the first sight of the interior of the House of Commons. I had indeed been told that it but ill accorded with the dignity of what has been termed the first assembly of gentlemen in the world, or with the importance of the subjects on which they were convened to legislate. But I was not at all prepared for such a place as I then beheld. It was dark, gloomy, and badly ventilated, and so small that not more than four hundred out of the six hundred and fifty-eight members could be accommodated in it with any measure of comfort. When an important debate occurred, but especially when that debate was preceded by a call of the House, the members were really to be pitied; they were literally crammed together, and the heat of the house rendered it in some degree a second edition of the Black Hole of Calcutta. On either side there was a gallery, every corner of which was occupied by

---

[3] Hansard, *Commons Debates*, 5th ser., cccxciii, cols 403–4: 28 Oct. 1943.

[4] The comparison with a chapel was made, among others, by Karl Moritz: 'a mean-looking building, that not a little resembles a chapel': *Travels in England in 1782 by C.P. Moritz*, ed. Henry Morley (1886), 42. See KW, v, 401–3 for the Wren alterations. There are descriptions of the 18th-century chamber in P.D.G. Thomas, *The House of Commons in the Eighteenth Century* (Oxford, 1971), 1–3, and elsewhere, supplemented now by the visualisation of the chamber created by the St Stephen's Chapel project at the University of York: see *https://www.virtualststephens.org.uk/* (accessed 29 Oct. 2018).

[5] Select Committee on House of Commons Buildings, *Report* (HC 1833, 269), question 298.

legislators; and many, not being able to get even standing room, were obliged to lounge in the refreshment apartments adjoining St Stephens, until the division, – when they rushed to the voting room in as much haste as if the place they had quitted had been on fire.[6]

The entire Palace of Westminster was regarded as a higgledy-piggledy slum, lacking grandeur, commodiousness, and convenience, although the chamber was the place in which the problem was most acutely felt. While, throughout the 18th century, architects and others toyed with plans to address the problem, most of these were grandiose schemes designed to create an imposing structure that would reflect Britain's national pride and imperial prestige. They rarely dealt in any detail with the practical deficiencies of the Commons chamber.[7] The most serious effort to consider major adjustments to the chamber of the Commons came, ironically, only in the three years before it was finally destroyed in the fire of 1834, in the work of two select committees, and the accompanying debates in the House. They also provide the fullest evidence of the practical difficulties presented by so constrained a site and so ill-adapted a building.

The man behind the appointment of the first of the committees was Colonel Frederick Trench. In proposing the enquiry on 12 August 1831, he complained about the insufficient seating room; the poor acoustic; the constant movement of members coming and going along the seats; and the inadequate seating for visitors.[8] Trench had an agenda: he was a would-be developer who had successively, and unsuccessfully, proposed schemes for the embankment of the Thames in 1824, a new royal palace in Hyde Park in 1825, and the removal of Smithfield Market from the City in 1828.[9] His plan was to promote a design by the architect, Benjamin Wyatt (who was closely associated, as he was himself, with the duke and duchess of Rutland), which he outlined in his speech on 12 August.[10] Wyatt's plan, to remove Wren's ceiling and the partition that divided the lobby from the chamber itself, was discussed at some length by the committee, but found little support.[11] The committee's report, presented to the Commons on 6 October 1831, the day before the rejection of the Reform Bill in the house of lords sent parliament into a new political crisis, did, however, conclude that it was impossible to make satisfactory improvements to the present House 'as would afford adequate accommodation for the Members, due regard being had to their Health, to general Convenience, and to the dispatch of Public Business'. The only practical solution was to build a new chamber.[12] In a debate a few days later, Trench concentrated

[6]J. Grant, *Random Recollections of the House of Commons from the Year 1830 to the Close of 1835* (1836), 1–2. For Grant, see the entry in *ODNB*.

[7]The exception was the schemes of 1733 and 1739, described in KW, v, 416–25. When Sir James Wyatt was undertaking the changes required by the addition of the Irish members in 1800 he was said (by his son) to have wanted to extend the House 'to the full length of the Chapel' (i.e., to include the lobby), but he was only allowed to undertake a much more limited expansion of the space: see Select Committee on House of Commons Buildings, *Report* (HC 1831, 308), question 20, and below, note 11.

[8]The committee was appointed on 8 August, without debate: Trench found an excuse to speak about it in the House on 12 Aug. 1831: Hansard, *Commons Debates*, 3rd ser., v, cols 1261–3: 12 Aug. 1831.

[9]See the entry on Frederick William Trench (?1777–1859), in *The History of Parliament: The House of Commons, 1820–1832*, ed. D.R. Fisher (7 vols, Cambridge, 2009) [hereafter cited as *HPC, 1820–32*], vii, 497–505.

[10]For Trench's sponsorship of Wyatt's plan, see (HC 1831, 308), question 95. For Wyatt, see *ODNB*.

[11]The scheme may have been an elaboration of Sir James Wyatt's of around 1800: see above, note 7.

[12](HC 1831, 308), p. 3.

on the merits of the Wyatt scheme which the rest of the committee had rejected, and suggested that the proposals be examined by a new committee in the ensuing session.[13] Contributions to the poorly-attended debate, in which most members were patently not interested, quickly became a collection of quirky and particular complaints: Henry Hunt grumbled about the draught from the window; the bombastic Charles Waldo Sibthorp attacked the corrupt press for failing to report his speeches; the radical Henry Warburton explained how the system of ventilation was based on a wrong premise; and the reactionary John Wilson Croker's apparently lengthy and unchallenged contribution vehemently and sarcastically condemned any idea of change.[14]

Though Trench himself lost his seat at the post-reform election of December 1832, his efforts had provoked an interest, particularly among radicals, that would flourish after the passage of the Reform Act and the influx of members who had less patience with the idiosyncratic ways in which the House did its business (among them the campaigning journalist, William Cobbett, who complained bitterly about it in a newspaper article written only a month or so after he had first sat in the House).[15] Joseph Hume, a member of the earlier committee and a persistent thorn in the side of successive tory administrations, revived the issue on 7 March 1833, moving the appointment of a new committee to examine proposals for building a new chamber, probably in the space between the present House and the river.[16] The committee took evidence from a series of prominent architects, reporting two months after their appointment with conclusions that repeated those of their predecessor concerning the impossibility of altering the present House, and recommending the erection of a new house of commons; it failed, however, to recommend a preferred design.[17] Hume drew attention to these conclusions in a debate in early July 1833: but his proposed resolutions, that the House should agree to replace the present chamber, and to address the king to give directions for the new building, were rejected decisively (though with a not unrespectable 70 votes). Despite his defeat, there were further discussions about the chamber in relation to a proposal to change the way votes were recorded.[18] Hume would, again, urge the necessity of action in August 1834, only eight weeks or so before the fire that broke out on 16 October 1834 and destroyed the chamber.[19]

2. *Herrings in a Barrel*

The proceedings of the 1831 and 1833 committees and the associated debates are well enough known. Yet they are often neglected, for the various proposals discussed by the committee would be superseded, after much fuss, by the Barry design that was eventually

---

[13] Hansard, *Commons Debates*, 3rd ser., viii, cols 554–7: 11 Oct. 1831.

[14] For John Wilson Croker (1780–1857), Charles de Laet Waldo Sibthorp (1783–1855), and Henry Warburton (1784–1858), see *HPC, 1820–32*, iv, 798–813; vii, 600–7, 632–6.

[15] *Weekly Political Register*, 2 Mar. 1833, pp. 524–5.

[16] Hansard, *Commons Debates*, 3rd ser., xvi, cols 370–4: 7 Mar. 1833.

[17] (HC 1833, 269), p. 3.

[18] See below, note 46.

[19] Hansard, *Commons Debates*, 3rd ser., xxv, cols 1029–31: 7 Aug. 1834.

executed.[20] But the two committee reports and the associated (if brief) debates are, at least implicitly, the best available analysis of what contemporaries saw to be the advantages and disadvantages of the Wren chamber.

The principal problem they identified was one of space. The house of commons was generally thought to be completely inadequate to hold, in any degree of comfort, the number of members who might be expected to turn up for big political debates and votes. Before the Anglo-Scottish Union of 1707, there was a maximum of 513 members in the house of commons. In preparation for the influx of the 45 additional Scottish members (bringing the total to 558), the side galleries were enlarged, so that each consisted of two rows of seats, rather than one, with their additional weight now supported on slender iron columns, rather than just brackets projecting from the wall. In 1739, William Kent thought the chamber could reasonably comfortably hold 300 in the body of the House (allowing a fairly generous 22ins per member), with an additional 120 spaces in the side galleries.[21]

The union with Ireland in 1800 brought 100 more members. In preparation for their arrival, James Wyatt reduced the thickness of the walls underneath the old windows in the side of the chapel, with disastrous effects on the medieval wall paintings behind Wren's wainscoting.[22] The result was that (according to James Wyatt's son, Benjamin, giving evidence to the 1831 committee) 342 could sit in the main body of the chamber, allowing 2ft per member, with a further 54 places available under the west gallery (the seats below the bar, which could therefore be seen as technically outside the House).[23] Presumably there were still 120 places in the side galleries, though these were not mentioned. Trench said in the subsequent debate that 2ft was quite generous: in the theatres, he pointed out, it was more common to allow 18 or 20ins.[24] But with the House now totalling 658 members, this was still far short of adequate. Joseph Hume, in his 1833 speech calling for a new committee, reminded members of an occasion a few nights before when 'every seat below the gallery was quite full, and yet only 366 Members had anything like accommodation'.[25]

Defenders of the chamber would frequently point out that it was very rare for it to be full. The highest number recorded in a division between 1690 and 1715 was 464, not far

---

[20] See C. Shenton, *The Day Parliament Burned Down* (Oxford, 2012) for the fire, and C. Shenton, *Mr Barry's War: Rebuilding the Houses of Parliament After the Great Fire of 1834* (Oxford, 2016) for the process of designing the new palace.

[21] Kent's figures occur in his drawings for the 1739 project in the Victoria and Albert Museum. His calculations assume a total of 550ft of seating: the same amount if only 18ins were allowed would have allowed for 367 members to sit in the body of the chamber. The typical width of an economy class airline seat is, apparently, 17 to 18.5ins. Benjamin Wyatt, questioned by the 1831 committee, allowed 24ins per member ((HC 1831, 308), question 27). Compare Temple Luttrell's highly optimistic view of 1777 that there was room for 500 members: Thomas, *House of Commons in the Eighteenth Century*, 127.

[22] KW, vi, 525–6.

[23] (HC 1831, 308), questions 39, 41. Kent's calculations (which assume 550ft of seating) did not include the galleries but did include the narrow seating beneath the west gallery. Wyatt's figures appear to indicate that there was space for about 100 more members after the alterations, which would tally with the number that needed to be accommodated, but difficult to reconcile with the limited nature of his father's alterations. See Thomas, *House of Commons in the Eighteenth Century*, 127 for the seats under the gallery, and 127–8 for the use of the seats in the side galleries.

[24] Hansard, *Commons Debates*, 3rd ser., viii, col. 555: 11 Oct. 1831.

[25] Hansard, *Commons Debates*, 3rd ser., xvi, cols 370–9: 7 Mar. 1833. Hume may have been referring to the series of debates on the suppression of disturbances in Ireland in late February and early March: perhaps on 1 March (when a maximum of 534 voted in a division) or 5 March (when 555 members voted).

short of the number of places available in the chamber and the gallery. But the House was usually far, far, thinner than this: one member noted in the 1690s: 'we seldom get an House with 11 or 12, and a House is only 40 if there is a great bear or some monster to be seen or baited' (it is not clear whether this was meant figuratively).[26] Croker told the 1833 committee that between 1800 and 1830 there were only 13 divisions in which 500 members participated, and only one in which more than 550 participated (the Reform Bill, which produced 608): 'Everybody knows that on such occasions the great pressure exists for only the few last hours of a debate: and it should be recollected that the space and ventilation which would be required for 600 Members in the month of July, would be found uncomfortable for an ordinary House of 200 or 300 Members in the month of January.[27] Opponents of change would from time to time observe that the seats could not be too crowded and uncomfortable, as many could be seen sleeping on them: were they made more comfortable, members were even more likely to doze.[28] Croker, again, in the debate on 11 October 1831 on Trench's report, was able to point to several members who had nodded off.[29]

Nevertheless, it was clear that during a crowded debate the chamber could be an extremely uncomfortable place. Hume's ally, Warburton, complained that if he sat there for more than two or three hours he was 'in a state of bodily torture'. The few members who sat on the front benches were in a more convenient position, as Warburton told the leader of the House, Lord Althorp, goaded by his insouciance about the whole issue.[30] The distance from the back of one seat and the front of the next was, Wyatt told the 1831 committee, 2ft 8ins, the same as that in a modern economy class airline seat.[31] The architect, Sir Jeffry Wyatville, thought 3ft was adequate, 'but four inches more would make a great difference as to comfort'.[32] Members had problems extricating themselves from their seats where the space between the back of one seat and the front of the next was so small, though it was worst of all under the gallery, where (according to Hume) the space was only one-half the ordinary width: 'The Members were, in fact, wedged in, almost like herrings in a barrel.[33] Croker facetiously dismissed the complaint: 'at present, many hon. Members kept their places from an indisposition to disturb their neighbours; and were sometimes induced to attend to a, perhaps, tedious duty, and listen patiently to a debate, from which, with easier means of egress, they probably would escape'.[34]

The issue was not just one of seating, but also of movement around the chamber. Trench, in laying out his case for the appointment of the select committee, complained about 'the constant interruption occasioned now by hon. Members rising and crossing each other, so

[26] *The Parliamentary Diary of Sir Richard Cocks, 1698–1702*, ed. D.W. Hayton (Oxford, 1996), 23.

[27] (HC 1833, 269), question 931.

[28] Hansard, *Commons Debates*, 3rd ser., xxv, cols 1029–31: 7 Aug. 1834.

[29] E.g., Hansard, *Commons Debates*, 3rd ser., viii, col. 558: 11 Oct. 1831 (John Wilson Croker).

[30] Hansard, *Commons Debates*, 3rd ser., xix, cols 63–4: 2 July 1833.

[31] (HC 1831, 308), question 30. Kent's plan of the chamber gives a measurement for the width of the benches and the distance between the seats, at least on the main run of benches at the side of the chamber, which bears out Wyatt's figure; see also (HC 1831, 308) question 173; (HC 1833, 269), question 747.

[32] (HC 1831, 308), questions 111–15.

[33] Hansard, *Commons Debates*, 3rd ser., xvi, col. 371: 7 Mar. 1833; Kent's 1739 plan does show a significantly smaller space between the seating under the gallery, though he does not give measurements.

[34] Hansard, *Commons Debates*, 3rd ser., viii, cols 559–60: 11 Oct. 1831.

as to escape through the north and south doors into the lobby, without passing through the House'.[35] William Cobbett was particularly exercised by it, complaining in the article he wrote in 1833 of 'the crowds about the Speaker's chair, while the private bills are going on, the everlasting trampling backward and forward on the floor; the interruption which men give to one another, in spite of their desire to avoid it; the calls of "order, order," incessantly recurring; all these absolutely distract men's minds, and they render it impossible for them to do that which it is their duty to do, and which they wish to do'. The Speaker was constantly being badgered by members asking him to sign pieces of paper authorising the admission of their friends and constituents to the gallery.[36] On occasions of particular excitement, the chamber would be packed. Macaulay described the House on 22 March 1831, as the tellers came to the table to announce the result of the division on the second reading of the Reform Bill, as 'thronged ... all the floor was fluctuating with heads like the pit of a theatre'.[37] A particular bottleneck was the space between the bar of the House and the doors into the lobby, where members would congregate and hold conversations: Hume, in 1833, referred to the crowd there being so great 'that it was impossible to pass in or out without the greatest inconvenience'.[38] The 1831 committee asked Wyatt for a scheme that would allow 'communication around the House', and the Trench/Wyatt scheme for enlarging the House involved a passage all around the chamber, 'from which doors should open upon every gangway; so that an hon. Member, in taking his place, need never pass over the floor of the House ... nor need there ever be that accumulation of Members at the bar, which now gave rise to such noise and interruption to the debate'.[39] Yet Croker, in responding to Trench, again poured scorn over the idea that it should be made easy for 'gentlemen of locomotive habits' to move about 'to the obvious interruption of the business of the House and the country'.[40]

The problem of overcrowding extended beyond the chamber itself, into the lobby beyond it. During a division, the lobby had to accommodate members spilling out from the chamber to register their vote. Wyatville was asked, in 1831, whether he was aware that between 300 and 400 members could need to be held in the lobby, and that 'in the greater part of the session the Lobby is filled with persons obliged to be there to meet Members on business, previous to the meeting of the House'.[41] The space was said by Wyatt, in his evidence to the 1831 committee, to be nearly square, of 30ft by 33ft.[42] Smirke calculated that the lobby together with the lower lobby and an adjoining passage had an area of 1,500 sq. ft, and could hold no more than 380 members, allowing them 2 sq. ft to stand: the lobby itself was about 900 sq. ft.[43] Wyatt referred to the stairs to the strangers' gallery in the lobby, which were often thronged with people waiting presumably for admission, exacerbating

[35] The doors were introduced in 1816 and can be seen in Hayter's picture of the reformed parliament, which shows a curtain at the back of the undergallery on both sides of the chamber, covering the doors: KW, vi, 530.

[36] *Weekly Political Register*, 2 Mar. 1833, pp. 524–5.

[37] Thomas Babington Macaulay (1800–59), see *HPC, 1820–32*, vi, 229.

[38] Hansard, *Commons Debates*, 3rd ser., xix, col. 61: 2 July 1833.

[39] (HC 1831, 308), questions 18, 132; Hansard, *Commons Debates*, 3rd ser., viii, col. 556: 11 Oct. 1831.

[40] Hansard, *Commons Debates*, 3rd ser., viii, col. 560: 11 Oct. 1831.

[41] (HC 1831, 308), questions 145, 147.

[42] (HC 1831, 308), question 84.

[43] (HC 1831, 308), question 175.

crowding in the lobby.[44] In order to accommodate the members spilling out of the House into the lobby during a vote, it was essential to clear the lobby of the public: the difficulty was illustrated by the occasion during the Gordon riots when a large number of people gathered in the lobby and the doorkeepers were unable to clear it, preventing a division from taking place.[45] In parallel with the discussions about alterations to the chamber were a series of debates and a committee concerned with more efficient ways of conducting divisions. That committee concluded that the only satisfactory solution was to build at least one more lobby. An alternative system of counting votes was tried as an experiment, but judged to have failed dismally.[46]

3. *Vapours of Noxiousness*

Macaulay, absurdly, likened the chamber to the hold of a slave ship.[47] Grant's comparison with the Black Hole of Calcutta was more traditional.[48] A reviewer in 1834, arguing that the house of commons should be peripatetic, attempted to suggest that the experience was worse in the Commons: those imprisoned in the Black Hole of Calcutta had 18ins square to stand on, whereas a member of the house of commons, if there were 600 people present, had not quite 19½ins.[49] The author (Henry Cole, then at the record commission and later the first director of the Victoria and Albert Museum) speculated that there had to be some 'hidden and mysterious influence' to explain the willingness of members to work amid 'vapours of noxiousness in every variety, from the gouty decrepitude of metropolitan courtiers, to the hale freshness of fox-hunting country squires'.[50]

The heat and the appalling stuffiness were generally held to be deeply injurious to health. Both Trench and Hume attributed the early deaths of 'several' members to the poor ventilation of the chamber.[51] The complaint had been made for more than a century. As early as 1702, Sir James Lowther was complaining of the 'almost intolerable' heat in the chamber.[52] The earl of Pembroke wrote to his son, Lord Herbert, in 1788 on the subject of his acceleration to the house of lords, remarking that the Commons was 'particularly unwholesome for you, stink, heat and late hours, etc.'[53] William Windham complained in 1785 that 'the

---

[44](HC 1831, 308), p. 8.

[45]*Annual Register* (1781), 222. I am grateful to Robin Eagles for discussion of this incident.

[46]For consideration of taking divisions, parallel to the debates on altering the chamber, see Hansard, *Commons Debates*, 3rd ser., xv, cols 1079–89: 21 Feb. 1833; Select Committee on Means of taking Divisions of House of Commons, *Report* (HC 1834, 147); Hansard, *Commons Debates*, 3rd ser., xxi, cols 239–45: 11 Feb. 1834; xxv, cols 131–7: 18 July 1834.

[47]*HPC, 1820–32*, vi, 230.

[48]The comparison lives on: see *http://www.radiotimes.com/news/2015-02-03/michael-cockerell-reveals-whats-behind-the-pomp-and-facade-of-the-house-of-commons/2/* (accessed 21 Oct. 2017), for David Blunkett referring to the modern division lobbies in the same way.

[49]*The Westminster Review*, xxi (July–Oct. 1834), 320 n.

[50]Cole's authorship is indicated in his memoir, *Fifty Years of Public Work of Sir Henry Cole, K.C.B.* (2 vols, 1884), i, 8.

[51]Hansard, *Commons Debates*, 3rd ser., viii, col. 554: 11 Oct. 1831 (Trench); xvi, cols 371–2: 7 Mar. 1833 (Hume).

[52]James Lowther (1673–1755), see *The History of Parliament: The House of Commons, 1690–1715*, ed. Eveline Cruickshanks, Stuart Handley and D.W. Hayton (5 vols, Cambridge, 2002), iv, 685.

[53]George Augustus Herbert, Lord Herbert (1759–1827), see *The History of Parliament: The House of Commons, 1754–1790*, ed. Sir Lewis Namier and John Brooke (3 vols, 1964) [hereafter cited as *HPC, 1754–90*], ii, 612.

heat of the House disordered my faculties and enfeebled my powers and brought on a state of inability from which I could never recover sufficiently to rise'.[54] William Lamb, the future Viscount Melbourne, blamed his inability to contribute to debates on 'apprehension or heat, or long waiting, or the tediousness of much of what I hear', which induced a 'torpor of all my faculties'.[55] Henry Hepburne Scott complained in 1830, to his sister, of the transition from 'being out all day to be now cooped up in the heated atmosphere of the House'.[56] The rather sickly Sir Henry Bunbury told his son the same year, after a few days in the House, that 'he had not yet found the heat of the House injurious to my health, though the lights, etc. make my head ache'. A series of late nights, however, had taken its toll by March, when he complained of the 'great heat, the crowd, and the prolonged attention'.[57] Warburton, in the July 1833 debate, suggested that in private, at least, members would tell him that the House was affecting their health, and he was convinced that several of his friends had lost their lives as a result of attendance in the chamber. Heat was not the only issue. Henry Hunt's complaint of the 'inconvenience which was felt from the west window when the wind was blowing in that quarter' suggested that the chamber was still not immune from draughts.[58]

Numerous attempts had been made to improve the chamber's ventilation ever since the 1692 remodelling. Wren had, in 1701, created holes in the ceiling at each corner of the House, above each of which, in the roof void, stood 'a truncated pyramid', a structure that could be opened to let the heat escape, though they would also cause draughts.[59] Dr Desaguliers's remedy in the 1720s was to link the pyramids to a fire that would draw up the air from below. Famously the scheme was frustrated by the housekeeper in possession of the attic space who would only light the fire when it was already hot in the chamber, thus creating the opposite effect of the one intended and making it even hotter.[60] In 1736, Desaguliers implemented a new system, based on one he had invented for clearing mines, and had adapted for use in hospitals and sick rooms.[61] Neither it, nor adjustments made in 1769, succeeded in solving the problem. Nor did changes initiated by a committee in 1791, that included opening up the area around the chandelier that hung from the centre of the ceiling to provide a new ventilation shaft.[62] A new scheme was designed by the French émigré and heating pioneer, the marquis de Chabannes, who enjoyed a certain vogue in London in the 1810s. Chabannes had been engaged to create new systems of ventilation in the Covent Garden Theatre, and it was his success with this scheme that presumably resulted in his being commissioned to design a new scheme in the

[54]William Windham (1750–1810), see *HPC, 1754–90*, iii, 649; see also Henry Flood (1732–91), in *HPC, 1754–90*, ii, 441.

[55]Hon. William Lamb (1779–1848), see *The History of Parliament: The House of Commons, 1790–1820*, ed. R.G. Thorne (5 vols, 1986), iv, 360.

[56]Henry Francis Hepburne Scott (1800–67), see *HPC, 1820–32*, v, 574.

[57]Sir Henry Edward Bunbury (1778–1860), see *HPC, 1820–32*, iv, 424.

[58]Hansard, *Commons Debates*, 3rd ser., viii, col. 556: 11 Oct. 1831.

[59]KW, v, 404; *CJ*, xiii, 413, 416: 19, 20 Mar. 1701.

[60]KW, v, 404–5; J.T. Desaguliers, *A Course of Experimental Philosophy* (2 vols, 1734–44), ii, 560–1. For Desaguliers, see Audrey T. Carpenter, *John Theophilus Desaguliers: A Natural Philosopher, Engineer and Freemason in Newtonian England* (2011), 142–5; Elizabeth Hallam Smith's essay in this volume.

[61]Morrill Wyman, *A Practical Treatise on Ventilation* (Boston, MA, 1846), 215–6.

[62]KW, v, 405; *CJ*, xlvi, 415.

Commons.[63] In a pamphlet he published in 1819, describing the scheme introduced the year before, Chabannes asserted that 'the temperature in the House of Commons will not in future exceed that of the atmosphere without, by more than 6 or 8 degrees under the galleries, and 10 or 12 above, on the most crouded nights'.[64] But Chabannes's scheme was no more successful than any of its predecessors, and alterations were still being sought in 1826 and 1829.[65]

Criticized as the Commons chamber was, it is perhaps fair to say that most public rooms which were as crowded as this one were subject to similar criticisms. W.S. Inman, who wrote a commentary on the issues of ventilation and audibility as a contribution to the discussions surrounding the design of new chambers, after the fire, pointed out that 'with the present inadequate systems there is scarcely a church or public assembly which on entering does not feel oppressive or offensive'; the experience of being inside the committee rooms in the Commons felt like being 'immersed in a hot-bed, or pine-pit'; and the problem was not only felt in Britain – 'the premature death of some eminent men at the American Bar has been imputed to the want of ventilation and dampness in the Supreme Court at Washington'.[66]

4. *A Bear Garden*

Audibility was a more complicated issue. Some people regarded the acoustic in the chamber as good. Croker told the 1833 committee that 'the good hearing in the gallery of the present House is produced by the shape of the ceiling'.[67] In the debate inspired by Hume on 7 March 1833, Philip Howard (an opponent of change) commented that the chamber was well adapted for hearing; he was, in fact, the only one recorded in the debate to mention the question of sound, the other points made being mainly to do with the lack of accommodation.[68] But in his speech of 1831, Trench remarked that while in one part of the House – the area around the Speaker – it was very easy to hear; at the other end, by the gallery, it was very different. 'The reason was', he said, knowledgeably, 'that the voice was wafted directly across the House by the draught of air from the windows, and was lost in the lantern above – it was thus abstracted not to return.'[69] His ally, Benjamin Wyatt, agreed, arguing that since proceedings in the chamber were so audible for those sitting around the cavity in the

---

[63] See Martin Meade and Andrew Saint, 'The Marquis de Chabannes, Pioneer of Central Heating and Inventor', *Transactions of the Newcomen Society*, lxvi (1994), 193–213. According to Smirke, in 1835, Chabannes had himself supervised the work: Select Committee on the Ventilation of the Houses of Parliament, *Report* (HC 1835, 583), question 542 (see this also for Humphrey Davy's involvement in ventilation schemes in the Commons). Chabannes described the principles of his scheme in J.F. de Chabannes, *On Conducting Air by Forced Ventilation, and Regulating the Temperature in Dwellings* (privately printed, 1818).

[64] J.F. de Chabannes, *Appendix to the Marquis de Chabannes' Publication, on Conducting Air by Forced Ventilation, and Equalizing the Temperature of Dwellings* (1819): 'Some Reflections upon the Causes of the Heat Felt in Large Assemblies'.

[65] KW, vi, 530–2.

[66] W.S. Inman, *Report of the Committee of the House of Commons on Ventilation, Warming, and Transmission of Sound: Abbreviated, with Notes* (1836), 9.

[67] (HC 1833, 269), question 937.

[68] Hansard, *Commons Debates*, 3rd ser., xvi, col. 378; 7 Mar. 1833.

[69] Hansard, *Commons Debates*, 3rd ser., v, col. 1262: 12 Aug. 1831.

ceiling (the ventilator), the sound must be escaping into it.[70] Joseph Hume seemed to agree that it was much more difficult to hear in the western half of the chamber (away from the Speaker). He told the House in August 1834 that 'Much of the disturbance and confusion which took place in the House, and which impeded the progress of public business, arose from the impatience of hon. Gentlemen who found it absolutely impossible to hear what occurred in the course of the debate.' 'If the noble Lord would only change his position in the House and sit a few yards further down', he added, addressing the leader of the House, Lord Althorp, 'he would find, that he would not be able to hear much of what was spoken in the upper part of the House [i.e., close to the Speaker]'. Colonel Davies complained on the same occasion that, when large numbers were present, only half the House could hear the debate.[71]

Another issue was the effect of the galleries on the acoustic. It was generally accepted that the space under the gallery was less than perfect, at least for speaking.[72] Benjamin Wyatt remarked that the galleries were 'very much against the perfect conveyance of sound, inasmuch as they injure the natural elasticity of the atmosphere, by confining the heat occasioned by the respiration of a number of persons, warmth of body and woollen clothes in that situation, all of which are calculated to impede the smooth progress of sound, by decreasing the elasticity of the atmospheric air'. It was put to Wyatt that the ceilings of the galleries might act as sounding boards, but he rejected the idea: it might have been true were the ceilings perfectly flat, but they were rounded, 'meeting the wall at an acute angle'.[73] The wainscoting was, however, thought to assist the sound, and both committees discussed the resonant properties of different woods at some length.[74]

It was clearly sometimes difficult to catch what was said in the chamber, but exactly why is less certain. The parliamentary diarists, on whose reports we rely for the content of the speeches before newspapers began to cover them systematically, rarely commented on the audibility of individual speakers or the chamber in general. But from the early 1780s at least, newspapers, with their reporters stationed in the public gallery, between 50 and 60ft away from the Speaker, were providing regular reports of debates.[75] They often struggled to hear, as indicated by an incident in the gallery in 1819. One of the reporters, the colourful Irishman, Peter Finnerty, was hauled before the House as a result of an altercation with a doorkeeper when he tried to sit in the front row of the gallery (the reporters were supposed to sit in the back row). Finnerty excused his anger with the messenger on the grounds that 'my mind was engaged in the most intense application to the individual who was then addressing the House, and whose sentiments I was most anxious to take down correctly'.

Where the newspapers' reporters were unable to hear speeches by members, it was necessary to provide some sort of explanation. They would routinely describe speakers as

[70] (HC 1831, 308), question 3.

[71] Hansard, *Commons Debates*, 3rd ser., xxv, cols 1029–31: 7 Aug. 1834.

[72] (HC 1833, 269), question 312.

[73] (HC 1831, 308), questions 56–7; cf. question 104.

[74] (HC 1831, 308), questions 100–1, 102.

[75] For discussions of the quality of reporting, and the aims of the newspapers, see Nikki Hessell, *Literary Authors, Parliamentary Reporters: Johnson, Coleridge, Hazlitt, Dickens* (Cambridge 2012), 133, 136–40, and for earlier reporters, see Christopher Reid, *Imprison'd Wranglers: The Rhetorical Culture of the House of Commons 1760–1800* (Oxford, 2012), 85–96; see also A. Aspinall, 'The Reporting and Publishing of the House of Commons' Debates, 1771–1834', in *Essays Presented to Sir Lewis Namier*, ed. Richard Pares and A.J.P. Taylor (1956), 227–57.

'inaudible'. In 1783, Sir Robert Herries spoke 'in a low and inaudible tone of voice'.[76] Mr Edwards, seconding the motion for the address in 1785, 'made some observations, which he had arranged on a piece of paper, but in a voice too inaudible to form any conclusion from'; making another 'observation' before the question was put, he was still inaudible.[77] Lord Mulgrave 'offered some arguments in support of his opinion, but not being such as commanded the attention of the House, the noise prevented our hearing them distinctly'.[78] Edmund Burke was described in 1787 as speaking 'in a voice almost inaudible, through a violent hoarseness'.[79] Inaudibility was frequently attributed to illness. In June 1820, Lord Palmerston explained the army estimates 'in so low a tone as not to be audible in the gallery'. The Hansard reporter added that 'Here the noble lord was seized with sudden indisposition, which for some time prevented his proceeding. He resumed his seat for a moment, then again rose and addressed the House; but after two or three ineffectual attempts to proceed, his indisposition seemed to increase, and by the advice of some of his right hon. Friends, he sat down without bringing the estimates to a conclusion.[80] Canning's speaking 'in a tone so low as to be scarcely audible' in May 1825, was similarly attributed to 'a severe indisposition'.[81] It could also be attributed to emotion: in May 1811, Colonel Palmer 'spoke under the influence of such natural feelings, as rendered him scarcely audible … here the honourable gentleman's feelings affected his tone of voice, as to render the rest of his speech inaudible'.[82]

Such problems were not peculiar to the house of commons: similar points were made about individual speakers in the upper House, too. In 1784, it was said, Lord Ferrars spoke 'as usual', in 'a low, inarticulate and inaudible' tone of voice.[83] The same year, Lord Balcarres was described as having 'in a pretty long speech, the heads of which he had prepared in writing, expatiated with much emotion, but in a tone of voice, low and inaudible, and unworthy of a hero, on the sufferings and the merit of the Scotch and their kindred, and descendants, who had been concerned in the affair of 1745'.[84]

The implication of incompetence or incapacity on the part of the speaker could cause offence, a slur of a lack of robust manliness (and occasionally, given the difficult relationship between members and the press, the offence may have been intended). A no doubt apocryphal story published in 1833 concerned Admiral Sir Isaac Coffin, who had ceased to be a member in 1826, appearing in a newspaper office 'in a great fury, with a newspaper crumpled up in the grasp of one hand, while a terrific oaken cudgel was brandished in the other', demanding to see the editor. It transpired that he had been teased by a succession of

[76] *Morning Post and Daily Advertiser*, 5 Dec. 1783.

[77] *Morning Herald and Daily Advertiser*, 26 Jan. 1785.

[78] *The Times*, 22 Feb. 1785, p. 2.

[79] *Morning Herald*, 10 Feb. 1787. See also the *World and Fashionable Advertiser*, 10 Feb. 1787, which says that Fox explained that Burke's illness made him perfectly inaudible.

[80] Hansard, *Commons Debates*, 2nd ser., i, col. 805: 2 June 1820.

[81] Hansard, *Commons Debates*, 2nd ser., xiii, col. 888: 26 May 1825.

[82] *The Times*, 31 May 1811, p. 2. Hansard adds: 'Here the hon. Gentleman's voice dropt, and he appeared to be greatly affected; having succeeded with some difficulty in uttering a few sentences, which we could not hear, he was at length overpowered by the violence of his feelings, and under the necessity of sitting down': Hansard, *Commons Debates*, 1st ser., xx, cols 349–50: 30 May 1811.

[83] *Morning Post and Daily Advertiser*, 31 July 1784.

[84] *Morning Post and Daily Advertiser*, 17 Aug. 1784.

friends in his clubs that morning on account of being described as 'inaudible in the gallery' in a debate the day before. 'I can stand a joke, sir', the admiral told the newspaper, 'as well as any man in England, but hang me if I stand this any longer. Sir, I tell you that I was never more wind and weather tight in my hull than at this moment, and d—n me if I couldn't hail the main-top in any hurricane that ever blew.'[85] Sibthorp, in 1831, also took offence at the claim that the reporters could not hear him, taking the opportunity to attack 'the corrupt, hired, and perverted Press'.[86]

The alternative explanation for the difficulty of hearing was the level of noise in the chamber, described in 1835 by Charles Dickens, a reporter for *The Mirror of Parliament*, as being 'a conglomeration of noise and confusion to be met with in no other place on existence'.[87] Colonel Davies told the Commons in 1833 that 'the appearance of the House was frequently rather that of a debating club or a bear-garden, than of a deliberative assembly. The noise was excessive, and Members, instead of attending to the proceedings, amused themselves with talking, or laying stretched at full length asleep on the benches.'[88] It was bound to affect the reporters' ability to take down members' words. Henry Smith, in March 1809, got up to complain that he had been described inaccurately in that morning's newspapers as saying he spoke in favour of a motion by the chancellor of the exchequer concerning the duke of York. He confessed that the House had at the time been 'very impatient, and this, perhaps, with the noise that prevailed, and the disturbed state of the House, might prevent the person who reported him from hearing distinctly what he said'.[89] The noise was 'so incessant' on an occasion in 1819 that the reporters were unable to hear anything of what was said by Sir William De Crespigny.[90] Some members seemed to take offence at this, too, since a high level of noise might indicate their irrelevance as far as most members were concerned. Michael Angelo Taylor grumbled, in 1813, of a description of him in a report of a debate 'as having been assailed with loud noise in the course of his speech. He appealed to the House if this was the case.'[91]

Some of the noise was simply the result of members having conversations, or leaving the House. The gathering of members around the bar of the House was often the source of noise in the chamber.[92] Colonel Davies complained in February 1827 of being unable to hear a debate on the army estimates because of the racket of members leaving the House.[93] But much of it was deliberately intended to interrupt and suppress a speaker. Mr Whitmore struggled in 1821 to express his opposition to duties on wheat over a bout of 'loud and general coughing'.[94] One old gentleman, reported Samuel Bamford, of his visit to the

---

[85] 'The Newspapers. Reporting, Editing, Speculating, and Proprietorships', in *The Metropolitan Magazine* (New Haven, CT), Jan. 1833, p. 20. I have not been able to establish the original source of this article, or its author. Sir Isaac Coffin (1759–1839) was well known as a character: see *HPC, 1820–32*, iv, 698–700.

[86] Hansard, *Commons Debates*, 3rd ser., viii, cols 556–7: 11 Oct. 1831.

[87] Quoted by Hessell, *Literary Authors, Parliamentary Reporters*, 136. It is not quite clear whether Dickens was referring to the pre-1834 or post-1834 chamber. It was probably both.

[88] Hansard, *Commons Debates*, 3rd ser., xix, col. 62: 2 July 1833.

[89] Hansard, *Commons Debates*, 1st ser., xiii, col. 423: 14 Mar. 1809.

[90] Hansard, *Commons Debates*, 1st ser., xli, col. 677: 2 Dec. 1819.

[91] Hansard, *Commons Debates*, 1st ser., xxiv, cols 518–9: 15 Feb. 1813.

[92] See, e.g., Hansard, *Commons Debates*, 3rd ser., viii, col. 559: 11 Oct. 1831 (Croker).

[93] Hansard, *Commons Debates*, 2nd ser., xvi, cols 570–86: 19 Feb. 1827.

[94] Hansard, *Commons Debates*, 2nd ser., xvi, col. 778: 1 Mar. 1827.

chamber in 1816, 'actually coughed himself from a mock cough into a real one, and could not stop until he was almost black in the face'.[95] A speech of Colonel Davies in 1823 was interrupted by 'so much coughing and confusion in the House, that the hon. Officer was audible at intervals only'.[96] Members could often be forced to abandon their speeches as a result. It was probably a mundane impatience with him for delaying the House rising, that forced Henry Goulburn to give up in 1825 on the Roman Catholic Relief Bill.[97] But Henry Brougham's speech on the corn laws on 8 March 1827 was systematically obstructed for political reasons. In the words of the reporter:

> The House manifested much impatience by coughing, and at length the noise through-out the House occasioned a total interruption to the hon. and learned member's speech. On its subsiding, he said, that he did not think that, upon so important a subject as this, it was decorous that it should go forth tomorrow to the world that interruption like this had been given; it would not be consolatory to the hungry multitude, nor was it creditable to the House, or likely to add to the reputation of a new parliament, that a vital question like the present should be clamorously prevented from being discussed. If, in the only stage he could have an opportunity of expressing his sentiments, there was a rooted determination on the part of some gentlemen in the House – [Here the noise from both sides rendered the conclusion of the sentence inaudible.] he hoped he was mistaken. The fault might be his: he might have discussed the question in a tedious and tiresome manner: he would much rather that he should bear the reproach, than that it should appear that there was an attempt to clamour down a speaker for the sentiments he expressed. … He really hoped that the gentlemen who interrupted him would abstain from further impediments: the effort would only affect themselves, and bring on colds and coughs tomorrow, from unnecessary exhaustion.[98]

Lord Cochrane complained, in 1817, that he had been unable to hear a word of a petition read out by the clerk because of the noise going on. Cochrane observed later on that 'he had often remarked, that when petitions were presented which did not accord with the view of those who were in the habit of voting with ministers, it was common to oppose the reading of them by making a noise in the House, which had frequently been so great, that sitting on that bench he could not hear them … he had on the present occasion attempted to read the petition himself, because the clerks (without any blame to them), had in many cases not read such petitions with a voice sufficiently audible to obtain that attention which they ought to receive'.[99] When Sibthorp – regarded as a buffoon, if a not unpopular one – contributed to a Reform Bill debate in 1832, 'he was saluted with a volley of cheers, which were repeated at the conclusion of every sentence, the intervals between being filled up with every variety of laughter and schoolboy noise – the cry of an owl and the mewing of a cat being, ever and anon, heard from the gallery'.[100]

[95] Samuel Bamford, *Passages in the Life of a Radical* (Oxford, 1984), 27.
[96] Hansard, *Commons Debates*, 2nd ser., viii, col. 1459: 30 Apr. 1823.
[97] Hansard, *Commons Debates*, 2nd ser., xiii, col. 61: 19 Apr. 1825.
[98] Hansard, *Commons Debates*, 2nd ser., xvi, cols 1080–2: 8 Mar. 1827.
[99] Hansard, *Commons Debates*, 1st ser., xxxv, cols 78–83: 29 Jan. 1817.
[100] *HPC, 1820–32*, vii, 605.

For those inclined to resist change, it was not the acoustics in the chamber that were the problem but the quality of the members. Croker brutally made the point in the October 1831 debate. 'Whenever a Gentleman rose to whom the House was desirous of attending', Croker insisted, 'he had always the power of making himself heard … He doubted whether any architectural alteration that could be made would ensure either the attention of the House when it was not disposed to listen, or the power of any Member of commanding that attention.'[101]

5. *Atmosphere and Inconvenience*

The inadequacies of the house of commons chamber had been felt for many years. But underlying the debates of the 1830s was at least some sense that things had changed, that what was tolerable 20 or 30 years before was not tolerable any more. For one thing, money was being lavished on other public buildings, including a royal palace, and it seemed difficult to justify the failure to spend any substantial sums on the seat of the British legislature. For another, radical MPs like Hume or Cobbett were prepared to demand better conditions. And for a third, the chamber was now fuller and busier than it had been 30 or more years before. The 18% growth in the number of members at the union with Ireland would already have made it significantly more crowded; meanwhile the highly-contentious debates of the late 1820s and beginning of the 1830s (as well as the increasing coverage of Westminster proceedings in the newspapers) would ensure the interest and presence of very many more of them than before. Members frequently referred to the numbers present in recent divisions during the discussions of the rebuilding of the chamber in 1831 and 1833. They also referred to those who were regular absentees, taking little part in proceedings, though it was clear that this was a smaller proportion of the House than it had been previously. Croker, who was not much interested in altering the chamber, but was interested in better facilities for members, argued that 'in old times such accommodations were less necessary; Members came and sat a few hours in their seats, heard the debate, voted and went away in reasonable time; but now a Member of Parliament, who attends his duty closely, spends 12 hours a day in the House, to say nothing of committees'.[102]

There was no shortage of ideas or expertise about addressing the inadequacies of the chamber. The work done in theatres and other places to improve ventilation or audibility over the last 20 or so years was much discussed by the 1831 and 1833 committees and their witnesses. James Saunders's *Treatise on Theatres* was cited by Decimus Burton and James Savage.[103] Architects reverted often to their work elsewhere, particularly in London theatres and auditoria: the rebuilding at the Haymarket,[104] at Drury Lane,[105] the Ancient Concert Room in Hanover Square,[106] the Court House at Chester,[107] and the auditoria at London

[101] Hansard, *Commons Debates*, 3rd ser., viii, col. 559: 11 Oct. 1831.

[102] (HC 1833, 269), question 952.

[103] (HC 1833, 269), questions 380, 1104.

[104] (HC 1833, 269), question 441.

[105] (HC 1833, 269), question 441.

[106] (HC 1833, 269), questions 509, 58: i.e., the Concert of Ancient Music established in 1776, by then established in the Hanover Square Concert Room.

[107] (HC 1833, 269), question 775 (likened to the chamber of deputies in Paris).

University,[108] and of the Royal Institution.[109] The quality of any of these experiments was frequently in dispute, however: John Deering remarked that all the authorities on the subject said that the theatre at Bordeaux was 'a model with regard to hearing', but people who had been there said that it was awful, 'and we find the foundation of its good character to have been, that its history was published by its projector'. He had had a similar experience with the Infirmary in Derby.[110]

Despite the acknowledged problems with the chamber, and the expertise available, there was no consensus on altering or replacing it, nor even how to do so. There were two essential problems with altering the house of commons, much discussed in the 1831 and 1833 committees. The first was the difficulty of creating more internal space on the existing site. Many of the solutions for making a broader chamber within the Palace of Westminster produced odd and unworkable results. Sir John Soane thought it impractical: though the chamber could be made longer, broadening it would effectively mean completely rebuilding the House and destroying 'a great national monument, that is the pride of the country'.[111] The second was that the obvious solution for lowering the heat in the chamber – by raising the ceiling – risked wrecking the acoustics. The committees of 1831 and 1833 concluded that the only solution would be to construct a new chamber: yet here they came up against not only the practical problems that had frustrated alterations (the highly constrained space within the palace complex), but also a profound resistance to the expenditure of public money on what could so easily be seen as an unnecessary, self-serving, vanity project, associated with a group of radicals whose constant interventions were profoundly irritating to many more conservative members.

And beyond the difficulty of settling on a satisfactory alternative, many members struggled to see what the problem was. Among them, perhaps, were the senior politicians, Westminster giants whose place on the front benches rendered them largely immune to the discomfort suffered by the lesser mortals crammed under the gallery or struggling to hear amidst the rabble gossiping around the bar. Exchanging views, insults or compliments over the table of the House that divided them, they were privileged to speak in what Churchill would refer to as the 'conversational style', while others tried to catch what they said from the gallery or the back benches. Some would go beyond a lack of interest in the problem to express a positive attachment to the existing chamber. Gloomy, cramped and suffocating, the old chamber of the Commons could naturally induce in many a claustrophobic sense of crisis and confrontation, a 'scene of noise, heat and contention', as Gibbon put it, bringing on nausea and headaches. For others, it created an intense, intoxicating and oddly intimate atmosphere, mixed with a resonant and powerful history. For them, men like Croker or Peel, the chamber, for all its inconvenience and lack of grandeur, had its own charm. Churchill identified 'a sense of crowd and urgency' as the great virtue of the chamber designed by Barry after the fire. The same could be said, for good or ill, of its predecessor.

[108] (HC 1833, 269), question 651 (John Deering).
[109] (HC 1833, 269), question 932.
[110] (HC 1833, 269), question 660.
[111] (HC 1831, 308), question 24.

Parliament as Viewed Through a Woman's Eyes: Gender and Space in the 19th-Century Commons

SARAH RICHARDSON

The 19th-century house of commons is traditionally viewed as a masculine space overlooking the presence of female tourists, waitresses, housekeepers, servants, spectators, and residents. This essay demonstrates that, even when formally excluded from the Commons, women were determined to colonize spaces to witness debates. In the pre-1834 Commons they created their own observation gallery in an attic high above the chamber, peeping through a light fitting to listen to parliamentary sessions. After 1834, they were accommodated in their own galleries in the temporary and new house of commons, growing increasingly assertive and protective of their rights to attend debates and participate in parliamentary political culture. Far from being exclusively male, parliament was increasingly viewed through women's eyes.

Keywords: Commons; gender; Ladies' Gallery; parliament; politics; space; women

1

On Saturday, 24 January 1885, Irish Fenians carried out the most audacious attack on the houses of parliament since the gunpowder plot nearly 280 years earlier. Luke Dillon and Roger O'Neil, so-called 'dynamitards', joined other members of the public visiting the Palace of Westminster, successfully setting off two cakes of dynamite near the Commons chamber and in Westminster Hall.[1] The first bomb exploded undetected in the Commons just after 2 pm but, thanks to the vigilance of the public and the police, the device in Westminster Hall was identified and was being removed before exploding, wounding two policemen and Edwin Green, a civil servant. The key eyewitness to the Westminster Hall events was Green's sister-in-law, an Irish woman, Miss Davies. Her dramatic account of the moment of the explosion was published by the *Pall Mall Gazette* on the following Monday:

> My sister and I were just outside the gates, and we fell together into the hole caused by the explosion … When we recovered from the force of the shock we could see nothing. It was pitch dark. Dust was flying about the Hall, and it was several minutes before it was light enough to distinguish anything … Mrs. Green and I lost our bonnets, muffs, and bags, and I had my skirt torn from my waist. My sister and I were covered with dirt, and my sealskin tippet was blown to pieces.[2]

---

[1] For more information on the Fenian dynamite campaigns in London, see Charles Townshend, *Political Violence in Ireland: Government and Resistance Since 1848* (Oxford, 1983); Shane Kenna, *War in the Shadows: The Irish-American Fenians who Bombed Victorian Britain* (Dublin, 2013).

[2] 'The Dynamite Explosions', *Pall Mall Gazette*, 26 Jan. 1885.

A couple of weeks later, a new periodical was launched aimed at 'women of education'.[3]
The Lady, founded by *Vanity Fair* proprietor, Thomas Gibson Bowles, devoted its opening
editorial on the disruption caused to lady visitors to parliament by the Fenian bombing
campaign, railing against the new 'police instructions' regulating visitors to the House and
concluding that 'I am not at all sure that I would not prefer the remote risk of dynamite'.[4]

The daring escapades of the Fenians had drawn the attention of the parliamentary authorities to the many and diverse visitors to parliament in this period, and in particular
the presence of women as visitors, such as Miss Davies and Mrs Green, or observers in
the Ladies' Gallery like the female columnist in *The Lady* who soon had a regular feature
entitled 'From the Ladies' Gallery'. Although authorities attempted to bring in more reg-
ulatory control of visitors, this was challenged and rebuffed by the women and some of
their supporters in the Commons. The phenomenon was nothing new. Women had always
been present in the 19th-century houses of parliament, as tourists, waitresses, housekeepers,
servants, spectators, and residents, challenging the idea of the institution as wholly masculine. Although one historian, Claire Eustance, asserted that 'Parliament before 1918 was
an exclusively male environment', in fact, parliament had regularly been viewed through
women's eyes throughout the preceding century.[5]

Much attention has been given to the encroachments of the militant women's suffrage
activists into parliamentary spaces in the early 20th century with an indication that these
were the first efforts of women to challenge the idea that the Commons should be a male
only space.[6] There were certainly high-profile examples: Emily Wilding Davison hiding in
a ventilation shaft; Muriel Matters chaining herself to the grille in the Ladies' Gallery; and
Annie Cobden-Sanderson standing on seats to deliver her protest in Central Hall.[7] However,
although suffrage campaigners, like the Fenians before them, targeted the institution of
parliament to ensure that their protests received maximum publicity, the female invasion
and occupation of parliamentary space had begun much earlier. This essay will argue that,
once women regained a foothold in the house of commons, and were able to witness
parliamentary debates, they successfully resisted all efforts to curtail their attendance, and
indeed, grew increasingly assertive of their rights as the century progressed.

2. *Their Own Spectators' Gallery: Women and the Ventilator*

Things did not look so promising at the opening of the 19th century. Women had been
excluded from the Commons since 2 February 1778 when, as was common when MPs
wanted to debate in private, a call was made for the House to be cleared of strangers.
However, on this occasion, once male visitors had departed, the galleries were completely

---

[3] For a discussion of the changing nature of female periodicals in the 1880s, see Erica Rapapport, *Shopping for Pleasure: Women in the Making of London's West End* (Princeton, NJ, 2001), ch. 4.

[4] *The Lady*, 19 Feb. 1885.

[5] Claire Eustance, 'Protests from Behind the Grille: Gender and the Transformation of Parliament, 1867–1918', *Parliamentary History*, xvi (1997), 108.

[6] Eustance, 'Protests from Behind the Grille'.

[7] Parliamentary Archives, HC/SA/SJ/10/12, item 26: police report noting Emily Wilding Davison had been found hiding in a ventilation shaft, 4 Apr. 1910; 'Suffragists in the House', *The Times*, 29 Oct. 1908; 'Women Suffragists at Westminster', *The Times*, 24 Oct. 1906.

filled with women, including the Speaker's wife, Grace Norton. Captain George Johnstone then called for the House to be cleared of *all* strangers, which was achieved after some considerable effort and a long delay in the proceedings of the Commons.[8] The role of the Speaker and his wife is significant. The Speaker, as well as presiding over debates, controlled all aspects of the administration of the Commons. He had the authority to admit or refuse admission to visitors and to order public galleries to be cleared. He, his wife and children, lived within the precincts of the Palace of Westminster and he was ultimately in charge of all parliamentary space.[9] Initially, following the open rebellion by women who refused to leave the Commons, the Speaker took a hard line, issuing a rule excluding them from the House. However, many powerful and well-connected women continued to lobby for admittance and there is some evidence that they ignored the regulations and continued to attend debates in the Commons either openly, or by masquerading as men. For example, Charles Moritz, a Prussian pastor and travel writer noted that, in 1782, visitors to the galleries of the Commons included 'not unfrequently, ladies'.[10] The legal historian, William Charles Townsend, who wrote a multi-volume history of the Commons, also commented on reports of women such as the duchess of Gordon and Mrs Sheridan sitting in the strangers' galleries dressed as men.[11] Margaretta Grey, cousin of the whig leader, Earl Grey, was reputedly so disgusted at finding she was not allowed to attend parliament that she made it a custom to obtain admission by dressing as a boy.[12] There continued to be a large number of women of high rank and status, often wives and daughters of members, who wanted to visit the Commons, with a growing number of MPs and officials who wished to exclude them. John Hatsell, clerk to the Commons in the late 18th century, summarized the problem:

> … ladies, many of the highest rank, have made very powerful efforts to be again admitted. But Mr Cornwall, and the present Speaker, Mr Addington, have as constantly declined to permit them to come in. Indeed was this privilege allowed to any one individual, however high her rank, or respectable her character and manners, the galleries must soon be opened to all women, who, from curiosity, amusement, or any other motive, wish to hear Debates. And this, to the exclusion of many young men, and of merchants and others, whose commercial interests render their attendance necessary to them, and of real use and importance to the publick.[13]

The terms of debate were thus set. Women were singled out by some parliamentary officials, MPs and commentators as unsuitable visitors to the Commons on the grounds of

---

[8] There is no official contemporary record of the incident. E.g., Almon's *Parliamentary Register* merely notes that the House was cleared for the debate. However, details may be found in J. Hatsell, *Precedents of Proceedings in the House of Commons; under separate titles. With Observations* (new edn, 4 vols, 1818), ii, 181 n; W. Charles Townsend, *History of the House of Commons from the Convention Parliament of 1688–9 to the Passing of the Reform Bill in 1832* (2 vols, 1843), ii, 460–1; P.D.G. Thomas, *The House of Commons in the Eighteenth Century* (Oxford, 1971), 149. The two former accounts are authorities cited by MPs in 19th-century parliamentary debates on the legality of women observing debates in the House.

[9] *Speakers and the Speakership – Presiding Officers and the Management of Business from the Middle Ages to the 21st Century*, ed. Paul Seaward (Chichester, 2010).

[10] Charles Moritz, *Travels, Chiefly on Foot, Through Several Parts of England, in 1782* (1795), 59.

[11] Townsend, *History of the House of Commons*, ii, 461–2.

[12] Glen Petrie, *A Singular Iniquity: The Campaigns of Josephine Butler* (New York, 1971), 24.

[13] Hatsell, *Precedents of Proceedings in the House of Commons*, ii, 181 n.

propriety but also because they may take up spaces which should properly be given to men whose attendance at debates was considered necessary and important. Although women were officially barred from the Commons, they continued to be allowed to view the Lords, first from behind the curtains either side of the throne and later in a new gallery designed by Sir John Soane in the 1820s.[14] This distinction between the Lords and the Commons persisted throughout the 19th century, reflecting the greater ceremonial function of the Lords and perhaps the increasing status of the Commons as the legislating chamber.[15]

However, the pressure by women to attend the Commons persisted, in spite of the Speaker's definitive ruling. Therefore, at some point in the early 19th century, a compromise was reached. A limited number of women were permitted to attend the House and listen to debates in what became known as the ventilator or lantern – a small attic space high above the chamber.[16] The exact date that women visitors started to utilise the attic space is unclear. Sarah Grand, in an interview she gave to the *Humanitarian* in 1896, implied that Elizabeth Fry was the first woman to be permitted to listen to debates there:

> there was quite a storm of opposition when she modestly asked to be permitted to listen to a debate in the House of Commons arising out of the prison reforms of which she was the initiator.

> Yes, I remember, and as a last resort she asked to be allowed to listen outside one of the ventilators of the House, and the country squires were up in arms, and said that it would crush the fabric of domestic life if it came to the ears of their wives and daughters that a woman had listened to a Parliamentary debate, even through a ventilator.[17]

Fry attended parliament and gave testimony to an enquiry on prisons in the City of London on 27 February 1818 and, if Sarah Grand's recollection is correct, this is the most likely occasion that she visited the ventilator to listen to debates.[18] There is corroborating evidence that women were able to access this space, from the diary of Lady Frances Shelley.[19] Just a couple of months later, on 18 April 1818, Lady Shelley, a confidante of leading politicians including Brougham and Wellington, was invited by Brougham to the House to listen to discussions on the Alien Bill. Permission for her to go to the ventilator had to be obtained

---

[14] Townsend, *History of the House of Commons*, ii, 461; Sean Sawyer, 'Delusions of National Grandeur: Reflections on the Intersection of Architecture and History at the Palace of Westminster, 1789–1834', *Transactions of the Royal Historical Society*, 6th ser., xiii (2003), 237–50.

[15] An analysis of spatial configuration and power structures in the modern houses of parliament has found that the Lords is designed for ceremony and the Commons for scrutiny. Similar arguments may be made for the 18th-century chambers: see Brigid Maclachlan, 'Scrutiny and Consensus in the Palace of Westminster', in *Proceedings of the Space Syntax Third International Symposium, Atlanta, 2001*, ed. John Peponis, Jean Wineman and Sonit Bafna (Ann Arbor, MI, 2001), 44.1–44.7. The distinction in organisational practice between the Lords and Commons has continued into the 20th century with initiatives such as the broadcasting and televising of debates.

[16] For further discussion of the ventilator space, see Sarah Richardson, *The Political Worlds of Women: Gender and Political Culture in Nineteenth-Century Britain* (2013), ch. 6.

[17] Sarah A. Tooley, 'The Woman's Question: An Interview with Madame Sarah Grand', *Humanitarian*, viii (1896), 161–9.

[18] Select Committee on State of Prisons in City of London and Borough of Southwark, and on Dartmoor Prison, *Report* (HC 1818, 275).

[19] *The Diary of Frances, Lady Shelley, 1818–1873*, ed. R. Edgcumbe (2 vols, 1913), ii, 7–11. My thanks to Amy Galvin-Elliott for drawing my attention to this source.

from the serjeant-at-arms, Colonel Seymour, who managed the attendance of male visitors to the strangers' gallery. Lady Shelley was escorted to the space in the roof of St Stephen's Chapel by the parliamentary caterer, John Bellamy:

> I found myself in a room about eight feet square, resembling the cabin of a ship. There was a window to admit air, two chairs, a table, and a thing like a chimney in the centre. This was the ventilator, which opens into the body of the House of Commons. Through it, the sound ascends so perfectly that, with attention, not a word is lost.[20]

At this point, it is clear that women's use of the ventilator was not a common occurrence. Indeed, Lady Shelley noted that later she was quizzed at a party on her '*secret* expedition – for it is not an acknowledged thing to go to the House, although it is suspected that Lady Jersey has done it on some great occasion'.[21] However, by the 1820s, women's presence in the Commons was being routinely reported by the newspapers. For example, the *Morning Chronicle* noted in 1822 that: 'it was no uncommon occurrence for a party of ladies, from seven to ten in number, to be assembled in this elevated station, chiefly around the centre Ventilator, over the chandelier, to hear the debates'.[22] Indeed, the reporter even acknowledged the space as the 'Ladies' Gallery'. A few years later, *The Times* expressed surprise at women's determination to attend debates in such inhospitable surroundings: 'They sit in a shabby room over the chamber when the debate is going on, seeing nothing and hearing imperfectly through the holes of the ceiling ventilators, inhaling the steam of an intensely-heated atmosphere, and scarcely recompensed for their disagreeable sufferings by one eloquent or witty sentence in the course of a long evening.'[23]

But, in spite of the discomfort, women persisted in visiting the ventilator to attend debates. Entry was restricted to the family and friends of MPs. Tickets were issued to MPs by the serjeant-at-arms and then passed on to female visitors. There were frequently ballots for the 25 tickets (although there were only 16 places able to view the Commons chamber) available each night, particularly for important debates such as those on parliamentary reform. One paper, reporting on female attendance at the discussion on catholic emancipation, commented that, 'so anxious was the Duchess of Richmond to secure a good place, that her Grace "took her seat" by half past two o'clock, an hour and a half before the meeting of the House!'[24] By 1832, the ventilator had become so well known that *The Court Magazine, or Belle Assemblée*, aimed at a female readership and edited by Caroline Norton, ran a series of four articles entitled 'Evenings in the Ventilator', a forerunner of the later feature in *The Lady*. The writer, identified as 'S.' (possibly Caroline's mother, Caroline Sheridan), represented herself as a seasoned observer of Commons' debates, comparing what she described as the halcyon days of Burke and Fox with the less eloquent speakers of the 1830s. She painted a vivid picture of the female space in the attic above the Commons chamber. As one article made clear, in the early days of the ventilator, women had clear access to the sights and sounds of the Commons by sitting around the ironwork that

[20] *Diary*, ed. Edgcumbe, ii, 8.
[21] *Diary*, ed. Edgcumbe, ii, 11.
[22] *Morning Chronicle*, 12 Oct. 1822.
[23] *The Times*, 14 Feb. 1829.
[24] *Hampshire Chronicle*, 23 Mar. 1829.

supported the brass chandeliers bringing light to the House. However, as they were wont to disturb proceedings by their chatter and even, on occasion, as the author of the piece admitted, throwing objects down to attract the attention of the MPs below, they were '*built out*' of an unobstructed view on the orders of a furious Speaker:

> a circular shed of sixteen sides or panels, protects the spot sacred to the memory of Bankes and my comb, and a small oblong square aperture in every panel serves to admit the heads of sixteen anxious females who creep, unseen and unheard, to see and hear – and do their best to stifle the voice of the House of Commons, by preventing its members from breathing freely. Green baize benches surround the shed, and afford repose to the wearied forms of dowagers and damsels.[25]

A sketch of the space just before the Commons burnt down in 1834, drawn by Frances Rickman, daughter of the clerk assistant in the Commons, corroborates this depiction.[26] Her drawing demonstrates that the 'shed' served to make listening to, and observing, debates most uncomfortable, as the women had to lean through the small windows cut into the structure. In 1822, in a letter to her friend, Sophy Ruxton, Maria Edgeworth elaborated upon the problems that women faced in viewing the chamber:

> In the middle of the garret is what seemed like a sentry-box of deal boards and old chairs placed round it: on these we got and stood and peeped over the top of the boards. Saw a large chandelier with lights blazing, immediately below: a grating of iron across veiled the light so we could look down and beyond it: we saw half the table with the mace lying on it and papers, and by peeping hard two figures of clerks at the further end, but no eye could see the Speaker or his chair, – only his feet; his voice and terrible 'ORDER' was soon heard. We could see part of the Treasury Bench and the Opposition in their places, – the tops of their heads, profiles, and gestures perfectly.[27]

As Maria Edgeworth's report made clear, the space was uninviting, poorly lit, and filled with rubbish and debris. Yet she ends her account by comparing the Commons favourably with the French chamber of deputies and concluding that the visit 'surpassed our expectations'. By making the environment as inconvenient and unattractive as possible, the Commons' officials hoped that female visitors would lose interest and concede their right to attend debates. However, women of all ranks and status were not deterred, many adopting affectionate nicknames for the space. Lady Shelley called it her '*soupirail*' and Harriet Grote, the 'Lantern'.[28] As the series of articles by 'S.' demonstrates, there was an immense appetite to listen to political debate by women with connections to MPs. She devotes much space to discussing the debating styles of different MPs, including Peel, Stanley, Althorp, Russell, and

[25] 'Evenings in the Ventilator, No. II', *Court Magazine*, i (1832), 77.

[26] See the cover image.

[27] *The Life and Letters of Maria Edgeworth*, ed. A.J.C. Hare (2 vols, 1894), ii, 66–7: Maria Edgeworth to Mrs Ruxton, 9 Mar. 1822.

[28] As a soupirail is a basement window, one assumes Lady Shelley was being ironic; *Diary*, ed. Edgcumbe, ii, 10. H. Grote, *The Personal Life of George Grote Compiled from Family Documents, Private Memoranda, and Original Letters to and from Various Friends* (1873), 83.

Brougham, confirming 'though we hear well, we do not see in the Ventilator'.[29] Indeed, there are many accounts detailing both the content, rhetorical style and mode of delivery of speeches by key MPs. Unless members were particularly quiet, mumbled, or had speech impediments, women spectators appeared to have no trouble in listening to debates – indeed it was primarily this that attracted them to attend. Elizabeth Wedgwood, writing to her aunt, Jessie Sismondi, is but one example: 'Macaulay's speech on the Reform Bill almost made me cry with admiration, and I expect his speech on so much more interesting a subject to be the finest thing that ever was heard.'[30] Her sister, Fanny Allen, was equally enthusiastic about an address by Brougham: 'He spoke for an hour and 10 or 20 minutes, and it was the most incomparable thing I ever heard. I could have screamed and jumped with delight.'[31]

It should also be noted that there were more frivolous reasons for visiting the ventilator. It was a good place to see and be seen. Accounts by Lady Shelley and 'S.' confirm that MPs would often come up to the ventilator to speak to the ladies present. Therefore, although it tended to be female *managed*, it was not a woman-only space. As with all aspects of Commons' procedure, the Speaker was ultimately in charge and thus, in the ventilator, the Speaker's wife took precedence. Ellen Manners Sutton, the Speaker's wife, attended debates on catholic emancipation on two occasions in 1829. The first time she processed through the lobby of the Commons accompanied by her train bearer, but that was considered too ostentatious for what was still a semi-official space. So, on the second visit, she came by carriage to the entrance in Old Palace Yard, but, as a reporter on a local paper pointed out, as she was still attended by the train bearer, she attracted a considerable amount of attention.[32] However, the Speaker himself did not acknowledge women's presence in the ventilator and rules such as clearing the galleries of strangers were not applied to them. Hence, the regular attendees of the space were always concerned that their access would be removed. After the last sitting of the unreformed house of commons in December 1831, 'S.' tabled her last bulletin for *The Court* magazine, expressing both anticipation and anxiety for the future:

> Shall I be able again to occupy my seat in the Ventilator? Will the sternness of new members insist upon our stricter exclusion; or, imitating the gallantry of the other house, will it admit us to see, and what many of us love better to be seen? I have sat out this session in my hiding place, certainly 'far above the great,' and I shall hope to be at the first evening of the next; when I may give such readers as are not tired of me some account of the new members. With what solicitude I shall hear the new voice from the chair call upon the member for Birmingham or Leeds … it is most unlikely that six hundred and fifty eight men of education sent there by fifteen millions of Englishmen, will not furnish much variety of information, and a large fund of entertainment to sixteen ladies in the Ventilator.[33]

---

[29]'Evenings in the Ventilator, No. IV', *Court Magazine*, i (1832), 188.

[30]H. Litchfield, *Emma Darwin: A Century of Family Letters* (2 vols, 1915), i, 234–6: Elizabeth Wedgwood to her aunt, Mme Sismondi, 27 Mar. 1831.

[31]Litchfield, *Emma Darwin*, i, 158: Fanny Allen to her sister, Mrs Josiah Wedgwood, 13 June 1824.

[32]*Devizes and Wiltshire Gazette*, 28 May 1829.

[33]'Evenings in the Ventilator, No. IV', *Court Magazine*, i (1832), 189. Unfortunately, this was to be the last column by 'S.' writing from the ventilator.

3. *Formally not Part of the Commons: The Ladies' Gallery*

Ultimately, it was not the newly-elected MPs who put an end to the ventilator but the fire that swept through parliament on the night of 16 October 1834, that destroyed much of the Palace of Westminster. The influential women who had populated the attic space were keen that they should continue to be accommodated in any new building. In 1835, their cause was taken up by the flamboyant MP, George Fitzhardinge Grantley Berkeley. He successfully pushed through a motion for a select committee to be established to consider whether there should be a Ladies' Gallery in the new house of commons. The committee met in July 1835 but no women provided evidence. The only witnesses were Walter Watts, a reporter for the *Morning Chronicle*, Sir Robert Smirke, the noted architect who was working on the parliamentary estate in the aftermath of the fire, and, rather bizarrely, John Bellamy, the parliamentary caterer. Unsurprisingly, Watts's evidence focused almost entirely on the experience of reporters in the old house of commons, with hardly any reference to the proposed Ladies' Gallery. Smirke provided a detailed plan for the gallery, which was to be positioned at the end of the strangers' gallery, partitioned off, and with its own staircase. Bellamy's testimony focused on the impossibility of women using the existing staircase to access the proposed gallery. The committee eventually resolved that 'a portion of the Strangers' Gallery at the North end of the House, not exceeding a quarter of the whole, and capable of containing 24 ladies, be set apart for their accommodation, divided by a partition from the rest of the Gallery, and screened in front by an open trellis work'.[34] Regulations were also devised detailing the process by which women could gain entry via tickets issued to MPs. Although women did not give direct evidence, they quickly made public their desire to establish a subscription to buy a commemorative piece of silver plate for Grantley Berkeley in recognition of his championing their cause.[35]

There continued to be considerable resistance to the construction of an official Ladies' Gallery in the new house of commons. Although Berkeley had succeeded in incorporating a design for the gallery into the plans for the new house of commons, opponents staged several attempts to sabotage its construction. For example, in August 1836, there was a motion to grant the £400 needed to build the Ladies' Gallery. A number of leading parliamentarians, including Lord Palmerston and Sir John Hobhouse, reiterated arguments against admitting women to attend and observe parliamentary proceedings including that it was indecorous, opened women up to the horrors of political partisanship and that it was a continental practice (that is, French) and therefore to some extent 'unEnglish'. Hobhouse argued that he had assumed the original vote on Berkeley's proposals had been a joke.[36] Even the Speaker, James Abercromby, spoke against, asserting that he had not had an opportunity to put his own viewpoint but that he was decidedly against. This is in spite of previous Speakers tacitly allowing women to use the ventilator as an alternative ladies' gallery. The motion to authorise a grant to build the gallery was defeated by 14 votes. The *York Herald* went so far as to allege that the vote against was 'intended to check the too great indulgence of female curiosity!!'[37] A further vote on a grant of supply to erect the gallery was, again,

---

[34] Select Committee on Admission of Ladies to Strangers' Gallery, *Report* (HC 1835, 437), p. 3.

[35] *Preston Chronicle*, 11 June 1836.

[36] *Morning Chronicle*, 11 Aug. 1836.

[37] *York Herald*, 13 Aug. 1836.

lost in June 1837 by 24 votes, but there must have been some behind-the-scenes wrangling to ensure that it was built. By May 1850, Hansard reported a debate on the new house of commons which discussed whether the new Ladies' Gallery situated behind the Speaker's chair should be dismantled to provide a larger general public gallery.[38]

In the meantime, women were keen that they should not be excluded from attending debates in the temporary house of commons. There was no official announcement, but a concealed compartment about 12ft by 9ft was constructed between the Speaker's and strangers' galleries and was known as the Ladies' Gallery.[39] The *Derby Mercury* reported in 1842:

> It is but little known that a small enclosure behind the strangers' gallery has been erected, 'under the rose,' for the accommodation of political ladies desirous of hearing the debates. A space about the breadth of a hand has been opened, through which the ladies peep totally unobserved. There is not room for more than 12 or 13 of the fairer sex, who are admitted by orders signed by Sir W. Gossett, the Sergeant-at-arms.[40]

The space was even less inviting than the ventilator, was exceedingly cramped, and had hardly any view of the chamber. Yet women continued to throng to parliament to listen to debates in spite of the best efforts of parliamentarians to exclude them. The 'secret' nature of the temporary Ladies' Gallery demonstrated the ambiguous nature of women's attendance at parliament. By not acknowledging their presence and screening them off, MPs could claim they were not an official part of the House. However, the fact that, even in the temporary Commons, a place had to be found for female visitors, demonstrated women's determination to be included in parliamentary space. Women participated fully in the May 1850 trials of the new house of commons. They were permitted to listen to the debates screened off, not by the grille which would later be erected to shield them from the chamber, but by a curtain of green gauze, giving them, as the *Morning Chronicle* reported, 'a shadowy look and cadaverous hue quite supernatural':

> The gallery for ladies is a great improvement upon the pigeon holes in the old house, and the appearance of the fairer sex within the walls of the house was quite startling. However, to the superstitiously inclined, the flitting of certain dim figures across an upper gallery had a yet more awe-inspiring effect. These figures seemed as shadowy and unsubstantial as spectres, but we believe they were flesh and blood strangers, and not the ghosts of Barebone's Parliament come to revisit the glimpses of the Speaker's eye.[41]

The visual ethereal effect was, however, somewhat marred by women's audible presence, as they chattered excitedly in their newly-constructed space.

The new house of commons was eventually opened by Queen Victoria on 11 November 1852 and the Ladies' Gallery was rapidly established as an important space for women to participate in the political culture of the nation. Historians have tended to echo the

---

[38] Hansard, *Commons Debates*, 3rd ser., cxi, cols 102–4: 11 May 1850.
[39] *Aberdeen Journal*, 14 Apr. 1847.
[40] *Derby Mercury*, 9 Mar. 1842.
[41] *Morning Post*, 31 May 1850.

criticisms of contemporaries, regarding the gallery as a symbol of male oppression, with Nirmal Puwar terming it 'an overcrowded, hot and suffocating bird cage'.[42] Certainly, many women visitors expressed their discontent with the new gallery. Fanny Allen, who had been a regular attendee to the ventilator, found it far inferior in terms of audibility, while Kate Field, an American journalist, likened it to a prison.[43] The heavy ornate grille placed in front of the gallery to screen the women off from the MPs in the chamber led many women to voice their disapproval. Anna Parnell wrote an article for *Celtic Monthly* subtitled 'Notes from the Ladies' Cage', commenting that, as women visitors were not visible, 'they can very easily be supposed not to exist'.[44] Others went further: Mabel Crawford, in a piece entitled ' "Purdah" in the House of Commons', viewed the latticework akin to the curtain or veil segregating physical space within muslim households, arguing that it was un-English and reduced British women to 'the low status of their sex in Oriental countries'.[45] This opinion was echoed by Zeyneb Hanoum, the pseudonym of a Turkish writer who exclaimed to a friend:

> But my dear, why have you never told me that the Ladies' Gallery is a harem? A harem with its latticed windows! The harem of Government! How inconsistent are you English! You send your women out unprotected all over the world, and here in the workshop where your laws are made, you cover them with a symbol of protection.[46]

Yet, in spite of these negative opinions, what has been under-appreciated by historians analysing the space is the steady build-up of female influence and confidence which ultimately led women openly to challenge parliamentary procedures. The existence of an all-female space in the house of commons, albeit one designed and controlled by men, assisted in the creation of a feminised political culture nurtured and developed in this exclusive area. In fact, the Ladies' Gallery became one of the arenas identified by Martha Vicinus for activists 'claiming male space for women's purposes'.[47]

The new Ladies' Gallery was enthusiastically adopted by women visitors to the Commons. Tickets (or orders as they were known) had to be obtained from sitting MPs, which meant that the vast majority of attendees were the wives, daughters, and friends of politicians. However, although the female audience was an exclusive one, it was also numerous. The papers regularly reported on the high number of women crowding into the gallery. The *Fife Herald* commented that parliamentary debates 'stimulated all – male, female, and ecclesiastics – to struggle for room, sitting or standing'.[48] So many people wanted to attend

---

[42] Nirmal Puwar, 'The Archi-texture of Parliament: Flaneur as Method in Westminster', in *Ceremony and Ritual in Parliament*, ed. Shirin M. Rai (2011), 15–29; see also Eustance, 'Protests from Behind the Grille'. For a more positive interpretation, see Richardson, *Political Worlds of Women*, ch. 6.

[43] Litchfield, *Emma Darwin*, ii, 113: Fanny Allen to her niece Elizabeth Wedgwood, 26 Dec. 1847; Mary Suzanne Schriber, *Writing Home: American Women Abroad, 1830–1920* (Charlottesville, VA, 1997), 152: Kate Field.

[44] Anna Parnell, 'How They Do in the House of Commons. Notes from the Ladies' Cage', *Celtic Monthly*, iii (1880), 469.

[45] Mabel Shannan [sic] Crawford, ' "Purdah" in the House of Commons', *Women's Penny Paper*, 24 May 1890, p. 363. See also Antoinette Burton, *Burdens of History: British Feminists, Indian Women, and Imperial Culture, 1865–1915* (Chapel Hill, NC, 1994), 88.

[46] Zeyneb Hanoum, *A Turkish Woman's European Impressions* (1913), 192.

[47] Martha Vicinus, *Independent Women: Work and Community for Single Women 1850–1920* (1985), 264.

[48] *Fife Herald*, 1 Mar. 1855.

the sessions discussing Gladstone's budget in April 1865, that the papers noted: 'It is said that every seat in the Speaker's and Ladies' Galleries and the Speaker's Ladies' Boxes was secured by promise before the recess, and that four hundred more orders are issued for the Strangers' Gallery than can possibly be accommodated.'[49] In fact, there were regular ballots for tickets for the gallery, leading parliamentary officials eventually to adapt the space to provide double the number of seats and a tea room for the comfort of the visitors. As noted above, the Ladies' Gallery was not the only place where women could observe parliamentary proceedings. A more exclusive vantage point was the Speaker's gallery usually open to ambassadors and other privileged visitors. There was a corresponding Speaker's Ladies' Gallery, a sectioned off area to the west of the Ladies' Gallery which often provided much needed extra seats for women in popular debates.[50] The regular parliamentary columnist for *The Lady* noted that: 'Mrs. Peel, the Speaker's wife, I believe, is the presiding genius over this exclusive little nest.'[51] The wife of the Speaker therefore wielded immense power in political circles and the parliamentary sketch writer, William Lucy, joked that: 'it is easier for a rich man to get into the kingdom of heaven than for any one less than an Ambassador to gain entrance into the Speakers' gallery'.[52] It was usually only the wives and daughters of cabinet ministers or other privileged offices who were allowed access; for example, Mrs Peel gave a seat to Catherine Gladstone so that she could listen to her husband's speech on home rule in 1886.[53] Not all visitors appreciated their honoured position. Mary Curzon, the vicereine of India, regularly attended parliament when in London but resented sitting in the 'usual foul air and fussing female rows deep in the Speakers Gallery'.[54] However, she recognized the importance of the gallery as a place where she could influence and inform key politicians and diplomats on Indian affairs relaying evidence and opinion to her husband and civil servants. In Curzon's time, at the beginning of the 20th century, the space was even named 'Mrs Gully's Gallery' – Elizabeth Gully was the wife of the incumbent Speaker – and was frequently occupied by Miss Balfour, Lady Harcourt, and Mrs Asquith.[55]

Between 1858 and 1878, there were parliamentary questions and debates on the Ladies' Gallery more than 20 times in the Commons. These fell into three categories: the vast majority were about the inadequacy of the accommodation; there were concerted attempts by MPs to have the grille in front of the gallery removed; and, particularly during the debates on the Contagious Diseases Acts, there was discussion on whether the Speaker had the right to remove the occupants of the gallery from listening to proceedings. The gallery itself was certainly overcrowded, stuffy and uncomfortable, with one MP likening it to the

[49] *Derby Mercury*, 26 Apr. 1865.

[50] The Speaker's Ladies' Gallery is shown on plans drawn up by Edward Barry in 1869 proposing alterations to the space: TNA, WORK 29/1465. 'Strangers in the House', *The Graphic*, 16 Mar. 1889, refers to the space as Mrs Speaker's Gallery. My thanks to Melanie Unwin and Mari Takayanagi for these references.

[51] *The Lady*, 15 Apr. 1886.

[52] Henry William Lucy, *The Gladstone Parliament, 1880–1885* (1886), 128.

[53] *The Lady*, 15 Apr. 1886.

[54] Nicola J. Thomas, 'Mary Curzon: "American Queen of India" ', in *Colonial Lives Across the British Empire: Imperial Careering in the Long Nineteenth Century*, ed. David Lambert and Alan Lester (Cambridge, 2006), 285–308: Mary Curzon to George Curzon, c. May 1901.

[55] Mabel Mary Northcote, 'The Ladies Gallery: Parliament as Viewed Through a Woman's Eyes', *Harmsworth London Magazine*, x (1903), 680.

Black Hole of Calcutta.[56] The lack of a waiting room also drew comment, as women were not permitted to enter the gallery until the Commons was in session (in contrast to the men in the strangers' gallery) with many women sitting on the staircase awaiting admission. When challenged, Austen Layard, the first commissioner of works, stated that it was not possible to open the Ladies' Gallery earlier because of the number of women who wished to attend and who would therefore arrive early to secure front row seats.[57] Women put pressure on the parliamentary authorities to adapt the space, both directly and indirectly. The fact that the gallery was always full and that there were regular ballots for attendance meant that MPs could not claim women were disinterested in politics but women also made direct representations which were included in parliamentary debates on the space. For example, in 1858, Henry Edwards, the Conservative MP for Beverley, recounted the bitter complaints he had received from female constituents about their lack of access to the Commons due to the limited accommodation.[58] The fact that an MP from the north of England was receiving objections demonstrated that it was not merely small, metropolitan elites who were keen to attend the Commons.

The most heated debates regarded whether or not the grille should be removed, with MPs on both sides invoking the authority of the women who populated the gallery. Austen Layard quoted at length a letter from a regular attendee to parliament arguing that the latticework gave women privacy and seclusion, meaning that they could dress and act as they liked. The opinion of this one anonymous woman was repeated in subsequent debates, with MPs in favour of keeping the grille arguing that the women themselves wanted to retain it.[59] The most common argument put forward for the retention of the grille was that women were not officially permitted to be in the Commons and the grating therefore served to maintain the fiction that they were not present. As one of the commissioners of works put it: 'it would be better that the House should not be exposed to such an influence'.[60] MPs continued to resist the removal of the grille, even when it was pointed out that women listened to debates in the house of lords with unrestricted views. However, there were increasingly vociferous attempts by women themselves to pressure parliament to open up the gallery. The radical voice of suffrage activist, Mabel Crawford, was joined by the more measured tones of Mabel Mary Northcote, daughter of the Conservative cabinet minister, the earl of Iddesleigh. Her informative article 'The Ladies Gallery: Parliament as viewed through a woman's eyes' was a comprehensive guide for female visitors to the house of commons but she opened with an attack on the grille:

> Why, then, should a woman, when she wishes to hear a debate in the House of Commons be relegated to a cage just under the ceiling, while man enjoys the use of a large and comfortable gallery immediately facing the Speaker? Why, too, should her charms – be they great or small – be hidden away in semi-darkness behind an elaborate grille, which

[56]Hansard, *Commons Debates*, 3rd ser., clxxv, col. 434: 12 May 1864.
[57]Hansard, *Commons Debates*, 3rd ser., cxcviii, cols 20–1: 16 July 1869.
[58]Hansard, *Commons Debates*, 3rd ser., cl, col. 1203: 31 May 1858.
[59]Hansard, *Commons Debates*, 3rd ser., cxcvii, cols 1582 8: 9 July 1869.
[60]Hansard, *Commons Debates*, 3rd ser., clxxvi, col. 496: 30 June 1864.

makes it practically impossible to see anything unless one has the good fortune to occupy the front row?[61]

Their voices remained unheeded until, in 1917, a group of distinguished women, including many wives and daughters of parliamentarians, seized the initiative and presented Sir Alfred Mond, the first commissioner of works, with a petition from occupants of the Ladies' Gallery calling for the removal of the grille.[62] MPs could no longer claim that women visitors were in favour of keeping the grating, and Mond, whose own wife signed the petition, orchestrated its removal.

The final area of debate among MPs concerning the Ladies' Gallery was on the issue of whether the women were actually considered to be present in the House or not. Of course, they were literally in attendance, but the authorities, led by the Speaker, could not acknowledge their existence, as they were not officially supposed to be there. This absurd fiction led to difficulties when MPs wished to sit in closed session. The call of 'I espy Strangers in the House', which led to the closure of the men's public gallery, did not apply to the women. The matter came to a head during the debates on the Contagious Diseases Acts – a topic close to many women's hearts due to a fervent campaign co-ordinated by the Ladies' National Association. Many MPs argued that discussions on prostitution and sexually transmitted diseases were not ones that respectable women should be party to and tried to exclude women from the debates. In July 1876, the Speaker, Sir Henry Brand, made the official position clear, after Philip Mitchell MP spied strangers:

> I wish to point out to the hon. Member before I act upon his notice that if Strangers are excluded from the House this will not affect ladies, because the Ladies' Gallery is not supposed to be within the House. Of course, if after that intimation the hon. Member persists in calling my attention to the presence of Strangers it will be my duty to act upon the notice.[63]

Women themselves recognized that the existence of the grille gave them advantages not open to other visitors to the House. Anna Parnell argued that women in the privacy of the gallery had privileges denied to other attendees. Rules applied to the strangers' gallery such as absolute silence were not enforced in the Ladies' Gallery.[64] Women were also considered to be absent even though they were present. Parnell detailed a number of occasions where the House had been cleared of strangers but the women remained, arguing that: 'it is not after all hard to understand why they so contentedly submit to imprisonment and seclusion'.[65]

Women were thus able to subvert what appeared to be restrictions on their access to the Commons for their own benefits and increasingly they made more open challenges by occupying or attempting to inhabit other areas of the House. For example, in 1871, Josephine Butler and Margaret Pennington managed to secure a vantage point at the entrance to the

[61] Northcote, 'The Ladies Gallery', 675.

[62] *The Times*, 16 May 1917.

[63] Hansard, *Commons Debates*, 3rd ser., ccxxx, col. 1554: 19 July 1876.

[64] Parnell, 'How They Do in the House of Commons', 469.

[65] Parnell, 'How They Do in the House of Commons', 469.

chamber to witness their petition to repeal the Contagious Diseases Acts presented to the House: 'Mrs Pennington and I were allowed to stand quite at the door, almost in the House, directly facing the Ladies Gallery (which was crowded with ladies).'[66] In 1890, Henrietta Müller, editor of the *Women's Penny Paper*, which styled itself as 'the only paper conducted, written, and published by women', applied to be allowed a seat in the press gallery. Her request was turned down by the serjeant-at-arms who warned that 'the consequences were too difficult to conceive'.[67] Although Müller's attempt to move into the press gallery was thwarted, it was becoming increasingly difficult for the parliamentary authorities and MPs to maintain the fiction that women were not officially allowed in the Commons.

It was against this backdrop that the regular column, 'From the Ladies' Gallery', was published in the new magazine, *The Lady*. The editor may have taken inspiration from occasional articles written in regional newspapers introducing readers to the experience of listening to parliamentary debates from the space. For example, in 1879, the *Evening Telegraph* published 'A Letter to the Ladies (by a Lady Correspondent) In the Ladies Gallery'. Their reporter commented that she had difficulty hearing distinctly or recognizing faces clearly.[68] The column in *The Lady* was humorous, written in the style of a parliamentary sketch, but also intended to inform with detailed synopses of debates running to over 1,000 words per issue. The comfort (or otherwise) of the gallery itself was a common topic and the author came down firmly on the side of keeping the grille after a parliamentary debate in 1885:

> Our beloved gallery itself was the subject of a debate – remarkably deficient in 'dash' and gallantry, considering the opportunities which it afforded – on Monday evening. Mr Sidney Buxton, who has constituted himself the champion of the Anti-grille Party in the House of Commons, moved a resolution in the following terms:- 'That in the opinion of this House, it is advisable to substitute for the present grating (or some portion of it) a railing so constructed as not largely to exclude sound, light, and air; and generally that the accommodation of the gallery should be improved.' … I am sure he is well-intentioned, and sincerely wishes to make the occupants of the Ladies' Gallery comfortable; but, as I remarked on a previous occasion, his zeal is altogether misplaced. We are quite comfortable at present, and no structural alteration in our 'nest' above the Speaker's chair can be an improvement. Mr Buxton is in error when he supposes that we cannot see as much of the House as we want to; and he is wrong, too, in his belief that we are likely to perish of asphyxia. In addition, we can hear all the good speeches. It is only when members drop their voices and mumble to themselves that their remarks fail to reach us, and then, I daresay, we don't lose much.[69]

The correspondent for *The Lady* also revealed women's growing confidence in colonizing parliamentary space for their own purposes. No longer satisfied with being contained in a gallery behind a grille, they began to occupy the lobbies and one MP's wife even '*bestowed*

[66]London School of Economics, The Women's Library, Josephine Butler Letters, 3JBL: letter from Josephine Butler to Margaret Tanner, 4 Apr. 1871.

[67]'Women in the Press Gallery', *Women's Penny Paper*, 22 Mar. 1890; see also Michelle Tuson, *Women Making News: Gender and Journalism in Modern Britain* (Urbana, IL, 2005).

[68]*Evening Telegraph*, 23 Aug. 1879.

[69]*The Lady*, 26 Mar. 1885.

herself in the smoking-room, and declined to be dislodged' arguing that she had a right to be with her husband.[70] Another woman viewed debates, not in the Ladies' Gallery, but in one of the glass-fronted boxes either side of the chamber, which, as she was 'attired in a scarlet opera-cloak, threw a novel and striking beam of colour, as it were, across the dull and tiresome decorum of the House'.[71] Change was also happening in the class composition of female visitors to parliament. As Mabel Northcote reported:

> In these democratic days all classes of the community experience no great difficulty in obtaining orders from their respective Members, and as a result the day tripper from Yorkshire and the factory girl from Whitechapel can rub shoulders with the leaders of London society.[72]

Although this might be an optimistic viewpoint, and it is unlikely that parliament was overrun with working-class women, nevertheless, as these reports make clear, it was not the exclusive masculine domain that many have assumed.

4. Conclusion

It is important, then, to take a critical approach to interpretations of parliamentary space in this period. It is true that the house of commons was an institution designed by men for men. Women had to fight for their right to occupy even small sections of the building, and even then were not considered to be officially part of the House. However, where women were in control of space they could subvert this authority and utilise areas to their own political advantage. In the ventilator and in the Ladies' Gallery women challenged parliamentary authorities, flouted rules, and made the spaces their own, eventually spilling out into the lobbies and terraces of the Commons, refusing to be contained. When MPs, the Speaker, and parliamentary officials tried to control women's access, they were thwarted, pressured into making numerous concessions in the size and the organisation of the space before eventually removing the grille of the Ladies' Gallery entirely in 1917. At first, it was the sheer number of female spectators attending the House which compelled parliament to change practices. But women grew increasingly confident and vociferous, writing newspaper columns and pamphlets, lobbying MPs, and openly contravening regulations. Women's presence changed the experience of parliament for all occupants as they reported on, and reacted to, particular debates. However, encounters with parliament also had an impact on the women themselves developing their identity as political subjects claiming a right to participate in the affairs of parliament. Increasingly, they addressed MPs directly, in particular on areas which affected women the most: employment rights, education and, of course, the vote. In a carefully constructed essay ' "Better and Happier." An Answer from the Ladies' Gallery to the Speeches in Opposition to the Women's Suffrage Bill, February 28th, 1908', Laura McLaren challenged the arguments of those politicians who spoke against the bill.[73]

---

[70] *The Lady*, 17 Mar. 1887.

[71] *The Lady*, 17 Mar. 1887.

[72] Northcote, 'The Ladies Gallery', 680.

[73] Laura McLaren, *'Better and Happier': An Answer from the Ladies' Gallery to the Speeches in Opposition to the Women's Suffrage Bill, February 28th, 1908* (1908).

She reminded MPs who claimed that women had limited 'physical force' that, on their way to the debate, they had put on shirts tailored and ironed by women, entered through the doors of parliament that had steps that had been scrubbed and cleaned by women, and eaten food prepared and cleared away by women: 'From the cradle to the grave, that man depended for his comforts on the physical force of women.'[74] The Ladies' Gallery, for McLaren, was an empowering space enabling her to represent women's voices directly to MPs and the pamphlet was littered with references to the space. The cultural implications of living and experiencing the spaces of parliament were central to providing women with political experiences and forging female public identities. Parliament as viewed through a woman's eyes was increasingly a place where their voices could not go unheard.

[74]McLaren, *'Better and Happier'*, 7.

St Stephen's in War and Peace: Civil Defence and the Location of Parliament, 1938–51

MILES TAYLOR

This essay takes a new look at the destruction and the rebuilding of the house of commons during the 1940s. It argues that behind the home front bravado of the Palace of Westminster steadfastly enduring the blitz lay secret plans for rehousing MPs away from aerial bombardment, contingency scenarios that were then updated after 1945 in the event of attack on London by atomic weapons. The essay also suggests that threats to the security of parliament, together with the necessity to rebuild the Commons, were turned by the coalition government into an opportunity to refashion parliamentary politics in such a way that the two-party system was restored, along the traditional lines of government and opposition that had become blurred since 1931.

Keywords: BBC; civil defence; Giles Gilbert Scott; house of commons; house of lords; Palace of Westminster; parliamentary reporting; Second World War; serjeant-at-arms; Winston Churchill

1

'We shape our buildings and afterwards our buildings shape us'. So declared Winston Churchill in October 1943, as he introduced plans to reconstruct the chamber of the house of commons, destroyed during the blitz of 1941, as an accurate replica of Charles Barry's gothic masterpiece. It would be oblong and not semicircular, Churchill explained, and it would be small, with fewer seats than there were MPs. In this way, the spatial requirements for parliamentary government after the war – when, as Churchill later put it, 'fury and faction and full vent will be given to the greatest passions' – would be reinstated.[1] In 1944, Giles Gilbert Scott, doyen of the late gothic style and scourge of modernism (perhaps unfairly so) was appointed to design the refurbished building. Five years and £1.75 million later, the new Commons chamber was opened, looking to all intents and purposes like its Victorian predecessor, which itself had aped the original medieval chapel of St Stephen's out of which the modern Palace of Westminster was wrought across the centuries.[2] As the country emerged from the Second World War into austerity and reconstruction, the restoration of parliament, with materials drawn from the four corners of the commonwealth, served as a vital tonic to the nation, a reminder of continuity and durability in an age of uncertainty.

[1] Hansard, *Commons Debates*, 5th ser., cccxciii, col. 403: 28 Oct. 1943; cdvii, col. 1006: 25 Jan. 1945.
[2] Gavin Stamp, ' "We Shape Our Buildings and Afterwards Our Buildings Shape Us": Sir Giles Gilbert Scott and the Rebuilding of the House of Commons', in *The Houses of Parliament: History, Art, Architecture*, ed. Christine Riding and Jacqueline Riding (2000), 149–60; Maurice Hastings, *Parliament House: The Chambers of the House of Commons* (1950), 185–92.

Except that during the Second World War and its aftermath, there was very little continuity in the alternative accommodation provided for the house of commons. Churchill himself delivered those famous speeches defending the sacrosanct layout of the Commons in the chamber of the house of lords, where MPs sat for the duration of the war and throughout almost all of Clement Attlee's Labour government of 1945–50. During the blitz, the Commons actually spent nearly 50 days around the corner from the Palace of Westminster, meeting in Church House, next to Westminster Abbey.[3] Moreover, both before and after the war, extensive civil defence planning was carried out, with a view to relocating parliament altogether to completely new locations, which featured very different speaking chambers. Emergency schemes for moving the Commons were also hatched after 1945 in peacetime, although they have escaped the attention of watchers of Whitehall during the early cold war.[4] Nor was this an era dominated by party 'faction' in the way championed by Churchill. Between the formation of the 'National' government in 1931 and the general election of 1945, the conventions of two-party politics were challenged by the coalition government and an effervescence of independent MPs and minor parties contesting and, on occasion, winning elections. Indeed, during the Second World War itself there was a marked swing against the two-party system, symbolised by the emergence of Common Wealth led by the ex-Liberal MP, Richard Acland, and via the airwaves by the writer, J.B. Priestley.[5] Seen in this context, Churchill's comments were uttered out of hope as much as out of conviction, a wishful assertion that the norms of bipartisanship would be re-established once the Commons had been rebuilt along traditional lines.

This essay takes a second look at the destruction and the rebuilding of the house of commons during the 1940s. It suggests that the home front bravado – the Churchillian rhetoric of parliament enduring the blitz – masks the fact that, from as early as 1938, there were secret plans for rehousing MPs away from aerial bombardment, contingency scenarios that were then updated after 1945 in the event of attack on London by atomic weapons. The essay also argues that the threat to the home of democracy, and the necessity to rebuild the Commons, was turned by the coalition government into an opportunity to refashion parliamentary politics in such a way that the two-party system was restored, along the old lines of government and opposition. What follows is in three parts. First, there is an account of the relocation of the houses of parliament during wartime, both what was planned and

---

[3] Jennifer Tanfield, *In Parliament, 1939–50: The Effect of the War on the Palace of Westminster* (House of Commons Library Document no. 20, 1991), ch. 4.

[4] Peter Hennessy, ' "Inescapable, Necessary and Lunatic": Whitehall's Transition-to-War Planning for the Third World War', *20th Century British History*, xxi (2010), 206–24; Peter Hennessy, *The Secret State: Preparing for the Worst 1945–2010* (2010 edn); Matthew Grant, *After the Bomb: Civil Defence and Nuclear War in Cold War Britain, 1945–68* (2010); Daniel Lomas, *Intelligence, Security and the Attlee Governments, 1945–51: An Uneasy Relationship?* (Manchester, 2017).

[5] On the 1930s, see Nick Smart, *The National Government, 1931–40* (Basingstoke, 1999); Geoffrey Fry, *The Politics of Crisis: An Interpretation of British Politics, 1931–1945* (Basingstoke, 2001), ch. 2. On the Second World War, see Angus Calder, *The People's War: Britain, 1939–45* (1969), 546–51; John T. Callaghan, 'Common Wealth and the Communist Party and the 1945 General Election', *Contemporary Record*, ix (1995), 62–79; Steven Fielding, 'The Second World War and Popular Radicalism: The Significance of the "Movement Away From Party"', *History*, lxxx (1995), 38–58; Paul Addison, 'By-Elections of the Second World War', in *By-Elections in British Politics*, ed. Chris Cook and John Ramsden (1997 edn), 130–50; Kevin Morgan, 'Away from Party and into "the Party": British Wartime Communism and the 1945 Election', *Socialist History*, xxxvii (2010), 73–95; Kristopher Lovell, 'The "Common Wealth Circus". Popular Politics and the Popular Press in Wartime Britain, 1941–1945', *Media History*, xxiii (2017), 427–50.

what actually took place during 1941, a narrative that draws on the hitherto unused papers of the Commons' serjeants-at-arms. Then, the analysis turns to the debates around what form of assembly might replace the blitzed chamber, looking in particular at the work of the select committee of 1943–4. Finally, the essay describes Scott's new house of commons, which eventually opened for business in October 1950, how it combined reverence for Barry's gothic ornamentalism with a series of technological and architectural innovations which ensured that parliamentary government could function in a modern age.

2. Destruction

The oldest parts of the Palace of Westminster were among the first to be hit in the blitz that raged during the Battle of Britain in 1940–1. There was just collateral damage at first, from the river and from around the abbey. Then, on 26 September 1940, Old Palace Yard was hit, with a crater 30ft wide left, and St Stephen's porch damaged. Worse was to come during the winter. On 8 December, Cloister Court and the nearby clerks' offices were bombed, the floor of St Stephen's crypt broken up, and the Commons' lobby struck by falling masonry. Several months later, on 17 April, there was a third major strike, affecting the same vicinity of the palace. Finally, on the night of Saturday, 10 May 1941, the Luftwaffe took out the Commons chamber, and most of the surrounding complex of rooms and lobbies. There were 12 separate hits, thought at the time to be deliberate.[6] A few days afterwards, Winston Churchill, the prime minister, inspected the destruction, an iconic image caught for posterity in a photograph published later that month. Little of the famous debating chamber, nicknamed 'St Stephens' in Victorian times, remained intact. Only the gents' toilets in the 'aye' division lobby were left, as well as the reporters' gallery and, ironically, the ladies' 'grille', from where women visitors had been permitted to view proceedings, and to which suffragettes chained themselves in 1908. The Bible from the Speaker's table also survived unscathed.[7]

The air raids over the palace were not unexpected. Everyone knew that the seat of government and the home of the legislature were prime targets. From September 1939, the sittings of parliament commenced in the morning and concluded in daylight to lessen the risk of loss of life. On taking over the government in May 1940, Churchill insisted that this schedule be kept secret lest they wished suddenly to have hundreds of by-elections on their hands. MPs and parliamentary staff took turns as lookouts as night-time at the palace was turned over to scanning the skies for attack.[8] Fortunately, parliament was never

---

[6]For the precise locations, see the bomb maps held by the Westminster City Archives, available at *http://www.westendatwar.org.uk/page_id__110_path__0p28p.aspx* (accessed 19 Sept. 2016); cf. Parliamentary Archives [hereafter cited as PA], HL/PO/LB/1/87–8: 'Account of the damage done to the Palace of Westminster during the years 1939–41'; Tanfield, *In Parliament*, ch. 3; Bryan Fell, *The Houses of Parliament: A Short Guide to the Palace of Westminster* (1950), 34, claimed that the raid was not deliberate.

[7]*Illustrated London News*, 17 May 1941, p. 641. Hugh Dalton, minister for economic warfare in Churchill's coalition, concluded his inspection of the damage by relieving himself in the 'aye' lobby toilets: *The Second World War Diary of Hugh Dalton, 1940–45*, ed. Ben Pimlott (1986), 202: entry for 12 May 1941. The ladies' grille is clearly visible in two depictions of the destruction: John Piper, 'House of Commons 1941', Parliamentary Art Collection, WOA 496; Frank Beresford, 'Demolition of the Blitzed House of Commons', (1945), Parliamentary Art Collection, WOA 184.

[8]Alfred C. Bossom, *Our House: An Introduction to Parliamentary Procedure* (1948), 185; Tanfield, *In Parliament*, 7; *Back-Bencher and Chairman: Some Parliamentary Reminiscences of Lord Hemingford, P.C. KBE* (1946), 220–1.

actually meeting at a time of a direct hit, which was just as well as there was nowhere in the immediate vicinity that offered shelter. The cellars were too cluttered and, anyway, too vulnerable. None the less, in much the same way as the royal family could 'look London in the eye' by staying put during the blitz, so, too, parliament primed the pump of patriotism by carrying on at Westminster when under fire. At the beginning of September 1939, the government chief whip, David Margessen, had assured the Commons that parliament would continue to meet in the capital, to boost the morale of the nation. As Churchill himself put it in another context in June 1940 (referring to Dunkirk), 'wars are never won by evacuation'.[9] In fact, by then, evacuation planning for parliament was already underway.

A short-term refuge for the house of commons was found, first, seven miles away in Willesden. Opposite the bunker in Brook Road, Dollis Hill, purpose-built in 1939 for a wartime government, was Willesden Technical College, opened in 1934. In December 1938, Edward Fitzroy, Speaker of the house of commons, signed off on plans to evacuate the Commons to the college. The college's assembly and dining hall was earmarked for the Commons chamber, with classrooms and laboratories allocated for committee rooms and offices. Houses in nearby streets were identified for billeting up to 650 MPs and Commons' staff. Lists were prepared of essential items to be taken too: Hansard, current blue books and the *Commons Journal*, procedural manuals, minute books for Commons' committees, various accounts and ledgers, five days' supply of stationery, 5,000 towels, and, more ominously, Edwin Pratt's study of railways in the First World War, Edward Lloyd's *Experiments in State Control*, and Josiah Stamp's *Taxation During the War*.[10] After all, even in emergency, the Speaker needed to turn to precedent.

Willesden only offered a temporary solution, however. Starting in the spring of 1939, a much grander scheme of evacuation developed covertly, overseen by Ivor Hughes, the deputy serjeant-at-arms of the house of commons, in conjunction with Edward de Normann from the ministry of works, and officials from the treasury. This move would have taken both houses of parliament to Stratford-upon-Avon, code-named 'HK', and nicknamed, like something out of H.G. Wells, 'The Destination'. This full evacuation of parliament was associated with the government's decision to transfer as much of the civil service out of London as possible, the so called 'Yellow Move', two-thirds completed by June 1940.[11] In this plan the Commons would have assembled in the Shakespeare Memorial Theatre, on the banks of the Avon, an art deco building completed in 1932, replacing the original theatre destroyed by fire six years earlier. The theatre of parliament would literally become parliament in a theatre. Or not quite. For the auditorium was proposed as the Commons chamber, with the parliamentary reporters seated on the stage, and the Commons' Speaker and his clerks seated at their table on the forestage. Seats in the dress circle were given over to 'strangers' or visitors. Offstage, the theatre's star dressing rooms were allocated to the prime minister and the whips, with Attlee having to make do with the theatre manager's bedroom for an office. Schedules were drawn up to accommodate

[9]Hansard, *Commons Debates*, 5th ser., cccli, cols 363–4: 3 Sept. 1939.

[10]PA, HC/SA/SJ/13/9: 'Evacuation scheme 1'. The books referred to were: Edwin A. Pratt, *British Railways and the Great War: Organisation, Efforts, Difficulties and Achievements* (2 vols, 1921); E.M.H. Lloyd, *Experiments in State Control at the War Office and the Ministry of Food* (1924); Josiah Stamp, *Taxation During the War* (1932).

[11]Robert Mackay, *Half the Battle: Civilian Morale in Britain during the Second World War* (Manchester, 2013), 33; Brett Holman, *The Next War in the Air: Britain's Fear of the Bomber, 1908–1941* (Farnham, 2014), 236–7.

MPs and parliamentary staff in local hotels and homes, the billeting co-ordinated by the whips.[12] The level of detail to which de Normann and Thomas went in planning the evacuation was impressive. MPs, peers and palace staff were issued with special labels for their luggage; reporting centres and pick-up points were organised to ensure that everyone was ready to move in an emergency, whether they were present in parliament or not when the bombs fell; and two special trains were prepared to leave from Paddington.[13] 'Unto the breach' of modern warfare the nation might go, but parliament would be ensconced far away in the heart of old England. As the war commenced in September 1939, *The Times*'s parliamentary correspondent expected this evacuation to happen within days. Throughout that autumn everyone kept their bags packed and ready, recalled Guy Eden, the *Daily Express*'s man at Westminster.[14] The move to 'HK' – to Stratford – never happened, although the theatre remained mothballed for most of the war just in case, actors only returning to the stage to mark the bard's birthday, inevitably, with a performance of Henry V.[15]

The first nine months of the Second World War proved to be a phoney war on the home front, with no sign of the anticipated all-out attack from enemy aircraft on London and other cities. When the first air raids came over London towards the end of the summer of 1940, Churchill wrote a memorandum setting out options for moving parliament, leaving the arrangements to Lord Beaverbrook, minister of aircraft production. By October, a new emergency venue for parliament had been identified: Church House, the meeting place of the Church of England Synod and headquarters for its principal councils and committees. Its secretary, Frank Partridge, the bishop of Portsmouth, initially suggested that Church House be made available, according to John Colville, to the war cabinet. But, soon after, Churchill and various parliamentary officials toured the site and, with their customary gusto, Thomas and de Normann set to requisitioning its rooms for parliamentary, instead of ecclesiastical, purposes.[16] Church House was a good choice. It was nearby: a brisk five minutes' walk away; it was modern to the point of pristine, having only been opened for use in June 1940; and it boasted a large assembly room, of the circular kind, the one unloved by British parliamentarians. Church House was the work of Herbert Baker, the prolific architect responsible, among many commissions, for government buildings in South Africa and, with Edwin Lutyens, in New Delhi in India, where he had designed the semicircular chamber of the new Parliament House. Baker was proud of the new Assembly Hall, describing, in the brochure published to mark the opening of Church House, how it had been specially adapted to enhance the acoustics and guarantee the audibility of all who spoke there.[17]

---

[12]PA, HC/SA/SJ/13/9: 'Allocation of accommodation'.

[13]PA, HC/SA/SJ/13/11: 'Meeting of whips in the Speaker's Library', 17 July 1939; 'Conference on evacuation held in Serjeant at Arms' room', 18 Apr. 1940.

[14]Arthur Baker, *The House is Sitting* (1958), 77–8; Guy Eden, *Portrait of Churchill* (1945), 65.

[15]*The Times*, 26 Apr. 1943, p. 8.

[16]Martin Gilbert, *Winston S. Churchill. Vol. VI: Finest Hour, 1939–41* (1983), 860; John Colville, *The Fringes of Power: Downing Street Diaries, 1939–1955* (1985), 202: entry for 16 Sept. 1940; *Back-Bencher and Chairman*, 217–18.

[17]For Baker, see Daniel M. Abramson, 'Baker, Sir Herbert (1862–1946)', *ODNB*; Thomas Metcalf, 'Architecture and Empire: Sir Herbert Baker and the Building of New Delhi', in Thomas Metcalf, *Forging the Raj: Essays on British India in the Heyday of Empire* (Oxford, 2006), 140–51; Roderick Gradridge, 'Baker and Lutyens in South Africa, or, the Road to Bakerloo', in *Lutyens Abroad: The Work of Sir Edwin Lutyens Outside the British Isles*, ed.

However, no one ever did. On 14 October 1940, Church House itself was partially affected by damage done by a bomb which hit adjacent buildings in Dean's Yard. The Assembly Hall suffered the most; its ceiling collapsed and a large crack was made in its perimeter wall. The air raid proved two things. That this modern building was reasonably robust and fit for occupation, and that MPs would be unable to step inside its semicircular Assembly Hall. Instead, the 'Hoare Memorial Hall', a rectangular room with its own gallery, across the way from the Assembly Hall, was hurriedly prepared for occupation by the Commons, with a smaller room, the 'Convocation Hall', at the opposite end of the building reserved for the Lords. Churchill thanked Partridge for the loan of Church House and, in November, the king opened parliament in the 'Convocation Hall', looking out on a room that, in its essential dimensions, appeared much the same as the chamber of the house of lords.[18] Had the Luftwaffe not intervened, the king might have been addressing a parliament in the round.

In total, the Commons spent 49 days meeting in Church House, or the 'annexe' to give its *nom de guerre*. The sojourn came in two phases. Six days at the end of 1940 and 19 during May and June 1941 at the height of the blitz. Then, at the beginning of 1943, when the danger from the air seemed to recede, the building was given over to the ministry of aviation, before coming back into parliamentary use during the summer of 1944, when 'flying bombs' (the V1 guided missile) began to plague London and the south-east of the country.[19] For four weeks in 1944, Church House became a home from home for the Commons. The latter stages of debates over the coalition's Education Bill, and most of the discussion of the Town and Country Planning Bill, took place there. Not without irony perhaps. These were secular measures enacted in a holy place. The former provided for collective christian worship in all state schools, but gave parents the right for their children to opt out. The latter granted local authorities new powers of compulsory purchase over church property.

Church House was never intended as anything other than a last resort for parliament. Its cellars offered security from enemy bombs that was not available in the Palace of Westminster.[20] However, most MPs and peers did prefer to remain by the river. Although the Commons chamber was wiped out in May 1941, the rest of the precincts of parliament remained relatively undamaged. Alternative spaces for the Commons were thus near at hand. St Stephen's Chapel, reconstructed by Charles Barry as a lavishly decorated hall, was suggested as one possibility for a temporary meeting place for MPs, the idea put forward by Walter Elliott, the former secretary of state for Scotland. Churchill rejected that notion, preferring the royal gallery, perhaps inspired by Daniel Maclise's paintings of the British at war with Napoleon adorning its walls.[21] Some MPs looked, instead, to the house of lords, partly affected by the May bombardment but in working order. Symbolically, perhaps, the

[17] *(continued)* Andrew Hopkins and Gavin Stamp (2002), 147–58; Herbert Baker, *Church House: Its Art and Symbolism* (1940), 10.

[18] PA, HC/SA/SJ/14/14: 'Notes of a meeting 28 October 1940'; Churchill Archive Centre, Churchill College Cambridge, Chartwell Papers, CHAR20/2A/99: Churchill to the bishop of Portsmouth, 13 Nov. 1940; R.J. Craven, *The Church House Westminster 1888–1988* (1988), 20.

[19] PA, HC/SA/SJ/13/14: John Anderson to the Speaker, 30 Dec. 1942; 'Move to Church House', 20 June 1944.

[20] PA, HC/SA/SJ/13/14: 'Church House Civil Defence', 5 July 1944.

[21] *Harold Nicolson. Diaries and Letters, 1939–1945*, ed. Nigel Nicolson (1967), 165–6: entry for 14 May 1941.

stained-glass windows in the Lords, depicting the kings and queens of England and Scotland, had been shattered to bits, although all the statuettes of the nobles who signed the Magna Carta were undamaged. The chamber was duly offered up by Churchill's friend and cabinet colleague, Lord Moyne, then doubling up as leader of the Lords.[22] The Lords was made good for the new occupants. The lord chancellor's woolsack was removed, and the Commons' Speaker's table and chair put in its place. The throne was taken away, too, and the dais covered with a curtain. And so the Commons nudged aside the Lords, which moved into the smaller robing room for the next nine years. MPs met in the 'other place' for their first session on 24 June 1941. Officially, the move was a silent one, although some newspapers did report the new arrangements. Churchill took it all in his stride, confiding to his son that: 'I never thought to make speeches from those red benches, but I daresay I shall take to it.'[23]

As it turned out, the Lords was not so incongruous, proving a better venue for debate in some respects, than the old Commons. There was more light there than in the gloomy chamber where MPs had met since 1852. Translucent 'cathedral' glass temporarily replaced the destroyed stained glass, and shafts of natural light filled the room.[24] More space, too. Although the Lords was exactly the same width as the old Commons (45ft), it felt wider, as there were fewer rows of benches on either side. The chamber was longer, too, by 12ft. Unlike the Commons, the Lords was more of a proscenium layout, with cross benches situated at the far end. There was one other notable difference, too. By design, the Lords had much smaller division lobbies. The two corridors for 'ayes' and 'noes' running along each side of the chamber were narrower than those in the Commons. In other words, the new home of the Commons was less conducive to two-party politics than its old one. The Speaker would later complain of the difficulty in controlling the longer chamber.[25] Conversely, in its temporary meeting place, the house of lords was packed tightly into a room measuring only 54ft by 37ft, with a lower ceiling. Contemporary depictions suggest that the Lords acquired the dense atmosphere lost by the Commons.[26]

The reporting of parliament was also enhanced by the emergency arrangements. Although restrictions were imposed on the media at Westminster during wartime, particularly around describing when and where parliament met, and during its secret sessions, parliamentary journalism was largely a beneficiary, not a casualty, of the war. At Church House, the gallery overlooking the 'Hoare Memorial Hall' provided room for a total of 77 reporters. Similarly, there was room made for the press in the gallery of the Lords, positioned over the dais usually occupied by the throne. In both temporary chambers – Church House and the house of lords – parliamentary correspondents now faced the Speaker, rather than looked

[22]*Manchester Guardian*, 15 May 1941, p. 3; Churchill Archive Centre, Churchill College Cambridge, Chartwell Papers, CHAR 20/21C/300–2: Churchill to Moyne, 22 June 1941.

[23]Gilbert, *Winston S. Churchill. Vol. VI: Finest Hour*, 1104–5: Winston Churchill to Randolph Churchill, 8 June 1941; *Manchester Guardian*, 16 May 1941, p. 5; *Back-Bencher and Chairman*, 216–17 (secrecy); Sydney D. Bailey, 'Legislative Buildings of the World – IV. The Palace of Westminster', *Parliamentary Affairs*, iii (1949), 267 (robing room); John Battley, *A Visit to the Houses of Parliament* (1947), 30 (curtain).

[24]See Bryan de Grineau's depiction of the Commons' debate on the devaluation of the currency, 27–9 September, *Illustrated London News*, 8 Oct. 1949, pp. 544–5.

[25]Select Committee on House of Commons (rebuilding), *Report* (HC 1943–44, 109-i), pp. 22–3.

[26]See Bryan de Grineau's 'The House of Lords Sitting in the Robing Room, 1948', Parliamentary Art Collection, WOA 2532.

down on his back, meaning that they could take in a wider optic of the proceedings.[27] The Commons' debates were now more audible too. A sounding board was installed for the purposes of amplification in the Lords, with fixed and hanging microphones added later, to compensate for the larger auditorium. Wired for sound, the new chamber also welcomed the BBC. For the first time, the BBC now enjoyed the same access to Commons' reporting as the print media. Previously, its reporters were only allowed in to each sitting by special permission of the Speaker.[28] Taking advantage of this new status, the BBC began developing plans for a less formal style of reporting parliament, replacing the dry, verbatim record with commentary and 'colour', an innovation that turned into 'The week in Westminster'.[29] All this while the nation was at war.

Churchill, too, reaped some benefit from the making do and mending of the Commons. Church House was nicknamed 'Churchill's club', due to the much fuller suite of rooms given to the prime minister compared with those he used in the Palace of Westminster. Indeed, back in the palace, Colville complained of the longer journey he now had to make between the Lords and the PM's office.[30] With the reinforced 'annexe' to Number 10, Downing Street, the cabinet bunker on Whitehall, as well as Dollis Hill, the prime minister and his colleagues were now the most protected assets of the nation. Such priorities continued in peacetime. Enlarging the cabinet's footprint of space would become a priority in the rebuilt Commons, as we shall see.

There was one more evacuation plan for parliament made during wartime: to Park Lane Hotel on Piccadilly, another newish art deco building, this time with two basement levels, one of which would provide a temporary chamber for the Commons, larger than any auditorium in the palace or in Church House.[31] It proved unnecessary. On 24 April 1945, the Speaker of the house of commons, Douglas Clifton-Brown, switched on once more the beacon light over Big Ben. Details of the 'annexe' arrangements at Church House, the temporary move to the Lords, and even the 'HK' plan for Stratford-upon-Avon, were revealed to the public. Nothing was said about Willesden College. Just as well maybe, as an enemy doodlebug fell nearby in September 1944 killing many residents.[32] The Palace of Westminster was back in business.

3. *Renewal*

The Commons required rebuilding. In October 1943, Churchill presented the coalition government's proposals for the reconstruction of the chamber. Setting up a Commons'

[27] PA, HC/SA/SJ/13/14 (Church House press arrangements): serjeant-at-arms to G.E. Christ, 14 July 1944; Baker, *House is Sitting*, 72–3.

[28] *Listener*, 14 Aug. 1947, p. 452.

[29] *Nicolson. Diaries and Letters*, 247–8: entry for 8 Oct. 1942; Quinton Hogg, *The Purpose of Parliament* (1946), 103–4. For parliament and broadcasting in general at this time, see Colin Seymour-Ure, 'Parliament and Mass Communications in the Twentieth Century', in *The House of Commons in the Twentieth Century*, ed. S.A. Walkland (Oxford, 1979), 537–9.

[30] Craven, *Church House Westminster*, 21; Colville, *Fringes of Power*, 352: entry for 24 June 1941.

[31] PA, HC/SA/SJ/13/14: 'Meeting at the Ministry of Works and Buildings', 29 Jan. 1941; J.Y. O'Brien to Charles Howard, 26 July 1941.

[32] Baker, *House is Sitting*, 86; *Manchester Guardian*, 26 Apr. 1945, p. 3; *The Times*, 8 Sept. 1944, p. 4.

committee to do the preparatory work, Churchill gave it precise instructions. Its remit would be to seek designs for a chamber that would be oblong and not semicircular, and with fewer seats than there were MPs. The first requirement served democracy. Churchill declared that 'in so many countries semicircular assemblies which have buildings which give to every Member, not only a seat to sit in but often a desk to write at, with a lid to bang, has proved fatal to Parliamentary Government as we know it here in its home and in the land of its birth'. The second requirement 'restored intimacy and the 'conversational style' to the Commons. MPs mostly loved what they heard Churchill say, queuing up to claim the oblong auditorium as an example of English genius, seeking a restitution of Barry's chamber (without the poor ventilation), and noting that the temporary accommodation in the Lords was too large. Modern experiments with rotunda shapes had not been a success, it was said: '[t]o address the London County Council', which met inside a marbled semicircular chamber in County Hall, completed in the 1930s, 'is to make a speech in a tomb'. However, there were dissenting voices, too, keen to break with convention. Earlier in 1943, Common Wealth had won its first seat in the Commons, the fourth independent MP elected during wartime. At one extreme was James Maxton, veteran of the Independent Labour Party. In the debate he called for parliament to start again and relocate somewhere away from London, 'built on a fine site, in good English parkland, as near to London as the kind of land can be got – some 20 miles out'. Others, including Nancy Astor and Viscount Hinchingbrooke, wanted to modernise the Commons' seating in such a manner as to reflect the diversity of parties and allegiance that had grown up since 1931.[33]

Churchill got his way, in so far as the 'select committee on house of commons (rebuilding)' was mandated to come up with a scheme for a traditional rectangular chamber. The decision to go for continuity over change looks on the face of it like a vindication of Churchill's commitment to parliamentary democracy and the traditions of parliament. Quintin Hogg, MP for Oxford and Churchill supporter, described his October speech as 'by far the most important of our constitutional system that has been made in years', a viewpoint echoed by other contemporary commentators quick to condemn the foreign innovations of the 'reformers' who wanted a French-style chamber of deputies.[34] In fact, Churchill had loaded the dice, and preset the terms of the select committee, expecting it to restore two-party politics by creating a structure, and, more importantly, an atmosphere, in the middle of the 20th century derived from the mid-Victorian era. Having said that, the committee was cross-party. Chaired by a maverick Conservative, Lord Winterton, and including the independent MP, Eleanor Rathbone (MP for the Combined Universities), the committee was not simply a rubber stamp. Churchill himself was not called to give evidence.[35] As the committee met through 1944, two more independent MPs successfully contested by-elections.

[33]Hansard, *Commons Debates*, 5th ser., cccxciii, col. 404 (Churchill); col. 411 (Maxton); col. 417 (Astor); col. 445 (Hinchingbrooke); col. 447 (tomb): 28 Oct. 1943.

[34]Hogg, *Purpose of Parliament*, 8; W.J. Brown, *Everybody's Guide of Parliament* (1945), 64–5; Alan Herbert, *The Point of Parliament* (1946), 34–8: 'reformers'; cf. Kevin Theakston, ' "Part of the constitution": Winston S. Churchill and Parliamentary Democracy', *Finest Hour*, cxxxvi (2007), 30–6; Kevin Theakston, *Winston Churchill and the British Constitution* (2004), 135.

[35]Earl Winterton, *Orders of the Day* (1953), 300–1, 309. Churchill Archive Centre, Churchill College Cambridge, Chartwell Papers, CHAR 20/138B/152–3: Churchill to Winterton, 6 Nov. 1944.

Winterton's committee mostly stuck to its brief as it set to work on rough outlines drawn up by Edward de Normann and his colleagues at the ministry of works. There was some disagreement over whether the plans for the chamber of the new Commons should look at increasing the overall number of seats for MPs, a compromise being that various options might be considered in the architects' plans. There would be no extension of the space between the two front benches, a *sine qua non* of the two-party system, not even by three inches. However, Eleanor Rathbone ensured that the committee did consider alternative seating plans, even within the very narrow terms of reference it had been given. She pressed Sir Gilbert Campion, clerk of the house of commons, on the rules around who could sit on the cross benches of the house of commons, situated on the public side of the bar of the Commons. Might these seats become home to independents, she enquired? Unhappy with his observation that independents were 'merely a passing phenomenon', Rathbone stuck to her ground. Campion was sent away to produce a memorandum on the cross benches. While by convention they had been reserved for MPs not yet sworn in, or for MPs wishing just to observe the debates but not speak, Campion conceded that they might be extended and used for other purposes, including for accommodating peers wishing to view proceedings.[36] It was not much of a concession, but Rathbone had made her point. By the beginning of April, the committee had completed its gathering of evidence, and tenders were invited, from which Giles Gilbert Scott's design was chosen as the recommended blueprint for the new house of commons. A small wooden model was made of the proposed chamber. By October his full designs were complete, the contractors lined up: Mowlem for all the stonework, and Oscar Faber as the consultant engineer for the reinforced steel and concrete framework of the new building.[37]

In January 1945, Churchill brought the committee's report back to the Commons, carrying on where his rhetoric had left off in 1943. To patriotism he now added a strong dose of partisanship, explaining that soon parliament would need to return to adversarial politics and regular whipped-in divisions. The temporary spell in the house of lords, he complained, had left the Commons 'short of the accommodation which we require to conduct heavy party fighting with the conveniences which were available in the other Chamber'. For the Labour Party, Frederick Pethick-Lawrence, a member of Winterton's committee, chimed in, lamenting just how long divisions had been taking in the house of lords. A conventional chamber was needed once more. In vain did John Dugdale, Labour MP for West Bromwich, protest that the decision to appoint Scott had been rushed, and styles other than gothic, for example the modernism of Gropius and Corbusier, could have been considered.[38] Oblong and gothic it was to be. As the Commons signed off on its new chamber, another committee, this time of both houses of parliament, met to consider the accommodation overall within the Palace of Westminster. Chaired by the former leader of the house of lords, Lord Stanhope, among other issues, the committee looked at ways to increase office accommodation in the palace, particularly for parliamentary staff and MPs. Clifton Brown, the Commons' Speaker, had his eye on the new spaces envisaged above the Commons chamber, while other witnesses giving evidence suggested turning over the Victoria Tower at the western end

---

[36](HC 1943–44, 109-i), pp. 57–62.

[37] Stamp, 'Sir Giles Gilbert Scott and the Rebuilding of the House of Commons'.

[38] Hansard, *Commons Debates*, 5th ser., cdvii, cols 1005–6 (Churchill); col. 1048 (Pethick-Lawrence); cols 1076–7 (Dugdale): 25 Jan. 1945.

of the palace for full occupation, or for erecting a new building over Westminster Bridge, on a site then occupied by St Stephen's Club, a Conservative hang-out since the 1870s. In the end, in its report of March 1945, Stanhope's committee made several recommendations along these lines, opting for new buildings both on Bridge Street for parliamentary offices and along Abingdon Street beyond the Jewel Tower.[39]

By the close of the war, the old Commons chamber was still a demolition site, but plans to raise a new one from the ashes were in place. Those designs were dictated by necessity for reconstruction, but also by party pragmatism, by the need to reassert control. For the 1945 election demonstrated no let-up in the momentum behind breaking the two-party grip. Independent candidates experienced their best ever general election. Including the three nationalist parties, there were 149 independent candidates altogether, almost half the total put up by the Liberal Party, with over 20 returned, roughly equal to the combined presence of the Liberals and National Liberals. The electorate was in a breakaway mood – the 'movement away from party'. Fielding candidates in every constituency for the first time in its history, the Labour Party urged voters to avoid independent candidates, who would leave the Commons incapable of registering the decisive majorities required for its legislative programme.[40] In that aim, Labour and Conservative were of one mind, whatever else divided their views.

4. *Reconstruction*

Work on the new Commons chamber began on 10 May 1945, four years on from the bombing, and was completed five years later. Superficially, Scott's new Commons chamber reproduced Barry's Victorian building, the key dimensions and features exactly as before. The roof had been raised, which meant that, although there was no increase in floor space, there was additional room for galleries for the press and for visitors. The division lobbies had been widened. There was symbolism of nation and empire throughout. Much of the woodwork in the new chamber came from English oak, from Shropshire trees planted specially in 1943. As promised at the time of its destruction, the new Commons was furnished from Commonwealth countries. The Speaker's chair was made from black bean wood from Queensland, Australia; the clerks' table from Canadian oak, the entrance doors of oak from South Asia (one from India, one from Pakistan); the Bar-rail was made of Jamaican bronze; the dispatch boxes of puriri wood from New Zealand.[41] However, the most ingenious changes were around the new chamber, rather than within, in the provision of offices and meeting rooms, principally for ministers and whips. In Barry's chamber these had been scattered across the Palace of Westminster. Now, they were brought in closer proximity to the house of commons. Faber's innovative frame, the first of its kind in Britain, allowed the chamber to hang and to be wrapped around with rooms on either side, and below. There

---

[39]Joint Select Committee of the House of Lords and of the House of Commons appointed to enquire into the accommodation in the Palace of Westminster, *Report* (HL 1944–45, 26–1), 10; (HC 1944–45, 64–1), xvii.

[40]Fielding, 'The Second World War and Popular Radicalism'; Labour Party, *Let us Face the Future: A Declaration of Labour Policy for the Consideration of the Nation* (1945), available at *http://www.politicsresources.net/area/uk/man/lab45.htm* (accessed 18 Sept. 2016).

[41]PA, HC/SA/SJ/9/50: 'Gifts for the new House of Commons'; *Illustrated London News*, 28 Oct. 1950, pp. 690–1.

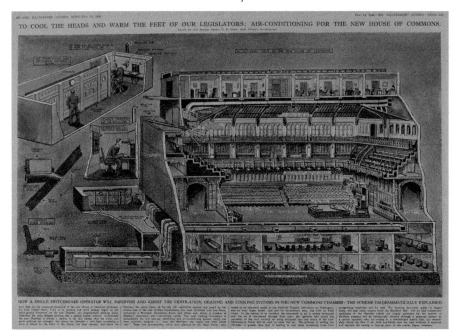

Figure 1: Cutaway Diagram Published in the *Illustrated London News*, 14 Feb. 1948, pp. 182–3. © Illustrated London News Historical Archive/Cengage Learning.

were now two new floors below, as David Reid's controversial ventilation system of the Victorian era was replaced by a more efficient one taking up less space (Figure 1). One of these new floors, directly under the Commons, was devoted to ministerial and whips' use, the second floor for MPs. Overall, in the refit, office and meeting space expanded by some 78%.[42]

Advances in technology were also hidden way from immediate view. The Commons chamber was now fitted out for amplification, with microphones inserted into the seating, so sensitive that one new MP in 1951 was able to hear the Speaker whispering to his clerks. A new electronic 'annunciator' was introduced to provide information about the day's business throughout the palace, and, crucially, to improve the summonsing of MPs to key divisions.[43]

The rebuilt Commons suited the resurgence of two-party control. The wartime coalition was one of the largest administrations to date. An American journalist counted 140 MPs under the direct charge of the Churchill-Attlee government, including all the ministers and parliamentary aides. Attlee's government formed in the summer of 1945 numbered 71. The phrase 'cabinet government' began to displace older notions of 'parliamentary government', coined in Victorian times. Attlee's new leader of the house of commons, Herbert Morrison, led the attack on antique parliamentary procedures that protected the sanctity of discussion

[42]'The New House of Commons', *Illustrated London News*, 21 Feb. 1948, pp. 564–5.

[43]*Illustrated London News*, 31 Dec. 1949; *The Backbench Diaries of Richard Crossman*, ed. Janet Morgan (1981), 39: entry for 30 Nov. 1951.

and the rights of back-bench MPs, bringing back the government powers of 'guillotine' over debates and stalled legislation. Veterans of parliament, including Campion, regretted the change of temper.[44] By 1950, the process was complete. Independents were eclipsed at the election of 1950, more or less a straight fight between the Conservative and Labour Parties.[45] At the end of that year, this new intake entered a chamber recalibrated for such a contest. In May 1951, the Lords returned to its home, its windows and roof repaired, new microphones and loudspeakers added, and the woolsack and throne reinstated.

Fear of the bomb did not go away with the end of hostilities. Secret planning to protect parliament in the event of enemy attack continued after the war. In August 1945, shortly after atomic bombs were dropped over Japan, the Attlee government decided to suspend civil defence for the nation at large. However, the 'houses of parliament civil defence committee', chaired by Victor Goodman, one of the clerks, carried on its business into the early 1950s. Largely responsible for co-ordinating Air Raid Precautions at the Palace of Westminster during the war, the committee now turned its attention to evacuation plans in the event of atomic attack. On 2 November 1949, two months after the Soviet Union successfully tested an H-bomb, Goodman met with the home secretary, Chuter Ede, as well as other parliamentary officials, and de Normann from the ministry of works, to discuss options for erecting 'citadel protection for a small chamber' capable of accommodating an average attendance of the Commons. The main difficulty in such a scheme, noted the meeting, was keeping it out of the public eye, especially if a large slice of taxpayers' money was required for its finance. A solution was suggested: bury the 'citadel' deep in the basement of the new buildings going up on the north side of Abingdon Street, at the corner of Great College Street, just a few hundred yards away from the palace. The whole row of 18th-century houses there had been destroyed in the blitz, and a new block, purpose built for parliamentary use – offices and meetings rooms – was now filling the cleared site. Where better to hide away a bunker for MPs than underneath their new home. Significantly, it was assumed that party politics would carry on underground. Charles Howard, the serjeant-at-arms, was directed, in particular, to look at ways of recording MPs' votes without the division lobbies, for which there would be no room.[46] With the approval of Attlee's cabinet, later confirmed when Churchill returned to office in 1951, Goodman's committee met on several more occasions, working on a 'first phase' to move both the Commons and the Lords to temporary accommodation within the palace in the event of war, and a 'second phase', taking both Houses into the 'deep shelter' across the way. Momentous as these plans may seem, Goodman's committee hardly worked with alacrity, mainly because the ministry of works delayed over completing the required surveys and costings.[47] By 1952, the committee had

---

[44] Albert Viton, 'The British Parliament in Total War', *Virginia Quarterly Review*, xxi (1945), 24. Front and opposition bench figures are taken from *The Times Guide to the House of Commons 1945* (1945), 3–6; cf. John P. Mackintosh, *The British Cabinet* (1962); Hans Daalder, *Cabinet Reform in Britain, 1914–63* (Stanford, CA, 1953); Gilbert Campion, 'Parliamentary Procedure, Old and New', in *Parliament: A Survey*, ed. Gilbert Campion (1952), 157.

[45] For the re-emergence of party, see Andrew Thorpe, *Parties at War: Political Organisation in Second World War Britain* (Oxford, 2009),

[46] PA, VGO/2/1: 'Protection for parliament in wartime', 2 Nov. 1949. For the Attlee government decision in 1945, see TNA, CAB 128/1: 23 Aug. 1945.

[47] PA, VGO/2/2: 'Minutes of the 7th meeting of the Defence Committee, Houses of Parliament', 27 Nov. 1951; VGO/2/2: 'Civil defence: Executive Officer's report (27 November 1951–4 February 1952)'.

wound up its affairs, and the 'citadel' scheme disappeared from the record. Britain by then had its own bomb, and the acceleration of nuclear weapons technology by the USA had tilted the balance of cold war firepower back to the NATO alliance. Protecting parliament fell down the list of national priorities. Indeed, parliament now needed protection at street level, not below. Later in the decade, policemen in Parliament Square looked on as tens of thousands of CND protesters filed past the Palace of Westminster en route up Whitehall to Trafalgar Square at the end of the famous Aldermaston marches.

5. *Conclusion*

Breaking with tradition, the house of commons assembled in St Stephen's Hall on 15 August 1945, for the state opening of parliament by the king, who gave his address from the throne in the Lords chamber, returned to the upper House just for the day. St Stephen's was fitted out for the occasion in the usual style of the Commons, with green seating on either side, and a temporary Speaker's chair and clerks' table placed at the western end. Later that day, Clifton Brown, the Speaker, pointed out to the Commons an interesting coincidence. One-hundred-and-eleven years earlier to the day, MPs had sat in the original St Stephen's Chapel for what proved the last time before the fire which destroyed the old palace two months later in October 1834.[48] It was a neat touch. Parliament likes reminders of its antiquity, the principle of precedent, and the comfort of continuity. Parliament returned to work in peacetime in a fit of nostalgia for the old ways, trumpeted in a new range of guides to the houses of parliament, and in the foundation of the Hansard Society in 1947. Yet, throughout the 1940s, as this essay has described, the Palace of Westminster experienced anything but continuity in its proceedings. In the space of 13 years, the Commons met in four different chambers, with contingency plans for three other emergency alternatives. The Commons oversaw the war from the 'other place', then, just as the whigs had done after 1834, Attlee's government delivered an age of reform from the house of lords. Time spent in Church House and in the house of lords reminded the Commons of what it missed about Barry's chamber. At the same time, two-party politics was challenged by independent MPs wanting a different way of doing business. Reconstructing the Commons after the war was both an act of restoration and of invention, as Churchill and his successors sought to reshape parliamentary politics to their own ends.

[48] *The Times*, 16 Aug. 1945, p. 4. There is a photograph of St Stephen's Hall readied for the state opening in Fell, *The Houses of Parliament*

The Palace of Westminster: Another Window of Opportunity?

LEANNE-MARIE COTTER ⓘD
AND MATTHEW FLINDERS ⓘD

The Palace of Westminster is in need of urgent, substantial repairs. This provides a 'window of opportunity' for change. This essay traces the restoration and transformation (or lack of) that the Palace of Westminster has seen in the last half a century, before assessing its current state, and considering whether parliament is fit for purpose. It provides a 'long-view' understanding of previous missed 'windows of opportunity'. The essay focuses on drawing insights from history in order to add a depth of understanding to the contemporary issue. An understanding of the preceding renewal and restoration projects enables us, potentially, to avoid some of the problems that have been previously experienced, and finally seize this opportunity to build a parliament which is fit for purpose.

Keywords: Augustin Pugin; Charles Barry; fit for purpose; Giles Gilbert Scott; Restoration and Renewal programme; window of opportunity; Winston Churchill

1

The Palace of Westminster is in urgent need of substantial repairs. The building is suffering from crumbling stonework, leaking roofs, electrical failures, exposed asbestos, and poor ventilation. There are also concerns about whether the building actually satisfies legal requirements in relation to air and water quality for staff and visitors, or Building Regulations for disabled access. The state of the building is so poor that the 2015 Independent Appraisals Report stated that 'the risk of catastrophic failure is increasing' and 'a major failing of the existing service infrastructure is inevitable'.[1] Rectifying this situation is expected to cost anywhere from £3.52 to £5.67 billion (possibly more) and take somewhere between six and 32 years to complete (possibly far longer). In light of the major Restoration and Renewal programme proposed for the palace, this essay offers a historically informed analysis of previous periods of parliamentary history in which matters of 'restoration' and 'renewal' have been addressed. The key questions guiding this essay are: What insights might this 'long view' offer the current Restoration and Renewal programme? How have similar challenges been addressed in the past? and What can we learn from the prism of the past?

This essay aims to provide a 'long-view' understanding of the restoration and renewal of the Palace of Westminster, by drawing on the themes of 'windows of opportunity' and 'lessons from history'. The essay is split into two parts. The first part provides an overview of

---

[1]Deloitte, *Palace of Westminster, Restoration and Renewal Programme, Independent Options Appraisal, Final Report, Volume 1*, 8 Sept. 2014, available at *http://www.parliament.uk/documents/lords-information-office/2015/Independent-Options-Appraisal-final-report-A3.pdf* (accessed 24 May 2016).

major redevelopment projects, and the second part focuses on the contemporary building and current Restoration and Renewal programme. In the first part, the first section focuses on the principles and values that underpinned its initial formation, the second section focuses on the devastation caused by the fire of 1834, and the subsequent debate about the following restoration process, the third section focuses on the Palace of Westminster after the German bombing in 1941, and considers the limited debate concerning the reimagining of the legislature to reflect the changing structure and nature of British parliamentary democracy. In the second part, the fourth section looks at the contemporary Palace of Westminster, tracing the restoration and transformation (or lack of) that the Palace of Westminster has seen since its rebuilding after the Second World War. The fifth and final section moves to address the major Restoration and Renewal programme that is currently under consideration, before highlighting the lessons which can be drawn from history. The aim of the essay is to gather insights from historical analysis, and to show how many of the debates and issues that the current Restoration and Renewal programme must confront have been experienced previously during past rebuilding projects. The historical analysis suggests a route to learn from previous mistakes, and embed this experience within the current debate.

2. *Major Redevelopment Projects*

The Palace of Westminster was never originally constructed or intended to be a functioning legislature. Instead, the building steadily underwent an organic transition from palace to parliament. Its function and structure evolved in an *ad hoc* manner, with new constructions being added as required. This resulted in the 'old' palace resembling a muddle of buildings, corridors and towers which, as will be shown below, was deemed by many as unfit for purpose.

In 1822, John Soane, as an official architect of the office of works, undertook several major alterations. This included a new royal gallery, a new library, new committee rooms, and alterations to the interiors.[2] However, the building struggled to adapt appropriately: the limited space, ageing design, and often ill-thought-through additions to the building created a sprawling maze of winding passages made of flimsy partition walls. This left many calling for an entirely new palace.

William Cobbett, pamphleteer, journalist, and later an MP, argued that Britain needed to look towards the United States, not only in the architecture of their Capitol building but also in the working environment it created:

> An Englishman would blush were he to see the House of Assembly of one of the states of America, not to mention that of the congress of the United States … The benches are built in a horse-shoe form; the Speaker's chair occupies the space, which the horse-shoe does not fill up, and the clerks of the house are seated at the table before him. Every member comes to his seat from an opening in the outside part of the horse-shoe. His seat is always the same seat, and he comes to it, and goes from it, without interrupting any other member … Every member has a little desk fixed before him, in his lodge, as it may be called, for the purpose of locking up his papers, or for the purpose of writing on.[3]

[2] Dorothy Stroud, *Sir John Soane Architect* (1984), 226.
[3] *Cobbett's Weekly Political Register*, 2 Mar. 1822, pp. 524–5.

In contrast, Cobbett described the negative influence that the overcrowded physical space of the house of commons had upon members: 'The *effects* of this want of room are many, and most detrimental to the proceedings of this assembly.' He went on to suggest that the conditions of the chamber were not fit for business and were preventing MPs from doing their 'duty':

> [t]he confusion, which arises out of it, beggars all description. The business is retarded by it; the crowds about the Speaker's chair, while the private bills are going on, the everlasting trampling backward and forward on the floor; the interruption which men give to one another, in spite of their desire to avoid it; the calls of 'order, order', incessantly recurring; all these absolutely distract men's minds, and render it impossible for them to do that which it is their duty to do, and which they wish to do. The House necessarily thus becomes a place for doing little business, and that little not well.[4]

Two select committees, in 1831 and 1833, were formed to discuss the condition of the Commons chamber. The 1831 select committee was established 'to consider the possibility of making the House of Commons more commodious and less unwholesome'. The reports produced by these select committees stressed how the chamber was inadequate, and that politicians were constrained and influenced by the physical space that they occupied. In 1833, the second select committee concluded that 'no alterations could make the present House fit for the convenient accommodation of the present number of Members, and that it was therefore expedient that a new House should be erected'.[5] This was the opinion not only of the committee, but also of a great many members of the House. The building was not only deemed inadequate, it was also deemed dangerous. In the late 18th century, a committee of MPs responsible for assessing the state of the palace reported that it posed a significant fire risk, and if a fire were to break out there would be colossal damage.[6]

Alternative sites, such as St James's Park and Hyde Park, were suggested for building a new parliament, allowing for a purpose-built building to be constructed. Advocates of this idea highlighted how a building designed specifically for parliamentarians would ease the pressures of modern parliamentary business, allow for effective governance, and better reflect the changing political landscape. They stressed that a new building would be able to include two chambers that could accommodate all members, as well as provide office space, and adequate committee rooms. However, the plans were rejected due to the cost and inconvenience.[7]

On 16 October 1834, fire broke out in the Palace of Westminster, quickly destroying many of its buildings. In theory at least, this provided the opportunity to recreate, redesign, and remould the arena of politics, into one that better represented the new parliamentary democracy that was taking form in the wake of the 1832 Reform Act. This may be

---

[4] *Cobbett's Weekly Political Register*, 2 Mar. 1822, pp. 524–5.

[5] Hansard, *Commons Debates*, 3rd ser., xix, cols 59–66: 2 July 1833.

[6] *House of Commons Sessional Papers of the Eighteenth Century*, ed. Sheila Lambert (147 vols, Wilmington, DE, 1975), v, 263–9.

[7] See Paul Seaward's essay in this volume.

considered as an opportune moment, as the 1830s was a decade of great changes for the British political system.[8] Several commentators regarded this as an opportunity to create a building that not only accommodated, but also represented, the new political landscape.[9] The chance to design a new parliament provided an opportunity to depart from a physical structure that reinforced the nation's hierarchical medieval elite past; this was an opportunity that was embraced by some, but resisted by others.[10]

While there were initial calls to relocate parliament, it was decided, in June 1835, that the 'new' palace should remain on the current site, thereby ending the debate regarding the relocation of parliament. Debate then moved to a focus on the architectural style of the building. To many, this posed an opportunity to break from the constraints of a building that physically reflected and reinforced a specific understanding of prestige and power. David Cannadine recounts that whig members viewed the fire as a cathartic break with a feudal past.[11] With the recent passing of the Reform Act in mind, they saw this as an opportunity for achieving further change and modernisation.[12] However, the tories viewed the fire as a more disturbing metaphor for the Reform Act, the descent of a centuries-old institution into chaos. They also argued for a legislature built in the Elizabethan – or neo-gothic – style and, rather than construing this as a bridge between a conservative past and a liberal future, they viewed it as representative of the permanence of the *ancien régime*, aesthetically celebrating the age of Good Queen Bess, the birth of the overseas empire, Shakespeare, *et ejusdem generis*.[13] Radical MPs were not unsurprisingly opposed to this position and argued for a neoclassical style symbolising a departure from the nation's outdated past.[14] The neoclassical approach, similar to that of the White House and the Capitol Building in the United States, was popular at the time and had already been used by Sir John Soane in his additions to the old palace.[15]

It is important to understand the context within which changes – or proposals for change – were taking place. At the start of the 19th century, liberal values began to spread across many of the political elite. This was particularly strong among the liberal tories, Canningites, whigs, radicals, and Liberals. As Peter Mandler observes: 'Governments in the age of reform required … an ability to satisfy popular opinion, or at least to be seen to respond to it'.[16] The importance of increasing the accessibility of parliamentary debates, the need for accountability, and duty of engagement, were raised during this period. This

[8] See, e.g., D.E.D. Beales, 'Parliamentary Politics and the "Independent" Member 1820–1860', in *Ideas and Institutions of Victorian Britain*, ed. R. Robson (1967), 1–19; David Close, 'The Formation of a Two-Party Alignment in the House of Commons between 1832 and 1841', *English Historical Review*, lxxxvi (1969), 257–77; I.D.C. Newbould, 'The Emergence of a Two-Party System in England from 1830 to 1841: Roll Call and Reconsideration', *Parliaments, Estates and Representation*, v (1985), 25–31.

[9] T.A. Jenkins, *Parliament, Party and Politics in Victorian Britain* (Manchester, 1996).

[10] David Cannadine, 'The Palace of Westminster as Palace of Varieties', in *The Houses of Parliament: History, Art, Architecture*, ed. Christine Riding and Jacqueline Riding (2000), 157.

[11] Cannadine, 'The Palace of Westminster as Palace of Varieties', 13.

[12] Cannadine, 'The Palace of Westminster as Palace of Varieties', 13.

[13] Cannadine, 'The Palace of Westminster as Palace of Varieties', 13.

[14] Cannadine, 'The Palace of Westminster as Palace of Varieties', 157.

[15] See above, p. 150.

[16] Peter Mandler, *Aristocratic Government in the Age of Reform, Whigs and Liberals, 1830–1852* (Oxford, 1990), 46.

gave way to ideas regarding the importance of accountability and communication with the public.[17] This was a critical decade for the role of the MP. As representation was expanding in terms of the franchise, so, too, were developments in political culture and procedures. Rix argued that this period saw a growing emphasis among politicians on being, or wanting to be, seen as accountable, and responsive to the public.[18] There were shifting perceptions of the relationship between politicians and the public they represented.[19] A desire, and a need, to improve scrutiny and communication, to showcase and open up the political stage, to systematise and publicise conduct, suggested an environment and space that would enable business to reflect this new vision.[20]

The relationship between the Palace of Westminster and the functioning of political society was transforming. The politician, as well as those they were representing, was changing and, as a result, expectations were altering. As Rix suggests, a new dialogue was created, one where communication was transformed and the need to inform the public of the activity inside parliament was recognized. As a result, both the function of the Palace of Westminster and the role of the politician were changing. For example, the house of commons was no longer simply used as a debating chamber for the political elite, but as a platform for addressing the nation. From 1830, the number of members who regularly spoke in parliament increased. Todd claims that, before 1832, there was a core of 150 but this had increased to 231 by 1841, and to 300 by 1861.[21] Similarly, Cox calculated that, in the 1828 session, 37% of MPs appeared in the Hansard Index, yet by the 1833 session 60% of members appeared.[22] This increase in participation was born from the new form of politics, and an increasing enthusiasm to be reported and seen by constituents. These changes led to a desire, among many, to create a parliament that was 'fit for purpose' and reflected the new political culture.[23]

However, neoclassical design was deemed to have connotations of revolution and republicanism, and was therefore rejected in place of a design that favoured conservative values and traditionalism. Any debate surrounding the need to learn from abroad or seek an alternative style was suddenly cut short on 15 June 1835 when the earl of Rosslyn, as lord president of the council, announced in the house of lords that 'the style of the building should be either Gothic or Elizabethan'.[24] The earl of Rosslyn went on to declare several specific requirements for the rebuilding which restricted redesign. On 14 July, a royal commission was appointed. The commission accepted the recommendations, and opened general competition for architects to design and rebuild parliament.[25]

---

[17] A. Aspinall, 'The Reporting and Publishing of the House of Commons' Debates, 1771–1834', in *Essays Presented to Sir Lewis Namier*, ed. Richard Pares and A.J.P. Taylor (1956), 239–40.

[18] Kathryn Rix, ' "Whatever Passed in Parliament Ought to be Communicated to the Public": Reporting the Proceedings of the Reformed Commons, 1833–50', *Parliamentary History*, xxxiii (2014), 453–74.

[19] Angus Hawkins, 'Parliamentary Government and Victorian Political Parties, c.1830–c.1880', *English Historical Review*, civ (1989), 638–69.

[20] Angus Hawkins, *Victorian Political Culture: Habits of Heart and Mind* (Oxford, 2015).

[21] Arthur Todd, *On Parliamentary Government in England* (2nd edn, 2 vols, 1887), ii, 401.

[22] Gary Cox, *The Efficient Secret: The Cabinet and the Development of Political Parties in Victorian England* (Cambridge, 1987), 53.

[23] Hawkins, *Victorian Political Culture*.

[24] Hansard, *Lords Debates*, 3rd ser., xxviii, cols 774–9: 15 June 1835.

[25] Hansard, *Commons Debates*, 3rd ser., xxxv, cols 398–418: 21 July 1836.

In February 1836, Charles Barry, with the help of Augustus Pugin, was chosen as the architect tasked with redesigning and rebuilding parliament. While Barry's own architectural style was classical, his winning proposal was a neo-gothic design that preserved the embedded conservative aspects of the status quo. Barry's plans, alongside Pugin's designs for the interior, 'projected a backward-looking, conservative, and exclusive image of the British constitution'.[26] At a broader level, according to Cannadine, the 'New' Palace of Westminster articulated a 'hierarchical image of the social and political order, stressing venerable authority, presidential subordination and true conservative principles'.[27] The foundation stone was laid on 27 April 1840, the house of lords was completed in 1847, the house of commons in 1852. However, the rebuilding of the whole palace was not complete until 1870.

The next period of significant change came as a result of destruction caused during the Second World War. On 10–11 May 1941, the Luftwaffe dropped two incendiary bombs on the Palace of Westminster, causing significant damage and destroying the house of commons chamber. Just as, after the Great Fire of London in 1834, this unfortunate event was presented as the opportunity to reshape institutions and procedures and, in turn, possibly change the nature of British politics. However, the debate was restrained and subdued. In a time of war, there was widespread desire for continuity and stability. Among both the politicians and the public there was a desire to rebuild what the Luftwaffe had destroyed, and demonstrate the strength and resilience of Britain. The focus was, as the prime minister, Winston Churchill, informed the Commons, to ensure 'that the work of our parliamentary institutions will not be interrupted by enemy action'.[28] It being a time of war and economic austerity, with the need to rebuild homes and generate industrial capacity, meant that there was little desire to drive through significant constitutional or aesthetic change. Moreover, Churchill quickly closed off the debate, stating that the rebuilding of the Commons should preserve 'all its essential features', and that the adversarial government structure should be retained. Churchill insisted that the new chamber be kept small in order to reinforce 'the conversational style, the facility for quick, informal interruptions and interchanges', that he believed made the Commons the greatest parliamentary chamber in the world.[29] He argued that its dimensions and structure were inseparable from the British political tradition, and therefore needed to be preserved. Churchill's preference for continuity over change, and demand that a reconstructed house of commons must retain 'all its essential features', dominated the direction of restoration and renewal.[30]

While the majority accepted Churchill's plans, there were some advocates for redesigning the Palace of Westminster to create a parliament that was both appropriate for the functioning of politics, and one that reflected contemporary political culture. For example, Nancy Astor (Conservative), was openly critical of the plan to rebuild 'like-for-like'. Astor claimed that the prime minister was 'thinking backwards instead of forwards'. She condemned the confrontational style of the Commons, claiming that: 'I have often felt that it might be better if Ministers and ex-Ministers did not have to sit and look at each other, almost like

[26] Cannadine, 'The Palace of Westminster as Palace of Varieties', 11.

[27] Cannadine, 'The Palace of Westminster as Palace of Varieties', 11.

[28] Hansard, *Commons Debates*, 5th ser., cccxciii, cols 403–73: 28 Oct. 1943.

[29] Hansard, *Commons Debates*, 5th ser., cccxciii, cols 403–73: 28 Oct. 1943.

[30] See Miles Taylor's essay in this volume.

dogs on a leash, and that controversy would not be so violent.'[31] This foreshadows some of the arguments put forth by feminist scholars such as Joni Lovenduski:

> [F]ormal and informal requirements for masculine dress, provision for hanging up one's sword but none for looking after one's child, admiration for Oxford Union styles of debate which will typically include jibes, taunts, farmyard noises and finger stabbing, in a Chamber where acoustics favour loud voices, the frequent use of sporting and military metaphors, the regularly reported experience of women MPs banned by staff from 'Members-only' areas are all manifestations of the gender regime of parliament.[32]

Consequently, those who highlighted the value of a less-confrontational layout, notably in the form of a semicircular seating arrangement, and argued that this presented an opportunity to update an outdated system, were quickly dismissed.[33] Churchill stated that 'Logic is a poor guide compared with custom',[34] and so preservation was favoured over progress. There were also those, such as James Maxton MP (Independent Labour Party), who was ardently opposed to Churchill's plan and called for the construction of a new parliament. Maxton stated:

> I should like to see premises built on a fine site ... in good English parkland ... as near to London as the kind of land can be got – some twenty miles out, I should say, is not an impossible distance and there I would erect the finest building that British architecture can devise.[35]

Among several MPs, there was the realization that this posed an opportunity to update the system in line with how politics and the role of the politician had advanced. Major Petherick MP (Conservative) made the case that MPs should have their own private offices:

> I think there is one amenity which the House of Commons has very gravely lacked in the past and that is private rooms in which Members could work and keep their papers ... In addition, it would be a very great advantage if it were possible for Members to receive guests in a private room. Often constituents come with troubles and wish to express them privately.[36]

Several other members also called for better accommodation, for example, Major Peto (Conservative) requested that MPs might be provided with typewriter and telephone:

> I am only a soldier, but I believe that in no business, however small, and certainly not in my constituency, would the board of directors, or the managing director, not have an

---

[31]Hansard, *Commons Debates*, 5th ser., cccxciii, cols 403–73: 28 Oct. 1943.

[32]Joni Lovenduski, 'Feminising British Politics', *The Political Quarterly*, lxxxiii (2012), 6997–7002.

[33]TNA, CAB 66/31/3: 'War Cabinet: Rebuilding of the House of Commons', Nov. 1942; CAB 128/2: 'Conclusions of a Meeting of the Cabinet held at 10 Downing Street, SW1, on Tuesday 20th November, 1945, at 11am'.

[34]Winston Churchill, *Closing the Ring: The Second World War*. Vol. 5 (1951).

[35]Hansard, *Commons Debates*, 5th ser., cccxciii, col. 412: 28 Oct. 1943.

[36]Hansard, *Commons Debates*, 5th ser., cccxciii, col. 422: 28 Oct. 1943.

office in which he could install a typewriter, a telephone and his files so that he could do his job properly.[37]

Sir John Wardlaw-Milne (Conservative) drew upon comparisons with Canadian parliamentarians in order to petition for facilities for members to meet in private with constituents:

Practically every Member of the Ottawa Parliament has his own room, or shares a room with another Member, in which there is ample facility for Members to meet and deal with correspondence and interview their constituents.[38]

However, these attempts to bring parliament into the 20th century were largely ignored. The new chamber was completed in 1950, designed by Giles Gilbert Scott, and strongly emphasized continuity. Pugin's gothic design was reproduced almost without change and Churchill managed to secure a duplication of the old Commons. Furniture and ceremonial objects were carefully reconstructed, including the clerks' table, the Bar-rail of the House, the dispatch boxes, the canopied Speaker's chair, and the petition bag hanging behind it.[39] The chamber was also intentionally too small to seat all members; 427 seats were included although there were 646 members, and the idea of moving to the hemicycle institutional design of many continental parliaments was fiercely rejected, again adhering to Churchill's desire to keep the existing intimate and confrontational layout, in a desire to maintain an adversarial and quasi-elite politics and close this particular window of opportunity.

3. *From 1950 to the Present*

In March 2015, Lord Lisvane (the clerk of the house of commons, 2011–14) stated: '[w]e could not be, and should not be, another generation of stewards of this unique building who shied away from their obligations'. In this simple statement, Lord Lisvane captured the politics of parliamentary restoration and renewal since 1950.[40] Indeed, the history of the parliamentary estate reveals growth and modernisation in relation to the provision of new parliamentary buildings and facilities (notably Portcullis House) but woeful underinvestment in maintaining the Palace of Westminster itself. Although an ongoing scheme of what has been termed 'aggressive maintenance' has been undertaken, there has been no general renovation of the building or its services since 1945.[41] This means that some elements of the building date back to the early 19th century. Since 1960, the Palace of Westminster has required constant and costly spending on specific projects that are usually commissioned on a reactive or emergency basis. Added to this are annual day-to-day repair and maintenance costs – estimated in 2015 as at least £150 million a year – that are necessary

[37] Hansard, *Commons Debates*, 5th ser., cccvii, col. 1012: 25 Jan. 1945.

[38] Hansard, *Commons Debates*, 5th ser., cccvii, col. 1010: 25 Jan. 1945.

[39] Charles T. Goodsell, 'The Architecture of Parliaments: Legislature Houses and Political Culture', *British Journal of Political Science*, xviii (1988), 287–302.

[40] Lord Lisvane KCB, *Constitution Unit Lecture, Monday, 16th March 2015*, available at https://www.ucl.ac.uk/constitution-unit/events/public-seminars/201415/RRlecture160315 (accessed 29 Oct. 2018).

[41] *Restoration and Renewal of the Palace of Westminster: Pre-Feasibility Study and Preliminary Strategic Business Case* (2012), available at http://www.parliament.uk/documents/commons-commission/PED-Modernisation-Report-Oct12.pdf (accessed 24 May 2016).

simply to keep the building running (i.e., they are separate from the costs of actually running the parliamentary processes).[42]

As the role of the MP and peers has changed throughout the second half of the 20th century, there has been a growing need for office space. As a result, the parliamentary estate increased, as accommodation was sought in neighbouring buildings. Eventually, this led to the acquisition of 6–7 Old Palace Yard in 1994, leasing part of Millbank House in 2000, the construction of Portcullis House in 2001, the acquisition of Fielden House in 2001, and the eventual acquisition of the whole of Milbank 'Island Site' in 2005. The changing role of politicians in modern politics meant that it could no longer be contained inside the Palace of Westminster; instead what had evolved was a much larger parliamentary estate with the Palace of Westminster at its core.[43]

The combination of a growing estate and an underinvestment in maintenance led to an extensive and expensive backlog of repairs by the 1990s. A number of internal inquiries set out the scale of the problem. In 1990, Sir Robin Ibbs's report highlighted that there was a large-scale backlog of essential maintenance, with an estimated cost of £220 million.[44] The report also revealed that members were greatly dissatisfied with their accommodation. In 1999, a further inquiry, led by Michael Braithwaite, concluded that the Palace of Westminster represented 'an inconvenient and expensive World Heritage Site'.[45] The review also discovered that around half of the maintenance backlog identified by Ibbs almost a decade previously had still not been undertaken, and further work (at a cost of around £285 million) would be required by 2007.[46] In 2007, in a review of house of commons' management and services, Sir Kevin Tebbit informed the house of commons commission that 'in the virtually unanimous opinion of those interviewed, the organisation put in place following the Braithwaite report had not proved satisfactory, and significant problems remained in the planning, management and control of the Parliamentary works programme'.[47] Again, 'the growing backlog in maintenance of the Estate, including the roof of the Palace and the basement mechanical and electrical project' was stressed. Lord Lisvane would later coin the now popular description of the basement as 'the cathedral of horror'.[48]

From this, a set of recommendations were made and accepted by the house of commons commission. In response to the Tebbit Review, there was a comprehensive restructuring of the management of parliamentary estates. In the house of commons, in an attempt to improve the management and maintenance of the parliamentary estate, a new director

[42]Deloitte, *Independent Options Appraisal, Final Report.*

[43]Hansard, *Lords Debates*, 5th ser., dcxv, cols 8–9WA: 10 July 2000; col. 437: 9 Mar. 2001; col. 1334: 21 Jan. 2002; Written Statement 17 (22 Mar. 2005), available at *https://publications.parliament.uk/pa/ld200405/ldhansrd/vo050322/text/50322-47.htm#wms* (accessed 30 Oct. 2018).

[44]On Ibbs, see House of Commons Commission, Review of Management and Services of the House of Commons, *Report by Sir Kevin Tebbit KCB CMG* (HC 2007, 685), Annex 4, available at *https://www.parliament.uk/documents/commons-commission/tebbit-review-2007.pdf* (accessed 30 Oct. 2018).

[45]On Braithwaite, see Review of Management and Services, *Report to the House of Commons Commission* (HC 1999, 745), para. 2.3, available at *https://publications.parliament.uk/pa/cm199899/cmselect/cmhccom/745/part02.htm* (accessed 30 Oct. 2018).

[46](HC 1999, 745), para. 7.12, available at *https://publications.parliament.uk/pa/cm199899/cmselect/cmhccom/745/part07.htm* (accessed 30 Oct. 2018).

[47](HC 2007, 685), para. 158, available at *https://www.parliament.uk/documents/commons-commission/tebbit-review-2007.pdf* (accessed 30 Oct. 2018).

[48]Lord Lisvane, *Constitution Unit Lecture.*

general of facilities for the house of commons, and a new parliamentary director of estates, responsible for the whole of the parliamentary estate, was appointed. In the house of lords, from 2009, responsibility for accommodation and works was transferred from black rod to a newly-appointed director of facilities.[49] However, after little improvement in services, in 2012 the management boards of both houses of parliament appointed a study group to 'review previous documentation relating to the modernisation of the building services of the Palace of Westminster, and describe the preliminary strategic business case for a general modernisation of the Palace'.[50] The scope of the study was extensive:

> [A]t this stage, *the full range of possibilities should be included from either a new build Parliament or a completely modernised Palace* at one end of the spectrum, to a programme of managed replacement and condition-based maintenance at the other.[51]

Long-term under-investment in the fabric of the building, combined with intensive use, has left the Palace of Westminster in need of major work. What historical insight does the period since 1950 offer us?

The first insight is really a general failure of parliament, despite numerous reports, investigations, and internal reforms, to respond to the challenge of physical dilapidation. The subtitle of Sir Barnett Cocks's *Mid-Victorian Masterpiece* (1977) was 'The story of an institution unable to put its own house in order', and this seems apt for the 40 years since publication as well as before.[52]

The second insight may offer an explanation for the first, in the sense that the issue is perceived by politicians to be toxic, given that spending money on politicians or political institutions is generally likely to produce a public backlash. The third, and possibly most significant, insight is that the gap between supply and demand *vis-à-vis* the Palace of Westminster has grown significantly. MPs now have significant numbers of staff, the expectations placed upon them in terms of being present and visible in the House have increased, the rise of the professional politician has necessitated more parliamentary support staff and new digital facilities, while the introduction and evolution of select committees has created new demands that could never have been anticipated in the middle of the 19th century. The core objective of delivering 'a parliament fit for the twenty-first century' in the Restoration and Renewal programme's goals recognizes that the Palace of Westminster has failed to keep pace with the demands of a modern legislature. The question then becomes one of the relevance of the 'long view' offered in this essay for the current reform agenda.

The Palace of Westminster is unfit for purpose. An assessment of the seat of government highlights two core problems: first, it is a 19th-century building with 20th-century modifications that does not meet the *standards* of a 21st-century *building*; second, it is a 19th-century building with 20th-century modifications that does not meet the *requirements* of a 21st-century *parliamentary democracy*.

---

[49]House of Lords, Annual Report 2007/08, HL Paper 152, p. 21, available at *http://www. publications.parliament.uk/pa/ld200708/ldbrief/152/152.pdf* (accessed 29 Oct. 2018).

[50]*Pre-Feasibility Study and Preliminary Strategic Business Case*, p. 4.

[51]*Pre-Feasibility Study and Preliminary Strategic Business Case*, p. 42 (emphasis added).

[52]Barnett Cocks, *Mid-Victorian Masterpiece: The Story of an Institution Unable to Put Its Own House in Order* (1977).

In 2012, the pre-feasibility report revealed that the scale of the challenge was actually greater than previous reviews had indicated. Basic structural components of the infrastructure had been neglected for almost half a century with significant neglect of mechanical and electrical systems (heating, water, ventilation, power, etc.) following the 1945 reconstruction.[53] The cost of the repair work within the palace, and concern about public opposition to this expenditure, had meant there was little incentive for successive governments to tackle the hidden issue of infrastructure maintenance. Instead, it appears that higher priority was given to visible aspects of maintenance, such as the condition of the stonework, in order to preserve the external façade, and on the acquisition and funding of new buildings for the parliamentary estate.

There have been repeated warnings about the infrastructure of parliament. Key findings from survey work undertaken in 2008 revealed:

> that the steam and condensate system was well beyond its normal life expectancy, that the chilled water system was hydraulically unstable, that the network of basement corridors and risers was heavily congested, that there were some other significant risks to health and safety, and that there was a serious lack of ventilation in areas of the basements due to the original ventilation shafts having been filled with building services over the years.[54]

A second team concluded that:

> without urgent and significant intervention a major failure of the existing service infrastructure is inevitable, which will disrupt the function of the Palace and is likely to require extended periods to recover the service.[55]

The study also highlighted that the building was at considerable fire risk. In 1992, in the wake of the fire at Windsor Castle, Sir Alan Bailey, after undertaking a report on fire protection measures in the royal palaces, suggested the need for a reconfiguration of the interior structure of the Palace of Westminster. He recommended that compartmentalisation be adopted; this passive fire protection method would help confine a fire by preventing its spread.[56] In 1992, the parliamentary fire safety committee accepted this recommendation. However, the review in 2008 not only found that this recommendation had not been fully completed, but also that later building works and additions had undermined the progress which had been made.[57]

The condition of the basement also created a significant hazard. Obstructed ventilation shafts, boarded windows and corridors, and congested mechanical and electrical services, plague the basement. There is an absence of smoke clearance provision and, as the basement corridors are also being used as storage areas, it poses difficult access for the emergency

---

[53] *Pre-Feasibility Study and Preliminary Strategic Business Case*, p. 33.

[54] *Pre-Feasibility Study and Preliminary Strategic Business Case*, p. 33.

[55] *Pre-Feasibility Study and Preliminary Strategic Business Case*, p. 17, quoting *Mechanical & Electrical Modernisation Project; Due Diligence 'The Way Forward'* (16 July 2008), p. 7, available at *https://www.parliament.uk/documents/commons-commission/PED-Modernisation-Report-Oct12.pdf* (accessed 30 Oct. 2018).

[56] *Pre-Feasibility Study and Preliminary Strategic Business Case*.

[57] *Pre-Feasibility Study and Preliminary Strategic Business Case*.

services.[58] In 2008, the insertion of a sprinkler system was suggested; however, the principal engineer concluded that such a system 'would be virtually impossible to install without first resolving the already grossly overcrowded corridors'.[59] While there have been no major fires in recent years, 40 minor fires have been detected since 2008.[60]

The Palace of Westminster also contains significant levels of asbestos. Specialist consultants assessing asbestos levels in 2007 stated: 'As a result of our inspections of the risers and ducts we became aware of significant dangers and risks to the health and safety of persons not only gaining access and working in risers and ducts but generally to all persons within the Palace of Westminster.' Although accessible asbestos had been encapsulated, they did not encapsulate where pipes pass through walls and voids, or under floors. There are also areas where the encapsulation was damaged, resulting in exposed asbestos.[61]

Steam presents another significant risk. Much of the palace's pipe system dates back to the 1930s and 1950s, and is now corroding, which results in seven to eight incidents of high-pressure steam leaks each year.[62] Drainage pipes and culverts also cause significant problems; pipes filled with wastewater, sewage and cooking by-products, are over capacity and eroded, leading to frequent blockages, vile smells, and sewage leaks into MPs' offices. Unblocking and repairing pipes and sewage systems is made more difficult by the fact that there are no blueprints for the system, therefore frequently it is unknown where pipes go, what they carry, or where they dispose waste. This is due to it being built and designed in the 19th century, inadequately updated to meet the demands of the 20th century, and therefore unable to cope with the realities of the 21st century.

The Palace of Westminster, built after the 1834 fire and partially rebuilt following the 1941 bomb, was considered outdated even before completion, and it is unable to meet the increasing demands of today. As was demonstrated above, as a building, the Palace of Westminster is almost beyond repair. However, as the home of parliamentary democracy, the Palace of Westminster is also failing. It has been unable to keep pace with the growing professionalism of politics.

The role of peers and MPs has changed significantly. Workload has dramatically increased, staffing has magnified, the role of communications and engagement has intensified, expectations from constituents have altered, the use of technology has increased, and the role of committee work has become increasingly significant. In short, the outside world has modernised and, in order for politicians to 'do politics', those practices need to come

---

[58] *Pre-Feasibility Study and Preliminary Strategic Business Case*, p. 20, quoting *Estate Wide Fire Programme Lot B: Palace of Westminster Hidden Voids and Compartmentation*, 17–20, available at https://www.parliament.uk/documents/commons-commission/PED-Modernisation-Report-Oct12.pdf (accessed 30 Oct. 2018).

[59] *Pre-Feasibility Study and Preliminary Strategic Business Case*, p. 20, quoting *Mechanical & Electrical Modernisation Project: Review Update* (Apr. 2008), available at https://www.parliament.uk/documents/commons-commission/PED-Modernisation-Report-Oct12.pdf (accessed 30 Oct. 2018).

[60] *Pre-Feasibility Study and Preliminary Strategic Business Case*, p. 42.

[61] *Pre-Feasibility Study and Preliminary Strategic Business Case*, p. 19, quoting Goddards Consulting *Summary Report on Health and Safety* (Jan. 2008), section 11.2, available at https://www.parliament.uk/documents/commons-commission/PED-Modernisation-Report-Oct12.pdf (accessed 30 Oct. 2018).

[62] Matt Chorley, 'Politics Stinks! Surge in Complaints about Parliament's Ancient Plumbing, with Sewage Pouring into MPs' Offices and Broken Toilet Seats "Biting" Staff on the Bottom', *Daily Mail*, 15 Aug. 2014, available at http://www.dailymail.co.uk/news/article-2712287/Politics-stinks-Surge-complaints-Parliament-s-ancient-plumbing-sewage-pouring-MPs-offices-broken-toilet-seats-biting-staff-bottom.html#ixzz4H6hD2pOJ (accessed 29 Oct. 2018).

into parliament. The modern parliamentarian engages directly with both the private sector and international political institutions, there is fluidity in which politics, business and public life are all conducted, and the Palace of Westminster has been unable to respond to these changes. This has been recognized and subsequently stated in one of the objectives of the Restoration and Renewal programme; namely, to 'Accommodate the needs of a twenty-first century parliament.'[63] As the 2015 Independent Appraisals Report stated: 'The building has to support the modern ways in which Parliaments work with informal as well as formal meetings, digital information and mobile devices.'[64]

In October 2012, the pre-feasibility report concluded that, without urgent and significant intervention, a major failure of existing service infrastructure was inevitable.[65] A subsequent report, the June 2015 Independent Options Appraisal, bolstered the argument that significant work needed to be carried out by stating that there was 'risk of catastrophic failure'. It stated:

> business continuity risk has continued to steadily rise and whilst the Members and users do not always see the full effects, building services issues are ever present and the risk of catastrophic failure is increasing. Examples include a burst water pipe flooding the Committee Room corridor and a component of the ceiling in the Lords Chamber falling into the benches below.[66]

In response to the Independent Options Appraisal report, a joint select committee was formed in July 2015. On 8 September 2016, the Joint Select Committee published its recommendations. The report concluded that the current ad hoc 'patch and mend' approach was no longer sustainable, that a major programme of works was essential, and that parliament must enable the next stage of urgent work to go by allowing a 'full decant', in order to reduce further risks. Committee member, Chris Bryant (Labour), said: 'All the evidence points to having to move out of the whole Palace simultaneously. That is the lowest risk, most cost-effective and quickest option.'[67] Initially, work was planned to start in the first quarter of 2020. However, on 24 October 2017, Commons' leader, Andrea Leadsom (Conservative), proposed the establishment of a new 'delivery authority' to assess the costs of the three options put forward to renovate the estate. It was stated that this would lead to a 12- to 18-month delay. The government initially declared that the vote would take place before Christmas 2017; however, the vote was pushed to 11 January 2018, and was again delayed, until the end of January 2018.

On 10 January 2018, Lord Norton of Louth tabled a written question asking when was the earliest date the two Houses could decant the Palace of Westminster if both Houses voted for that option and what was the estimated cost to the public purse for repair and

[63]Deloitte, *Independent Options Appraisal, Final Report*.

[64]Deloitte, *Independent Options Appraisal, Final Report*.

[65]*Pre-Feasibility Study and Preliminary Strategic Business Case*, p. 42.

[66]Deloitte, *Independent Options Appraisal, Final Report*.

[67]Joint Committee on the Palace of Westminster Restoration and Renewal of the Palace of Westminster, *Report* (HL 2016–17, 41; HC 2016–17, 659), available at *https://publications.parliament.uk/pa/jt201617/jtselect/jtpow/41/4102.htm?utm_source=41&utm_medium=fullbullet&utm_campaign=modulereports* (accessed 30 Oct. 2018).

maintenance of the palace in the period until decanting took place.[68] On 23 January 2018, Lord McFall of Alcluith produced a written answer stating that the earliest would be 2025 and that, over the next five years, the cost of repairs and maintaining the palace would exceed £400 million.[69] Finally, on 31 January 2018, the house of commons considered two motions. The first, seeking a 'full and timely' decant, as well as the establishment of a delivery authority to manage the work, was carried by 236 votes to 220. The second, that three options be costed in detail and brought back to parliament in 12–18 months for a decision, was not voted on. MPs also voted against a call for a future review to consider relocating parliament away from the Palace of Westminster permanently.[70]

Under the plan for a full decant, the Commons and Lords would move off site in 2025 for an estimated six years, with the Commons moving to Richmond House on Whitehall and the Lords to the Queen Elizabeth II conference centre, near Westminster Abbey. For the third time in 200 years, a 'window of opportunity' has opened, and the country has a chance to create a parliament that is truly fit for purpose, and able to accommodate generations to come.[71]

4. *Conclusion*

An assessment of previous restoration and renewal projects offers four key insights for those charged with future restoration and renewal processes. First, there is a pressing need to ensure that governance arrangements for overseeing restoration and renewal are clear and accountable. A significant challenge for Barry was the fragmentation of responsibilities for various elements of the parliamentary estate. There was no 'single client interface' and, instead, Barry was forced to negotiate with an array of offices, boards and commissions. Added to this was the manner in which Barry's freedom to deliver the project was hampered by the creation of a range of authorities appointed by the government, commissioners or elements of the parliamentary estate to oversee his work. The most extreme case of this issue was when a heating and ventilation engineer was appointed to assume control of those elements of the rebuilding project, in January 1840, without Barry even being consulted. The result was not only a lack of professional independence for Barry in undertaking his role but also a case of 'MAD' (multiple accountabilities disorder) whereby he was personally responsible for a project over which he had limited actual control. As a result, he increasingly spent the greater part of his time answering demands for information and explanations or appearing before parliamentary committees, than actually overseeing the creation of

[68]Lord Norton of Louth, 'Palace of Westminster: Repairs and Maintenance: Written question HL4602' (10 Jan. 2018), available at *http://www.parliament.uk/business/publications/written-questions-answers-statements/written-question/Lords/2018-01-10/HL4602/* (accessed 30 Oct. 2018).

[69]Lord McFall of Acluith, 'Palace of Westminster: Repairs and Maintenance: Written answer HL4602' (10 Jan. 2018), available at *http://www.parliament.uk/business/publications/written-questions-answers-statements/written-question/Lords/2018-01-10/HL4602/* (accessed 30 Oct. 2018).

[70]Houses of Parliament, Restoration and Renewal, *MPs Vote to Leave the Palace of Westminster during Essential Restoration Works*, 31 Jan. 2018, available at *https://restorationandrenewal.parliament.uk/mps-vote-to-leave-palace-of-westminster.html* (accessed 17 July 2018).

[71]'MPs Set to Leave Houses of Parliament for £3.5bn Restoration', *Guardian*, available at *https://www.theguardian.com/politics/2018/jan/31/mps-set-to-leave-houses-of-parliament-for-35bn-restoration* (accessed 17 July 2018).

the new palace.[72] Contemporary decision makers need to learn from this, and ensure that governance arrangements for overseeing restoration and renewal are not vague and hidden, but clear and accountable.

Second, parliamentarians need to accept the cost of restoration, and support the project. History has shown that there has been anxiety over spending significant sums of money rebuilding parliament, due to anticipated negative public reaction; therefore, politicians have either approached it with caution or attempted to ignore it altogether. The post-fire restoration and renewal of the Palace of Westminster after 1834 took place in an age of austerity. Therefore, the government was acutely aware of the possibility of a public backlash against the costs involved in the rebuilding. While Barry estimated a cost of £724,986 over six years, in the end the project cost over £2 million and took more than three decades to complete. Most politicians were content either to attack the project or to explore ways of reducing its costs and downplay its significance. The unwillingness of politicians to be associated with the project was particularly obvious on 27 April 1840, at the ceremony to mark the laying of the foundation stone for the 'new' palace, which no members of the government attended. A similar story can be told of the post-war rebuilding after 1945, again in an age of austerity, when politicians were unwilling to accept, or publicly admit, to the amount of time and money that was required.[73]

This is also demonstrated in the underinvestment in the maintenance of the building, which Cocks describes as like wanting 'champagne on beer money'.[74] Historical insight highlights that proper and full investment is necessary. Attempts to cut corners and seek 'the cheapest option' will not produce the standard of building needed to house parliament. Rather, underfunding and lack of integration of new technologies is a false economy that will lead to higher future maintenance costs. Linked to the above, there has been a desire to have a trouble-free approach to reform and restoration. If we are to create a parliament building that is truly fit for purpose, which engages the public, that is representative of current culture, and properly designed and delivered, then the degree of infrastructure investment required and the scale of the project needs to be fully acknowledged and accepted.

Third, there needs to be a full assessment of what is needed to create a parliament 'fit for purpose'. The restoration and renewal of the Palace of Westminster needs to be used as an opportunity for change. Decision makers need to consider the changing form of 'doing politics'. History has shown that there has been reluctance for change and a refusal to assess what is needed. Instead of embracing change, parliament adopts an evolutionary style of reform and progression. This view favours abstract ideas of 'tradition' and 'heritage' over those of progression and opportunity. This, in turn, can lock in a system that is outdated and damaging. Although there has been criticism, by some MPs over the centuries, about the time taken to create a parliament fit for parliamentarians, the public, and the politics of the day, these have been dismissed by decision makers. Little consideration has been given to the need to create a building that underpins the principles of advancing democracy. Instead, there has been a desire to lock in a system that reinforces an elite model of adversarial

[72]Cocks, *Mid-Victorian Masterpiece*, 42.
[73]C. Shenton, *Mr Barry's War: Rebuilding the Houses of Parliament After the Great Fire of 1834* (Oxford, 2016).
[74]Cocks, *Mid-Victorian Masterpiece*, 42.

politics. When opportunities arose to redesign the building fundamentally, emphasis was placed on continuity rather than change. History has demonstrated that there has been a deep reluctance to seek transformation and create a truly purpose-built parliament.

In terms of contemporary implications, there is the danger that what will emerge is a 'like-for-like' replica of the current Palace of Westminster which will be outdated before it is completed. The rebuilding of the Palace of Westminster should be seized upon as an opportunity to build a parliament that is not only fit for purpose but also one that is able to facilitate generations to come. Ambitions should be higher, there needs to be a desire to bring the parliamentary building up-to-date with modern politics and culture, not lock in an archaic system. In previous rebuilding projects, the nature of politics was ignored, and what was created represented previous traditions and customs, and did not facilitate a modern way of doing politics, thus creating a parliament that was unfit for purpose. The restoration and renewal of the Palace of Westminster offers a chance to transform the way we do politics. It offers a chance to remove the archaic fabric of a building that reinforces outdated norms and behaviours. One of the programme's objectives is to deliver a parliament that is fit for the 21st century. That requires decision makers to consider how the design and architecture of the legislature shapes the culture within. There needs to be a debate about the role the palace plays in embedding outdated and unacceptable behaviour that does not reflect the contemporary culture. Many have accepted Winston Churchill's statement that, 'we shape our buildings and afterwards our buildings shape us'. However, we should reflect on the response by Captain Somerset de Chair (Conservative), MP for Norfolk South Western: 'That is very true, but do they shape us so very well?'[75]

To date, there has been limited debate around using restoration and renewal as an opportunity to change the culture within the palace. This is a missed opportunity. We need to consider how the palace embeds outdated power dynamics, and affects the behaviour of its inhabitants. We need to consider how we can use this as an opportunity not just to repair a crumbling building, but to accommodate the needs of a modern legislature. This requires discussion around the layout of the chamber, the needs of its inhabitants, as well as the public's interaction with the building. As it has been argued, at previous moments of restoration and renewal, these conversations were attempted, but quickly dampened, leading to a parliament that was unfit for purpose before it was complete. Decision makers need to learn from history and avoid making this mistake once again.

Fourth, there needs to be a full and open debate, in order to have a full assessment of what is needed and create a parliament 'fit for purpose'. History has shown that there is a reluctance to have an open debate and learn from abroad. Instead, emotive notions of British culture and tradition have triumphed. The history of parliamentary rebuilding between 1945 and 1950 highlights the emotive power of narratives of British identity, culture and history that place the Palace of Westminster at their core. As Judge states, Britain is a parliamentary state where not only does all power reside in parliament but the dominant model of parliamentary design within this heritage is very much attached to a small adversarial chamber, a labyrinthine network of dark oak-panelled corridors, etc.[76] Current decision makers need to learn from history and not get distracted by the preservation of tradition

---

[75]Hansard, *Commons Debates*, 5th ser., cccxciii, cols 463–4: 28 Oct. 1943.
[76]David Judge, *The Parliamentary State* (1993).

and culture, but, instead, have an open debate about what a parliament that reflects modern day Britain should look like. An assessment of previous restoration and renewal projects also highlights the role and capacity of the executive, notably the prime minister (in the case of post-war rebuilding), to close down reform debates. It needs to be accepted that, in order to create a parliament fit for future generations, discussion, debates, and decisions, need to be truly open and not constrained by notions of tradition.

At present, there is little attempt to cultivate debate regarding the multi-billion pound project of rebuilding parliament. For example, the *Call for Evidence* published by the joint committee on the Palace of Westminster in late November 2015 did not 'open-up' or invite debate.[77] The *Call for Evidence* only asked four questions, two concerning scope, and two focusing on delivery, and did not encourage opinions on the wider issues and questions. Similarly, in late 2018, the draft legislation to establish an arm's-length delivery authority contained no mention of public engagement and approached restoration and renewal as little more than a large and heritage-focused rebuilding project. Put slightly differently, the plans emphasized 'restoration' of the past but not renewal with a view to the future and this was emphasized by the chair of the shadow sponsor board when she subsequently appeared before a joint committee of both Houses in January 2019.[78] In order to create a parliament that re-engages a disengaged public, the views of the public regarding what they want from their parliamentary building need to be explored.

Similarly, there seems to be little attempt to learn from abroad. As history demonstrates, following the fire of 1834 and the bombing in 1941, any debate surrounding learning from abroad was rejected. On each occasion, there was little attempt to consider, accommodate, or integrate a modern way of thinking that spoke to the public, as found in other legislatures. Instead, inaccessible, incomprehensible, and often undemocratic rituals and symbolic activities, which are derived from Britain's historically elitist approach to politics, were further embedded into the system.

Current decision makers need to learn from history. Rather than a closed debate which reinforces a system that is disconnected from the public, we need to have an open debate in order to re-engage with the public. Decision makers should acknowledge the needs of a parliament in the 21st century and consider the lessons that can be taken from abroad. The challenges highlighted above are embedded in history, and risk casting a long shadow over the current Restoration and Renewal programme. It is crucial that we understand the 'long view' of the Palace of Westminster and the building and rebuilding of our parliament, in order to learn from past mistakes and inefficiencies, and this time seize the opportunity in full.

[77]Joint Committee on the Palace of Westminster, *Call for Evidence*, 30 Nov. 2015, available at *http://www.parliament.uk/documents/joint-committees/Palace%20of%20Westminster/Call-for-Evidence-Palace-of-Westminster.pdf* (accessed 29 Oct. 2018).

[78]Draft Parliamentary Buildings (Restoration and Renewal) Bill Committee. Oral Evidence, Wednesday 9th January 2019, available at *http://data.parliament.uk/writtenevidence/committeeevidence.svc/evidencedocument/draft-parliamentary-buildings-restoration-and-renewal/oral/94813.html* (accessed 14 Jan. 2019).

Index